MOUNT HOPE BAY

ORIENS

RIO

HOPE

POCASSET

AQUIDNECK

SCALE OF MILES

0   ¼   ½   ¾   1

MOUNT HOPE

MOUNT HOPE

A New England Chronicle
by GEORGE HOWE

NEW YORK
The Viking Press
1959

P   N   B

LIBRARY OF CONGRESS CATALOG CARD NUMBER: 59-5643

SET IN CALEDONIA AND BASKERVILLE TYPE FACES AND
PRINTED IN THE U.S.A. BY THE VAIL-BALLOU PRESS, INC.
ILLUSTRATIONS LITHOGRAPHED BY THE MURRAY PRINTING CO.

CONTENTS

THE ILLUSTRATIONS

The author is indebted to a number of individuals and organizations for the illustrations from their collections included in this volume. The sources which should be acknowledged are American Antiquarian Society for "King Philip" and "Benjamin Church" from the book *Paul Revere's Engravings* by Clarence Brigham; Samuel Church Wardwell, Harbor Master of Bristol, for the water-color "The brigantine *Macdonough*"; Grace Abbot Fletcher for the water-color "Ship *General Jackson*"; John Winthrop deWolf for the silver flagon in his collection; Marie F. Smith for the photograph of the marker of the original town alarm post; Francis Colt deWolf, Jr., for the portrait of Mark Antony deWolf; Dr. Halsey deWolf for the portraits of Abigail Potter deWolf, John deWolf, Jr., and James deWolf; Russell G. Colt for the portraits of Charles deWolf, General George deWolf, William deWolf, Theodora Goujaud deWolf Colt, S. Pomeroy Colt, and "An orgy at the Casino"; John W. Burrows for the portrait of William Henry deWolf; Bachrach for the photograph of Russell G. Colt; W. Robert Jones for the photograph of George deWolf's Mansion; Moss Photo, New York, for the photograph of Ethel Colt Miglietta; the Providence *Journal-Bulletin* library for "The Fourth at Bristol, 1910"; the Bristol Historical Society for the drawing "Old-time Bristol" by Wallis E. Howe; the City Art Museum of St. Louis for the painting by John Greenwood, "Sea-captains carousing at Surinam." "Melinda Mitchell" is from the book *Indian History and Genealogy* by E. W. Pierce; the diagram of a slaver's half-deck from *Africa and the American Flag* by Commodore Andrew Foote, reproduced from an English engraving of 1808; "Baranov's fort at Sitka," by Dr. George Langs-dorff, from *Voyage to the North Pacific* by John deWolf; the pictures of Henry deWolf and John deWolf from *The De Wolf Book* by Calbraith B. Perry; of General Ambrose E. Burnside from *The Story of the Mount Hope Lands* by Wilfred H. Munro; "The Battle of the Peasefield," "The Great Swamp Fight," and "The death of King Philip" from *Old Times in the Colonies* by C. C. Coffin. "*Vigilant* versus *Valkyrie*" is from a Currier & Ives print. "Bristol Harbor, 1856," is from an engraving by D. P. Newell. The endpaper map in the front of the book is by courtesy of Charles B. Rockwell and was painted for him by Wallis E. Howe. The map on the rear endpaper was drawn by Rus Anderson. The Library of Congress historical collections have been of great assistance.

ILLUSTRATIONS

MOUNT
HOPE

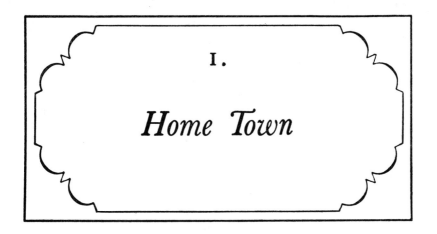

I.

Home Town

From Stamford, Connecticut, to Machias, Maine, the coast of New England is studded with former seaports that have turned their backs to the sea. Some earn their livelihood from textile mills, some from truck farms, and others from summer boarders; those which are nearest to the old way of life, like Gloucester, Massachusetts, from codfishing and lobster-trapping. Some are almost deserted, like Machias; some have become suburbs of the spreading cities, like Salem, Massachusetts, and some, museums, like Mystic, Connecticut; some, like Stamford, are cities themselves. Some, like Norwich and Hartford, are far inland on rivers that once were navigable; others, like Newport, Rhode Island, lie open to the ocean. Their founders were Englishmen, almost without exception. Their populations now are the happy mixture called American. Though to the tourist one may look just like another, the mailboxes and shop signs carry names which are French or Polish in one town and Portuguese or Italian in the next. Similar though they may be now, they differed sharply in the days when they were cut off from one another by forests or impassable roads, and their only highway to the rest of the world was the sea. New York itself was isolated then. Some of the seaports were actually islands, like Nantucket; others, though on the mainland, were so remote as almost to be islands too.

Speaking of his home town in Rhode Island, Bishop Mark Antony DeWolfe Howe (1808–1895) said:

> The villagers of Bristol, having little intercourse with the outside world, became in many respects a peculiar people, and of these, the few who differed from their neighbors were decidedly eccentric.

All were queer, he meant, but some were queerer.* When he delivered this opinion, his home town was two hundred years old already, and had a population of five thousand. Now it is three-quarters of a century older and two and a half times as crowded. Even now, people are always going through Bristol, not *to* it. If they drive down Hope Street, they see the lacy architecture of a slave trader's mansion and the massive stonework of the Town Hall, and the end of an archway of elms which vaults the length of High Street. If they take the Back Road from Providence they see a radar station on the hilltop where an Indian king was slain, and a Nike battery on the site of General Ambrose E. Burnside's banquet hall, and catch the reflection of a thousand mill windows in Fall River, over Mount Hope Bay in Massachusetts, before they cross the Mount Hope Bridge toward Newport. The twenty thousand tourists who watch Bristol's famous Fourth of July parade get only a day's glimpse of its history in the Continental uniforms of the Train of Artillery, and only a hint of its seaborne commerce in the Star boats of the Yacht Club regatta.

The seal of Rhode Island is the word HOPE, surmounted by an anchor. The state is the smallest in the Union, and Bristol is the seat of its smallest county, but there is no town in New England with a prettier setting or a more lurid history. It lies halfway between Newport at the mouth of Narragansett Bay and Providence at the head, on a two-pronged peninsula, shaped on the map like

---

* Lunacy, in the strict sense of aberration induced by a full moon, is not recorded in Bristol. But Mrs. Thurber, in the Bungtown quarter of the rival town of Warren, would once a month refuse to take more than a dime a dozen for her eggs, and, if she found a stick of kindling with a knot in it, would chuck it over the fence to get rid of the Devil. The waning of the moon, however, always brought her around.

a lobster claw half ajar. On the east, Mount Hope Bay divides Rhode Island from Massachusetts; on the south, the mile-wide channel still called the Ferry (though there have been no ferryboats for thirty years) divides it from the island which gives the state its name; on the west, the main waters of Narragansett Bay lead up to Providence.

Bristol harbor lies between the two jaws of the lobster claw. The bigger jaw is the town itself, with its wharves, like teeth, jutting into the salt water. The smaller is the peninsula of Poppasquash. Between the two, like the lobster's bait, lies Hog Island. Mount Hope, like the knuckle, rises two hundred feet into the sky behind the claw. Bristol is earthbound on the north alone, where the rival town of Warren, like the lobster's wrist, joins it to the body of the USA.

The origin of all these names is uncertain. On the stony beach at the north side of Mount Hope, by the water's edge, is a boulder of the soft, enduring rock which geologists call graywacke. It is seaweed-brown below tidemark and weather-gray above. Its slanted top, broken off in some unnoticed disaster of the past, is carved with a crude boat and a line of angular letters—if they are letters—in an unknown tongue. The learned Professor Wilfred H. Munro, who, in the last century, knew more about Bristol than everyone else put together, claimed that the Vikings carved it five centuries before Columbus discovered America; that they visited the monticule on a cruise from Iceland, picked grapes on it, and named it Hóp— which means a fiord fed by a river at one end and open to the sea at the other. The inscription, he said, could be translated:

HALLV STRAYS HIMSELF AND IS LOST HERE.

The Indians, he believed, garbled the Norse name Hóp to Montaup, and the English to Mount Hope. What grapes grow there now are not worth picking, that is sure, and other historians doubt that Norsemen ever came to New England, anyway. Perhaps the rock was carved by the Indians, though they had no written language, or perhaps by the English boys of Bristol, to fool professors. It was carved, whoever the author, a long time ago, for the blurred inscription was there as far back as 1818, to puzzle and inspire such scholars as William Richmond, a poetic lawyer who will be quoted later.

The name Poppasquash is just as unsatisfactory. Colonel Merton "Chezzie" Cheesman of the Train of Artillery, who lived there, insisted on spelling it Pappoosesquaw, on the theory that the Indians hid their women and children at its tip when the English attacked Mount Hope in 1676. Others have spelled it Poppysquash because Proprietor Byfield, when he moved in soon after, planted the first flowers and vegetables in town.

As for Hog Island, the lyrical Mrs. Henrietta Brownell, in her novel *God's Way Man's Way* (1885), submits that the Indians called it Chessawannoc, which, scholars say, meant "many clamshells." Captain Jim deWolf, the town's richest slave trader, owned Hog Island once. In a burst of poesy, he called it "my plum pudding set in a silver bowl." When he died in 1837, he left it to his Perry son-in-law. His will defines it as "that well-known island called Hog, hereafter to be called Perry." For a few years the charts marked it "Hog or Perry Island," but then gave up the effort to obey him, for the irreverent Bristolians called Perry "Captain Hog" behind his back. One local wit named his hog Captain Perry. There has always been more prestige than profit to owning Hog Island, anyway. Until fifty years ago Ray Arnold's family were the only people aboard it; they lived in a single house, three generations of them, until they grew tired of solitude and moved to the mainland. Even on Hog Island, though, there has been adventure. It is recorded that once, when the lighthouse ran out of oil, one of the three Mrs. Arnolds warned a ship off the shoal by outshouting the storm with her powerful pair of lungs.

On a fall morning the harbor between the twin peninsulas can be as calm as a pond, the wake of a quahog skiff stretching a line of blue the full length of the silver water; and as silent too, the flat surface rising and falling a little with the tide, echoing the cry of seagulls and the whir of mill spindles. In summer the southwest

breeze, every afternoon at two, threads up the channel from Newport and the ocean beyond, spangling the harbor into a million diamonds and dropping a blanket of lethargy on mankind till the sun
drops behind Poppasquash. In Saint Michael's Episcopal Church,
Minister Locke once preached an hour-long sermon to explain why
the sou'wester made him sleepy every afternoon and had so dulled
his invention that week that he could think of nothing *else* to preach
about—and why the bleak northeaster, when *it* blew, "keened him
up." He repeated the sermon from year to year. They say a Bristol
man left in the middle of it to catch a clipper for the Alaska gold-
fields; and that when he came back, twenty years and a million dollars later, at the same hour of a Sunday morning, he walked into
the same sermon at the very same sentence.

The sou'wester is also reputed to be aphrodisiac, as witness this
letter of 1825 from Ike Peck in Virginia to his convalescent brother
Nick at home:

—Dear long-lost unforgotten brother:
You are now in the town of girls, geese and onions. Bristol is a
fine place to pick up one's flesh, but don't misunderstand me, I pray.
You may recover there as well as any place on the earth, or better.
Fine sea-breezes, bathing and very fine chowder. Very pretty girls
and plenty of them. I hope and trust, though, that you will carry
yourself moderately among the kind consenting creatures wherever
you may find them. Do not hold too fast to that which is good.
When I went home two years ago, you remember, I had the ague
and fever. From a skeleton, I was up to full health in a jump, almost
as fast as you could say Jack Robinson. Well, what did I do? Why,
I carried myself very properly and moderately, as I always do. The
change was so rapid in all my feelings that I found it exceedingly dif-
ficult to forbear. Nothing but great prudence and the native fortitude
of my character kept me within bounds. In a week or two you will
be like a well-fleshed stallion, very dangerous at times. Be moderate.
If so, how great your victory over the flesh and the Devil!

When ships were smaller than they are today, and the sea was
America's highway, Bristol harbor was the town's livelihood. The
town began existence at its edge, and spread inland through the

years. In 1819 as many as one hundred sail were Bristol-owned: West India freighters, seaweed sloops, slave ships, and assorted smugglers. It was prophesied that the port would outgrow New York. No vessel drawing more than 16 feet can now lie at the docks, though they used to take 20 feet. The harbor is outgrown. When the destroyers visit for the Fourth, they have to anchor far out by Hog Island. The old wharves have rotted from the top down, or been unplanked by hurricanes.

Once in a while, at the neap tides of the fall equinox, the ocean itself roars up into the harbor. The September gales have drowned homebound sailors in sight of Saint Michael's belfry. The big blow of 1815 drove William deWolf's brig *Juno,* 160 tons, upwater from his wharf, taking the sloop *Toadfish* with her. Together they hurdled the wharf of Deacon Royal Diman, and brought up against a new brig of Captain Sam Wardwell's, sending her to the bottom. The buoys in the harbor were all uprooted. The south end of Thames Street washed away, the whole length from Constitution Street to Burton Street. A storm-tossed fishhawk dropped a tautog in the front yard of the impecunious Baylies sisters, who had not eaten for three days, and four Poppasquash boys were drowned crossing the sluice of the old windmill at the head of the harbor.

The gale of 1869 sank every ship in the harbor, uprooted 197 elm trees, toppled the Baptist steeple, and let Bridget Ellersly's pig into Saint Michael's.

Mrs. Ellersly was a reprehensible Irish widow who listed her profession as "washwoman." She sold whisky in her kitchen, to the disgust of all the Yankees who didn't drink it, and of some who did. There was not much the police could do about her, for the whole department consisted of one-armed Captain Hoard. Like everyone else, the widow kept a pig in her back yard for the fall slaughter. (In one year, the Bristol *Phoenix* reported, the thirty-seven families on Constitution Street laid down fourteen thousand pounds of pork, which works out to nearly four hundred pounds a family.) When the two-day September gale abated, Minister Locke of Saint Michael's, who had only just been called to town, ventured up

Church Street from the rectory to see what damage it had done to his new freestone church. He found the big door blown in, and a pig happily hurdling the box pews from a stance on the new turkey-red pew-cushions. The widow was a poor woman; he knew that the pig was hers because it was so skinny at a time when most pigs were fattening up. He tried to shoo it out, but hunger had made it more agile than he. The pew-ends were just the right height for a pig, and just wrong for a parson. He could not catch it. At last he gave up and strode up the street, over the fallen branches, to her shibeen.

"Mrs. Ellersly," he said sternly when her red eye peered through the crack of her kitchen door, "do you own a pig?"

"I did, Reverend," she told him, "but what with the blow I've seen nor tail nor squeak of him for the two days gone, and where the poor darling is now I don't know at all."

"Well, I know where he is. He's in Saint Michael's Episcopal Church, and I request that you call him home at once."

Mrs. Ellersly drew herself up. Before shutting the door in the young minister's face, she told him, "That I will not, Reverend. If he's turned Protestant, he's no pig of mine."

In the gale of 1938 the Methodist steeple went. The empty tanks of the gas company swept up to Mill Gut on a fourteen-foot tidal wave, and 'Tave Leclair's twenty-footer, the *Go On,* rode over Miss Isoline Barns's seawall to land with her stern cradled on the piazza. The hurricanes come more often now. In the last one the buoys stored on the Coast Guard dock floated up-harbor and pounded Bob Tasca's auto showroom into matchwood. A lady was drowned off the boat works trying to save her yawl, and her husband, with his leg broken, was pulled out of the breakers by four townsmen whose names are not known and who are too modest to let them be known.

On the other hand, the winters are not as cold as they used to be. Not so long ago hundreds of children gathered at the top of Cooke's Hill each winter afternoon, and coasted all the way down Constitution Street on reaches and Flexible Fliers, with the tassels of their stocking caps flying behind them and their metal shoe-tips ready to brake their speed in case some cranky housewife had sprinkled ashes on the snow or a horse should come trotting past the corner of Wood Street. Crowds gathered to skate on the ice-ponds —Reynolds', Circular, and Big and Little 'Fessor's. Sometimes the harbor itself froze over. Then the boys could skate all the way to Hog Island or Poppasquash. In 1780 a ship of Captain Charles deWolf's was ice-locked in the Ferry; he walked out to her and dragged her bags of gold dust home to his wharf on a sledge. After the Revolution, Lafayette's barracks were sledged across the harbor ice from Poppasquash to town, set up on brick foundations, and sold off as dwelling houses. One of them still remains on High Street.

(Houses were always being moved round town in the days before electric wires made it impossible. Spencer Rounds, in 1906, moved off the State Street dock three houses that he had moved onto it thirty years before. I remember seeing a two-story building, chimney and all, creeping along Hope Street on rollers behind his horse-winch, while its occupants ate dinner inside and chatted with the passers-by.)

A fellow who was used to sailing his skiff two nights a week across the breadth of Narragansett Bay, to see his girl in Warwick, had to make the trip afoot instead one winter when the harbor froze. He must have loved her to trudge that seven-mile journey over and back each Wednesday and Saturday, all winter long, in the dark, across the treacherous slushy salt-water ice. In 1837 the snow at Sam White's Lane (it is called Chestnut Street now) was so deep that a tunnel was dug through it for the Providence stage. Ox-drawn sleds filled with men and boys cut their way through High Street with floating banners and merry bells. Looking from her second-story window, spry Mrs. Elizabeth Dimond, eighty-four years old, composed this poem upon the scene for her friend Abby Smith down street:

> O Abby dear, have you the scene surveyed
> And view'd the beauteous carpet Nature's made?
> Not only in one spot its beauty shone,

But every building wears a milk-white dome.
How did you like the grand majestic throng,
Waving their banners as they wade along?
Their noble bells they call a grand review,
To see this beauteous carpet cut in two.

To judge from the old stones in the North Burying Ground, and from the obituaries in the *Phoenix*, which, like its neighbor, the Warren *Gazette*, appears twice weekly, Bristol people seem to live longer than most. In 1840, sixty years after the Revolution, there were still fifty veterans on the pension rolls. Captain Daniel Morice was born in 1764; his daughter Arselia Babbitt did not die till 1927 —a life span of 163 years for the two generations.

They enjoy their old age more, too. My father drew a meticulous picture of Bristol houses at the age of eighty-eight. In 1909 the publishers of the Boston *Post*, for an advertisement, ordered seven hundred canes of the finest Gaboon ebony, with engraved gold heads. They sent one to the Council of every New England town, asking that it be given to the oldest citizen, and handed down on his death to the next. I doubt if one of those canes is left, except the one in Bristol. Old Dan Coggeshall, State Senator for fifteen years (he is only ninety-one, but they call him Old Dan to distinguish him from Young Dan, the Postmaster), has it now, but doesn't need it for support. (Since this was written, Old Dan has been called to a reluctant rest, and the cane has descended to John Usher on the Neck, whose first Bristol ancestor came to town as a missionary in 1727.) Minister Locke, one of my grandfathers, was asked to fill Saint Michael's pulpit for a single Sunday in 1867; he stayed over until his death at eighty-three in 1918. Bishop Howe, the other, was old enough to have pulled a pig out of the water by its tail in the gale of 1815, and died in 1895 at the age of eighty-seven. Only recently Alice Bell Morgan of Bristol, in her eightieth year, appeared in a flowered hat on a television show, and won $32,000 for her knowledge of finance. When the young interlocutor asked her for a tip on the market, she told him sternly, "In Bristol we don't fry our eggs till they are laid."

And when Sally Mutton, at the end of the last century, was pronounced dead, her husband held off the undertaker with a shotgun, forced hot milk between her lips, and brought her to; she survived him forty years.

You feel the harbor even when you are out of sight of it. Turn over in bed, and you know whether your face is toward it or away, from the fan on your cheek when the breeze is up, and the scent of the clambanks when the tide is out, and the moan of buoy and gull when the fog is down. From the sky, whence only airplanes and fishhawks watch the town, it would look like a herd of cattle clustered at a drinking-hole, and the intown roofs, peeping up among the vaulted elms, wait thirstily behind the big ones at the brink. Inland, the goldenrod grows yellower than anywhere else. Elderberries are plump on their clusters. In Tanyard Woods the mayflower blushes in the spring among the curly tobacco ferns, and the cardinal flower blazes in summer. Snakes hide in the huckleberry bushes there; and amethysts, says legend, are imbedded in the quartz at Ferry Point. The uplands are stony and the lowlands are boggy; but Bristol harbor has been compared for beauty to the Bay of Naples by our own Neapolitans themselves, with Mount Hope its miniature Vesuvius.

"Bristol touches the sea," exclaimed the Fourth of July orator in 1843, "and thereby the world!" Then, there was no railroad to the city and no bridge to the Island. You reached one by stage and the other by horse-ferry. The railroad, which came in 1855, went in the gale of 1938. The town was hitched narrowly to the rest of America, but seaward the world spread before it.

Bristol was at the end of the line. You had to make a point of going there. It was not on the way to anything, for traffic between the city and the Island was easier by land through Massachusetts than by the ferry. The town was secluded on its land's-end—that is why the slave-smugglers liked it—and a town can grow peculiar, just like a person, from loneliness.

Peculiar, I should say so! For instance, Dr. Neylan, who brought me into the world, had taught gymnastics in New York before he set up as an obstetrician in Bristol. For fifteen years he had been a professional acrobat. He had trained animals with John Robinson's Show and the Great Eastern. But the Train of Artillery trusted him enough to make him their surgeon, so my parents trusted him with their firstborn.

Perhaps the whole world was eccentric in the days when it had to hoist all its water from a well, and, to travel fifteen miles, had to walk to the stage office a day ahead, write its name on a slate, then wait at home till the driver blew his horn in front of its door; when it had no heat but a fireplace and no plumbing but an outhouse and no light but a candle.

The Yankee character is a perpetual battle between conscience and cupidity. The old-timers were generous and skinflint, irreverent, pious and scandalous, antlike for work and catlike for fighting. They loved sport and laughter, and they never took themselves too seriously. The teams in the old YMCA bowling league, for instance, who often came to blows over the ninepins, gave themselves such names as the Canvasbacks, the Honk Honks, the Pinticklers, and the Neversweats. Bristol had a tennis club as far back as 1876, a yacht club in 1877, a choral society in 1891, and a golf club in 1897. It now has clubs called the Recordacoes da Patria and the Società Principessa Elena. It is more like a club than a township, anyway.

How they fought! At the Neck, where Warren and the rest of the world is tethered to town, pitched battles used to rage between the Bristol Clams and the Warren Mussels. The Mussels' insulting warcry was:

> The Bristol boys they have no sleds,
> They slide downhill on codfish heads;
> The Bristol girls they have no combs,
> They comb their hair with codfish bones.

As soon as the horse-chestnut pods opened in the fall, Bristol girls gathered the biggest and hardest and saved them till winter for the boys, who embedded them in snowballs for the battles. As if another town wasn't enough to fight, Bristol fought itself. There have been fist fights at Town Meeting (as in the days of Charles II, you must own property to be admitted, but $143 is enough), and bloody noses over the election for such offices as Inspector of Stove Pipes, Surveyor of Fences, and even Night Soil Agent. The boys south of State Street—it was called Pump Lane then, from the long-handled town pump at the corner of Hope—used to taunt the boys north of it with their chant:

> Downtown gentlemen,
> Uptown rats,
> Goree niggers and
> Poppasquash cats,

to which the uptown boys shouted:

> White cockade and a peacock feather,
> The uptown boys will fight together.

There was a truce between the Clams and the Mussels every fall, at general muster of the militia on Bristol Common. The Mussels came down under a white flag, and even visited with the Clams at home. The only insult they had to bear was the cheer of the Select School, as the high school used to be called:

> One-two-three-four-five-six-seven;
> All good people go to Heaven.
> When they get there they will yell
> B-R-I-S-T-O-L.

In the end the Mussels won the battle by stealing the battlefield. At the state election of 1872, Bristol voted red-headed Lawyer Turner into the Assembly. It woke up one morning to find that he had put through a bill to give Warren two miles of the Neck. When it turned out that the renegade had been born in Warren there was more sympathy than anger for him in Bristol: what could you expect of a Mussel? The Mussels held a torchlight celebration. They posted a sign on the pole at the railroad crossing, which had been the former boundary between the towns. Arrows marked WARREN pointed both ways, and a placard was tacked below it reading: *From the Flood to now, Warren to Bristol four miles; from now to Judgment Day, two miles.*

How they worked! Charlie Dimond, who is ninety at this writing, used to drive cows to pasture for a neighbor when he was ten—two miles in the morning and two at night. He earned 30 cents for those 28 weekly miles. His mother took it out in milk at 3 cents a quart. She fed her eight children a quart apiece, and had two left over for the chickens. In the winter Charlie slept in the garret with his brothers. Come summer, she would chase them all outdoors, barefooted, for who could afford shoes for eight children, even if she was a sea-captain's daughter? They spent the long vacation days in the fields, living from breakfast to supper on turnips and carrots and swamp-apples.

In 1904 *Town Topics*, the scandal-sheet of the era, called Bristol "a more or less unhappy family of fourteenth cousins." It meant the deWolfs, the Great Folks, as the rest of town called them—although even as late as 1904 half the people in town still had a drop of deWolf blood. Most of the deWolf mansions have burned down or been demolished, but on Hope Street one still stands which shows about what the rest of them were like. The deWolf stillhouse, seven stories high, was carried away in a hurricane. Their wharves and counting-houses have all disappeared too, except for Captain Jim deWolf's brick bank, which is now a bar, and for the indestructible wharfhouse on Thames Street where he emptied and reloaded his slavers and privateers. It is built of stone blocks brought from Africa in ballast, and its cambered beams are as sturdy as a ship's timbers.

In his day Bristol harbor was a nest of slavers, privateers, and miscellaneous smugglers, or what the deWolfs themselves called "free traders." Nowadays its only lawbreakers are the tongers of undersized quahogs. A man can rake thirty dollars' worth of quahogs in a day, about the price of a prime slave on the African coast no more than a hundred and fifty years ago; and recently, when the

Coast Guard cutter rammed an illegal quahog skiff, the dockside watchers were as indignant as their ancestors of 1799 when her predecessor captured a slave ship.

(The quahog, pronounced "cohog" in Bristolese, is the hard-shelled cousin of the succulent softshell, or clambake, clam. It lives in deep water, while the softshell burrows in the beach between high tide and low. Fifty years ago the quahog was considered unfit for anything but chowder, but since New England waters warmed up, the softshell has almost disappeared, and the quahog is the nearest thing to it that is left.)

The Bristol cousinship now embraces names like Angelo, Mora, and DeCosta. The town is still a family, but a larger one, and, as families go, a happy one. Bristol has always been more like a clan than a municipality. In 1808, it is recorded, Captain Jim deWolf spotted Charlie Clark of Bristol leading a parcel of calicoed slave girls down a Charleston street to auction, and called out from the piazza of his hotel, "Charlie, where are you going with those girls, and how's everything at home?"

Not long ago a Bristol boy was walking down a street of shuttered houses in Providence when he heard his name called by a soft voice he remembered well enough from the next desk at Byfield School.

"Don't come in, Jim; just tell me, did they have a good parade at home last Fourth?"

In 1928, when I had lost my American passport in Europe, the immigration officer in New York let me land without it because I knew Emma Rounds, who sings alto in Saint Michael's choir. He had been sweet on her years before when he played baseball for Newport against Bristol. And in 1953 Jerry Donovan, with the 77th Division in the Philippines, hitched a ride with a truckload of GIs. The man in front of him was reading a paper that looked familiar to Jerry. It was the Bristol *Phoenix*. The fellow was John Troiano, the Hope Street tailor. They had not known each other at home, but made up for it then.

Immigrations have changed the old Bristol accent, which was never just the same as in Boston, or even in Providence or Newport. The word "harm," which is pronounced "ham" in Boston, is pronounced "hem" in Bristol. Many of the twelve thousand citizens still say "ayer" for "yes," and "hobbeeya?" for "how are you?" and "cookih" for "cookie" and "bot" for "boat." Charlie Dimond pronounces his own name "Chelladaymon." The Wardwells used to be called "Wardle"; the Coggeshalls are still called "Cogzle" and the Gladdings "Gladn." Nobody but an outsider would sound the second "h" in Herreshoff. Bristolians even spell the same name in different ways: there are Dimans as well as Dimonds, and Munros and Monroes, and deWolfs, D'Wolfs and DeWolfes. Some Perrys are Yankee and some are Portuguese. Half of the present-day Kings were originally Joaquins from the Azores. My boyhood chum was Albert Cicerchia, whose father, from Turin, grew violets in a greenhouse on Garfield Avenue. Some Yankees pronounced it Chicherea, to rhyme with Korea, and some Chicherary, to rhyme with Tipperary. Neither is right. For a few years the family had to call itself Ceven, which a Yankee *can* pronounce; but they are back to Cicerchia now, for Yankees are learning how to speak Italian.

The Town Council meets each Monday night in the largest room of the Burnside Memorial Town Hall, sitting in captains' chairs of worn oak. The pressed-brick fireplace of that chamber has never been blackened by smoke since it was laid up in 1883. Against the oak wainscot are ranged the ever-growing files of wills and deeds and mortgages. Fluorescent lights glare down on the portraits of long-dead town clerks, and on the dusty hatchment of General Ambrose E. Burnside, for whom the hall is named. Over the bookcase hangs a portrait of Benjamin Franklin, sewn in needlepoint by the wife of Peter Gladding, who was Town Clerk from 1847 to 1882. On top of the case, at the ends, stand the bronze trophies of the King Philip Little League and the Little-bigger League, presented by Coca-Cola. At the center, till lately, reposed a Mason jar of alcohol. Embalmed inside it floated the blanched ear of one citizen, wrenched bleeding from its socket by another. The attacker expiated his mayhem, and the Chief of Police, after the trial, set the victim's ear right in the Council Room as a warning against crime. Someone stole it, however, a year or so ago, and no reward has been offered for its return.

Joe Bruno, the last president of the Town Council, is the grandson of a pioneer from below Naples. His successor is Bill Sousa, the first Portuguese-American to hold the job. The last State Senator, Anthony DaPonte, was born in Ponta Delgada. He was beaten for re-election by a lady who is descended from Yankee sea-captains. John Church, who was Town Clerk for thirty-seven years, is sixth in descent, or thereabouts, from Benjamin, who drove the Indians off Mount Hope in 1676. Leah Young, his assistant, is the granddaughter of the sea-captain who brought the first Portuguese to town. When she reads out the voting list, she pronounces those same Portuguese and Italian names in the Yankee accent that he used himself, at the time when everyone else in town was Yankee too.

Bristol is part of New England, but unlike New England. Half its population descends from Italy or the Azores, but it is not like them either. Providence to the north was settled for conscience' sake by the Baptists, and Newport to the south by the Quakers. The first settlers of Bristol were real-estate speculators. They set up the town frankly as a "port for trade." It was a little foreign to New England, even before the foreigners came. Like a club, it has a continuing and overlapping history. The Town Clerk's office is its clubhouse, where the dead belong as well as the living.

This account introduces some of the elders to their descendants. It is taken from yellowed parchments and crumbling newspapers, from taciturn hermits and talkative politicians. From one lady in a house knee deep, all twelve rooms of it, with old Christmas cards, tin cans, and the skeletons of cats. From another, blind, deaf, paralyzed, cleanly and beautiful, on her Gatch bed at a nursing home in Warren, who mumbled into my microphone, "It's bad enough to live in Warren, George, but think of having to *die* in Warren!"

From a philosopher who lives alone in a henhouse, a junk dealer born in Poland, a bishop, a banker, and a ball-player. There was not one who did not have the feeling of belonging to a club.

All the way from Massasoit, King of the Wampanoags, to Bill Sousa of the Council, the town has been like that. There was a time when nearly all Bristolians were related, when the slaves on Goree took their masters' names, when "as pretty as a Bristol girl" was a common phrase, even in Warren, and "shipshape and Bristol fashion" was a familiar compliment anywhere on the seven seas.

The hurricanes have done a lot to alter the town's face, and mankind is always doing more. The population has changed even more than the landscape. But the town will not change at heart till Judgment Day, that biggest blow of all, sinks it in Bristol harbor.

2.

King Philip

PROFESSOR MUNRO'S Norsemen may be mythical, but there is no doubt about the Indians. In December of 1620, when the Pilgrims landed at Plymouth, thirty-five miles east, Mount Hope was ruled by Massasoit, King of the Wampanoags. The Wampanoags were a branch of the Algonquin nation; the name of the tribe means "Eastern People," and his own name means "Great Chief." He was chief of all the lesser sachems from Cape Cod to Narragansett Bay. He lived comfortably, in a tent-village which he called Pokanoket, north of the hill, above Norsemen's Rock. His lodges, framed on poles, were covered with reed mattings sewn together with hemp and bound tight at the smoke-holes with walnut bark. Having a flap at each end, they caught the breeze, whichever way it blew. The biggest of them, the longhouse, stretched a hundred feet. The village was built at the foot of Mount Hope, not on top of it, in order that the smoke of the campfire might not be mistaken for signals. His southern land, now the town, he called Cawsumsett.

When the fishhawks arrived in March, Massasoit knew that scup had moved up the bay. When the bud of the white oak had reached the size of a mouse's ear, his squaws planted corn, laying a ripe herring at each hill for fertilizer. They hoed with quahog shells. His braves, who scorned labor, stalked deer on Poppasquash with bow and arrow, and netted tautog in the channel. There were soft-shelled clams in the mud at low tide for the digging, and eels, quahogs, and scallops offshore for the treading, all of which were brewed into a chowder called nasaump. Groundnuts, which are the roots of the wild bean, needed no labor at all; and huckleberries grew wild in the clearings. Over open fires the squaws broiled roe, boiled succotash, baked cornbread, and refined the sugar of the maples. Winter was a season of semi-starvation, but meat and fish, tanned in the sun the previous summer, saw the tribe through. (The Indians never learned the use of salt to preserve their meat, though they were surrounded by sea-water.)

Fifteen miles inland, at what is still called Fowling Pond, Massasoit had a winter game-preserve. He might shift camp a little when his firewood gave out; even now heaps of clamshells, marking a campsite, are sometimes dug up behind Mount Hope. But with fair weather he always returned to his hill. Mount Hope was his home and his throne.

On March 22, 1621, with his brother Quadequina and sixty of his braves, he visited the Pilgrims at Plymouth. The royal party walked all the way from Mount Hope; horses were unknown to them. The *Mayflower*, which had brought the Englishmen from England the previous autumn, still lay in the harbor; she was not to return till April 5. The King's hair, high in front and long behind, was greased, and his face was painted with the royal mulberry. He looked like the gypsies whom the English saw at home. He wore mooseskin moccasins, deerskin leggins, and a squirrel coat with the fur inside. A string of bone beads hung at his neck. He carried a knife in his coatstrap and a wooden tomahawk in his hand. As interpreter he brought one of his subjects named Squanto. Seven years earlier an English raider named Hunt had kidnapped Squanto from the coast and sold him to slavery in Spain. He had escaped to London, where he had learned English, and from London, as recently as 1619, he had escaped back to his own country.

Squanto stood beside the King on a rise above the Pilgrims' stockade at Plymouth.

"Welcome, Englishmen," he called down to them.

Governor Carver must have been astounded to hear his own language from a red man. He sent his young secretary, Edward Winslow, up to the hill with presents in his hand: a knife, a jewel for the ear, a pot of "strong water," a good quantity of biscuit, and some butter. They were gratefully accepted.

"Do you dare to walk among us alone?" Squanto asked Winslow.

"Where there is love there is no fear," the secretary answered.

Winslow was detained on the hill as a hostage, while Massasoit followed Squanto down to the stockade. The newest cabin in the colony was made ready to receive him. It was not much better than the royal longhouse at Mount Hope. A green rug had been laid on the earth floor, with three or four cushions on it. Driftwood blazed in the clay fireplace. The room was lighted by paper windows, and, when darkness fell, by bayberry dips. Little Miles Standish, with a file of six men, presented arms. To the sound of a trumpet and drum, Governor Carver himself entered. He bent his chin over Massasoit's hand and kissed it. He gave him a great draught of strong water, whereat the King's whole body broke into a sweat. He had never tasted liquor before. Massasoit sat all afternoon beside the Governor, trembling with fear. Before he started home he had put his mark to a treaty of alliance with King James I of England. The white men who had landed on his shore, with cuirasses instead of leather for armor, with muskets and cutlasses for weapons instead of arrows, with sailboats and rum and tobacco, were lucky allies for him. He called them Wautoconoag, which means "Men Who Wear Clothes."

Massasoit was a portly and dignified sachem of forty-one, grave of countenance and spare of speech. Once he had been subject to the Narragansetts, westward across the bay. A four-year plague, beginning in 1617, had so reduced his tribe that they were making ready to subdue him again. Once there had been three thousand Wampanoags; now there were hardly more fighting men than the sixty who attended the King to Plymouth. As a later governor put it snugly, "Providence was visible in thinning the Indians to make room for the English."

The dour John Winthrop in 1634 gloated that "The natives are neere all dead of the small poxe, so as the Lord hathe cleared our title to what we possess."

But the Pilgrims, so far, were the only Englishmen north of Virginia. They had hardly survived their first winter in the new world, and had nothing to lose by making friends with the Indians.

Four months later they sent an embassy to Mount Hope to return Massasoit's visit. They brought him a horseman's laced coat of red cotton, though he still had no horse, and a necklace of copper beads to serve as a passport for future visits. Since warm weather had come, the King had reversed his squirrel coat so the fur was on the outside. Not being forewarned of the visit, he had to do his hasty best. For the reception he donned his turkey-feather mantle, tied at the throat with twine. The English, squatting on skins outside his wigwam, shared the dried beef which the squaws brought from the storepit, and two tautog shot by the braves with bow and arrow. The King had forty guests that afternoon: two Englishmen and thirty-eight Indians. They smoked his pipe of hemlock and ground-up ivy. They played the dice-game which their host called Hubbub. They watched, in the flowery words of Lawyer Richmond,

> While at a distance on the greensward plain
> Elastick youth would drive their sports amain;
> The hairstuffed deerskin at the wicket bowl,
> Run with the wind to reach some distant goal,
> Toss high the quoit, or, limb with limb entwined,
> Essay the powers of skill and strength combined.

These are fancy words, but the Indian boys probably showed off their skill at skipping stones, for Bristol boys have been showing off to strangers that way ever since.

The English ambassadors slept that night on the same plank bed with the King, his wife, and two of his chiefs.

"We were worse weary of our lodging," they reported to Plymouth, "than with our journey. What with the savages' barbarous singing (for they are wont to sing themselves asleep), with lice and fleas within door and mosquitos without, we could hardly sleep all the time of our being there."

Claiming they must keep Sabbath at home, but actually "much fearing if we should stay any longer we should not be able to recover home for want of strength," they started back the next day, and rode into Plymouth on Saturday night.

In December, when the Pilgrims gave thanks for their first year of survival, Massasoit returned the visit. His braves killed four deer, and the King contributed them to the first Thanksgiving dinner.

Two years later, Winslow heard that Massasoit was on his deathbed. He visited him again. He found the royal wigwam so crowded with mourners that he could hardly elbow his way inside. Beside the pallet stood the King's wife, his brothers Quadequina and Akkompoin, and his medicine men.

Massasoit, who suffered from constipation, had not eaten for two days. He lay among the howling sorcerers with his eyes closed. His sight had gone.

"Kéen Winsnow?" he asked faintly, meaning "Art thou Winslow?" Indians could not pronounce the letter L.

"Ahhé," Winslow answered for yes.

"Matta néen wonckanet namen, Winsnow." ("Ah, Winslow, I shall never see thee again.")

But Winslow had brought with him from Plymouth "a confection of many comfortable conserves." He forced it between Massasoit's stiffening jaws with his knifeblade. When the King had swallowed a little of it, the ambassador washed out his mouth and scraped his furry tongue. Next day he sent couriers to Plymouth for some chickens, for poultry was unknown to the Indians. While they were gone, he brewed a vegetarian pottage out of strawberry leaves and sassafras—all he could find in March—which a squaw ground up with a little corn and boiled in a pipkin. He strained the broth through his own handkerchief and fed it to the King. The next meal was goose soup, thanks to a pretty bull's-eye of his blunderbuss at 120 yards. (The Indian word for goose was "honck.") The soup restored the King's eyesight but was too rich for his stomach. He vomited, and bled for four hours from the nose. But after the nose-bleed he slept for six hours. When he waked, Winslow washed his face and suppled his beard. By the time the chickens arrived, the King was well enough to order them saved for breeding instead of being slaughtered for broth. His friends came from as far as a hundred miles to see the miracle of his recovery and listen to his praises of his English friends.

Massasoit begat three sons—Wamsutta, Metacom, and Suconewhew—and two daughters, one named Amie and one whose name is lost. He lived to see his two older sons marry two sisters from across Mount Hope Bay. Weetamoe, the wife of Wamsutta, was in her own right Queen of Pocasset, the hillside which is now Tiverton, Rhode Island.

Over the rest of his long reign, he recklessly ceded tracts of his depopulated kingdom to the Pilgrims in exchange for weapons, horses, rum, and currency. This currency was wampumpeage, in two denominations. Wampum, the black, was ground from the dark eye of the quahog-shell, and peage, the white, from the neck of the periwinkle. A New England penny was worth 3 beads of wampum or 6 of peage. Large transactions were handled in fathoms of 360 beads apiece, strung on thongs. A beaver skin, for instance, generally traded for 18 feet of peage or 9 feet of wampum. It took more time for the squaws to grind and bore the quahog than it did to grind the periwinkle, which is the reason wampum commanded a premium, and what better basis for the value of money has ever been found?

Massasoit was equally friendly with the Puritans, who landed at Boston ten years after the Pilgrims landed at Plymouth. When Roger Williams fled from Salem in 1636, he made him a gift of what is now the town of Seekonk, Massachusetts. In 1649 he sold to Miles Standish a tract of 49 square miles around the present Bridgewater, for a consideration of 7 coats, 9 hatchets, 8 hoes, 29 knives, 4 moose skins, and 1½ yards of cotton cloth. In 1653 he sold Hog Island, only an hour by canoe from Mount Hope, to Richard Smith.

The English converted some of the Wampanoags to Christianity, and a good many more of the inland Nipmucks. Massasoit clung to his traditional gods: Kichtan for good and Abemecho for evil. He believed vaguely that Heaven lay in the southwest, the direction of fair-weather winds. Kichtan had made the first man and woman out of stone; when they proved unsatisfactory, he destroyed them and made another couple out of a tree. The Pilgrims' story of Noah and the flood was not much different. He was willing to let the Nipmucks, and even his own Wampanoags, accept the English God, provided he did not have to give up his own. He did not object when John Eliot, the Apostle to the Indians, carried Sassamon, his secretary, to study the new religion at Harvard, nor even when his own youngest boy, Suconewhew, went there too. But for himself, he was too old to change.

Other sachems were more receptive. When the Pilgrims asked them "to worship ye only true God, which made Heaven and earth, and not to blaspheme Him," one of them answered wistfully, "We do desire to reverence ye God of ye English, and to speak well of Him, because we see He doth better to ye English than other gods do to others."

Another chief, after a second epidemic, complained, "What is the matter with us Indians that we are thus sick in our own air, and these strangers well? 'Tis as if they were sent hither to inherit our lands in our steads. But the reason is plain: they love the great God, and we do not."

Born to the narrow freeholds of England, the settlers coveted the Indian lands. The deeds, written in English, were witnessed and recorded in the General Court at Plymouth. They took over the choicest fishing-grounds and cleared the woods of game. When their trade goods had long been spent or drunk up, the land was still theirs. Even so, Massasoit was so grateful to his allies that he petitioned the General Court at Plymouth to assign English names to his two older sons. The Pilgrims would not grant them Christian names, and the only two close relatives from pagan history who came to mind were the warrior kings of Macedon. In 1656 Wamsutta became Alexander, Metacom became Philip. The brothers were flattered by the comparison. Aware that the Greek name Philip means "a lover of horses," the Governor gave the young prince a black stallion. (The Pilgrims first imported horses in 1625.)

At best, Indian names confuse the historian. They were just as troublesome to the Pilgrims. A victory, a wedding, or a funeral was excuse enough for a Wampanoag to change his name. Massasoit himself, at various times, had five names. Queen Weetamoe, in early life, was called Napumpum. When an Indian's name was unpronounceable, the Pilgrims gave him one that a Christian *could* pronounce. The name of Wootenekanuske, the wife of Philip, they shortened to Nanuskooke, which is still not short enough. Washawanna, one of Philip's fighters, they called Bill. They changed the name of Petononowet, who was one of Weetamoe's husbands, to Peter Nannuit. When that still sounded too long, they just called him Ben. The real name of Tobias, mentioned later, was Poggapanoffoo.

The English called their converts Praying Indians. They made them bailiffs and marshals in the villages around Boston, let them attend court and serve on juries, and even placed some of them over the white constables. The copper-skinned magistrate of the Praying Village at Natick issued this mandamus to his white assistant:

> You, you big constable! Quick you catch um Jeremiah Offscow, strong you hold um, safe you bring um before me—Waban, Justice of Peace.

When a new magistrate asked Waban what he did when the non-praying Indians got drunk and quarreled with one another, he told him, "Tie um all up and whip um plaintiff, whip um fendant, whip um witness."

The converted Indians hung around the fringes of the settlements, helping the English cultivate their corn, butchering their hogs in the fall, and digging clams or treading eels for them in exchange for food and rum. The English settlers at Weymouth, a village between Plymouth and Boston, complained that the Indians plucked their food from the kettles before they could get at it themselves.

Most of the sachems resented the conversions, and the tolerant Roger Williams at Providence agreed with them. In 1654 he wrote the Puritan governor of Massachusetts Bay:

> At my last departure for England, I was importuned by the Narragansett Indians to present to the high sachems of England that they might not be forced from their religions, and, for not changing them, be invaded by war. For they say they are daily visited with threatenings by [Praying] Indians that come from about the Massachusetts, that if they would not pray, they should be destroyed by war. Are not all the English of this land generally a persecuted people from their native land? and hath not the God of peace and Father of mercies made the native more friendly to us in this land than our countrymen in our own? Are not our families grown up in peace amongst them? Upon which I humbly ask how it can suit with Christian ingenuity to take hold of some seeming occasions for their destruction.

II

Massasoit died in 1661, at the venerable age of eighty-one. The haughty Alexander, his oldest son, succeeded him. The Pilgrims at once ordered him to Plymouth, to show proof that he would be as loyal as his father. They offered him a horse for the hot midsummer trip. Since they did not offer one to Queen Weetamoe too, he declined it and walked beside her, at the head of eighty braves, the whole long march of the Plymouth trail. The Pilgrims' suspicions, which seem to have been well founded, so outraged him that he broke into a burning fever before his trial began. Fuller, their doctor, gave him a "portion of working physic," but it made him worse. Weetamoe got their permission to take her husband home for treatment by his own medicine men, leaving their two sons with the Pilgrims as hostages. She suspected Dr. Fuller had poisoned him.

Alexander's braves hoisted him on their shoulders and started westward through the woods. On Taunton River they saw that his end was near. Beaching their canoes, they laid him on a grassy mound beneath an oak tree. Weetamoe cradled his head as he died. He had reigned only a year.

Philip succeeded his brother. He was twenty-four years old. On the rock now called King Philip's Throne, on the east side of Mount Hope, he donned the nine-inch stole of wampum, fringed with red deerskin and embroidered with beasts and birds, the headband with two flags behind, the breastplate engraved with a star, and the scarlet cloak which were his "royalties." Paul Revere's crude portrait of him, engraved a century later from imagination, and a hostile one at that, shows him as a square-set man of medium height, with a faint beard, standing before Mount Hope in his regalia, with bare legs above his moccasins, a musket in his hand, and a tomahawk and powder-horn at his feet. But it is likely that he was taller than most of the English, and doubtful that, at his age, he wore a beard.

One of Philip's hands was scarred from the explosion of a pistol. He had undergone the tests of manhood. He had spent the winter alone in the forest with only a bow and arrow, a hatchet and knife to defend himself against the wolves and wildcats. He had drunk the juice of poisonous herbs, with the medicine men standing by with emetics in case of danger, until he had proved himself immune. Legend says that, with the Devil to help him, Philip could throw a stone across the harbor from the crest of Mount Hope to Poppasquash, two miles away.

Like Weetamoe, he believed that it was English poison and not a broken heart that had killed Alexander. He was determined to avenge his brother. So fierce were his loyalties that he had once pursued the Indian called John Gibbs all the way to Nantucket Island, across forty miles of open water, because he had spoken ill of the dead Massasoit. Somehow the traducer escaped him in the dunes, but Philip would not leave the island till the English gave him all the money they could scrape together. It came to nineteen shillings.

King Philip's mark

Though Massasoit had been too old for Eliot to convert, and Alexander too indifferent, Philip at least gave him a hearing. In the winter of 1663–64, just after his accession, he sent to the Apostle for "books to learn to read and to pray to God." They did not persuade him; soon afterward, meeting the Apostle, he shook him by the coat-button and told him, in the Nipmuck dialect they both understood, "I care no more for your gospel than for this button."

By Massasoit's treaty, the English had agreed to respect the Indians' land. There was certainly enough for both. The treaty made it illegal for an Englishman to buy land from an Indian without the consent of the General Court at Plymouth. This rule was designed to protect the Indians from fraud, for it had never occurred to them that they owned the land anyway; they simply occupied it. Massasoit's generosity, and the greed of the colonists, made the law impossible to enforce. When Philip belatedly saw that he was not sharing his territory with the white men, but losing it to them, he determined to keep what little was left. His English friend John Borden reports that he told him, "But little remains of my ancestors' domain. I am resolved not to see the day when I have no country."

One of his surviving letters to the Governor of Plymouth Colony, probably in the hand of John Sassamon, shows his state of mind:

KING PHILIP desire to let you understand that he could not come to the Court, for Tom his interpreter has a pain in his back, that he could not travil so far, and Philip sister is very sick. Philip would entreat that favor of you and aney of the majestrates, if aney English or Enjians speak about aney land, he pray you to give them no answer at all. This last somer he made that promis with you, that he

would sell no land in 7 yers time, for he would have no English
trouble him before that time. He has not forget that you promis him.
He will come as sune as possible he can speak with you, and so I rest
                                  Your verey loveing friend
                                       Philip, dwelling at mount hope nek.

To the much honored
Governor, Mr. Thomas Prince
dwelling at Plymouth.

In 1671 he confirmed his father's treaty at a conference in the
Taunton meeting house, where the English sat on one side of the
aisle and the Indians on the other. Later in the same year he even
agreed to pay tribute to the Pilgrims, but did all he could to evade it
by pleading poverty:

> I am willing and do promise to pay unto the government of Plym-
> outh one hundred pounds in such things as I have, but would en-
> treat the favour that I might have three years to pay it in, forasmuch
> as I do not have it at present. I do promise to send unto the Gover-
> nor, or whom he shall appoint, five wolves' heads, if I can get them;
> or as many as I can procure until they come to five wolves yearly.

The settlers no longer needed the friendship of Indians. Three
times they summoned Philip, as they had summoned Alexander, to
answer charges of conspiracy. The first time, he meekly gave up
the seventy guns his braves had brought with them. The braves
were disgusted, for they had almost forgotten how to hunt with
bow and arrow, and even though they did not know how to repair
the guns themselves, there was a friendly English blacksmith
named Uriah Leonard, near Fowling Pond, who was always ready
to forge their spare parts from the bog-iron nearby—though he
broke the law when he did so.

In return for the seventy muskets, the settlers promised that all
future charges should be arbitrated by the Puritans of the Province
of Massachusetts Bay. The Puritans were richer, more numerous,
and sharper than their Pilgrim brethren at Plymouth, but Plymouth
had the advantage of seniority and was respectfully referred to as
the Old Colony. The Puritans deferred to the sanctity of the Pilgrims,

who, in return, were forever asking their help and advice. A saying grew up that the Plymouth saddle was always on the Bay horse.

The second time the Pilgrims complained, Philip went to Boston direct and convinced the Puritans that the charges against him were unfounded. The third time, he wrote angrily back to Plymouth, "Your governor is but a subject. I shall treat only with my brother, King Charles of England. When he comes, I am ready."

By 1671 there were perhaps forty thousand Englishmen in all New England, and only half as many Indians.* Before long there would be none at all, unless the English were driven out. They were beginning to surround Mount Hope itself. They had built a garrison house on Swansea to the north, and settled in numbers on Aquidneck, or Rhode Island, to the south, across the channel. Queen Awashonks of Sakonnet, whose kingdom adjoined Queen Weetamoe's, had sold land on the east side of Mount Hope Bay, within sight of King Philip's lodges, to an English carpenter named Benjamin Church. Philip himself, in spite of his resolution, sold off the present New Bedford in 1665, and in 1670 granted one hundred acres only a mile west of Pokanoket to a certain John Gorham. In all, he sold some thirty-five square miles in the nine years after his brother's death, at an average price of elevenpence an acre. But legally Mount Hope was still sovereign Indian territory, hemmed in on the north by the Baptist colony of Providence Plantations, on the south by the Quakers of Rhode Island, on the east by the Pilgrims themselves, and on the west by Narragansett Bay.

Philip had many grievances. The English let their cattle destroy the Indian cornfields, which were never fenced. In any lawsuit, they took the word of a single Praying Indian against that of twenty unconverted ones. As Philip told John Easton, a Quaker who ferried over from the Island to pacify him, "The English are so eager to sell the Indians liquor that most of the Indians spend all in drunkenness, and then raven upon the sober Indians."

The Pilgrim clergy kept one eye on Heaven and the other on

---

* The population of the four colonies is estimated at: Connecticut, 10,000; Rhode Island, 4000; Plymouth, 5000; and Massachusetts Bay, 17,000.

earth. This land, they sincerely believed, belonged to God. He had chosen them to bring it back to Him, and the Indians with it, if they would come. The Indians did not share this view—not even the Praying Indians.

The Wampanoags alone were too weak to attack the English, but Philip dreamed of an alliance with other tribes, from the Kennebec to the Hudson. They had never united before; it was their jealousies which had given the English their power, as the English themselves well knew. In the winter of 1674–75 he dispatched John Sassamon, his Praying Secretary, across Mount Hope Bay by canoe, with half a dozen others of his council, to draw the Squaw Sachem Awashonks into his conspiracy. She had an army of three hundred. She honored his envoys with a ceremonial dance. But as it began the unreliable Sassamon, with one of her own council named Honest George, slipped down to Church's farm to warn him of the plot. Church, unarmed, alone, and uninvited, followed them back to her wigwam. He found Awashonks herself, in a foaming sweat—the phrase is his—leading the dance. When he walked through the tent flap, she broke off the festivities and called him before her.

Church was a married man of thirty-five. If his Bristol descendants favor him, he was not bad-looking. Awashonks was the widow of a chief called Tolony. Her age is unknown now, and was perhaps a secret even then. She had a grown son named Peter, so can hardly have been younger than her uninvited guest. Church does not boast, but it is clear that he pleased her.

Inside the lodge, King Philip's men crowded around him "in the posture of war." Their faces and chests were painted with totems of yellow and red. Their hair was trimmed to a coxcomb. Some wore rattlesnake skins down their backs. Their shotbags and powderhorns hung from their shoulders. Church felt the shotbags and asked what they were for.

"To shoot pigeons with," was the mocking answer.

Church turned to the Queen in their presence and told her, "If Philip is resolved to make war, the best thing for Your Majesty will be to knock all these Mounthopes on the head and shelter yourself with me for protection. For my part, I desire nothing more than peace, yet if nothing but war will satisfy them, I believe I shall prove a sharp thorn in their sides."

His boldness drew him a promise that Awashonks and her army would at least be neutral if war should come. Enraged at her defection, Philip had the treacherous Sassamon murdered. (Among other knaveries, he had drawn up a will for Philip, who could neither read nor write, which left all the Mount Hope lands to himself.)

Philip's assassins bludgeoned Sassamon on the shores of Middleboro Pond. There was still ice on the pond that March of 1675. To pretend he had drowned on a hunting trip, they pushed his corpse under the ice and left his gun and a brace of ducks on the bank nearby. The English caught them anyway, and tried them before a mixed jury of white men and red. William Sabin of Seekonk was foreman. The Reverend Increase Mather from Boston attended the trial. (To the Plymouth colony, Increase and his son Cotton were the very voice of God.) He reports that Tobias, one of the three accused Indians, was proved guilty by the fact that Sassamon's body bled afresh when he approached it. All three were convicted. Two were hanged. The third was reprieved for a month, then shot.

The execution enraged Philip. He claimed that foreigners had no right to punish Indians who murdered other Indians. Worst of all, the trial exposed his conspiracy. Now he dared wait no longer to attack, though he was not quite ready for war. He spent the rest of the spring, afoot or in a canoe or astride his black horse, hurrying among the tribes as far west as the Connecticut River, bribing and cajoling them to join him and rid the country of the English forever. His father's old enemies the Narragansetts, across the bay, promised him four thousand fighting men, though it is doubtful they had that many. The Nipmucks from the west promised to attack the exposed English settlements along the Connecticut.

Philip held a two-week war dance atop Mount Hope. The visiting chieftains, the medicine men, and the oldest squaws squatted in a ring around the bonfire. The braves stood behind them, and the rabble milled on the outskirts. Each brave, as the name of an English settlement was called out, picked up a firebrand, danced around the circle in a mock battle with the flame, and finally conquered the town by quenching the torch in the earth.

In 1836 an Indian preacher with the strange name of William Apes wrote a eulogy on Philip. He states that Philip delivered this speech at the war dance:

> BROTHERS! You see this vast country before us, which the Great Spirit gave to our fathers and us; you see the buffalo and deer which are now our support. Brothers, you see the little ones, our wives and children, who are looking to us for food and raiment; and you now see the foe before you, that they have grown insolent and bold; that all our ancient customs are disregarded; the treaties made by our fathers and us are broken, and all of us insulted; our council fires disregarded, and all the ancient customs of our fathers; our brothers murdered before our eyes, and their spirits cry to us for revenge. Brothers, these people from the unknown world will cut down our groves, spoil our hunting and planting grounds, and drive us and our children from the graves of our fathers and our council fires, and enslave our women and children.

But since buffalo have never been sighted on Mount Hope, it is probable that the Reverend Mr. Apes made up the speech himself.

Philip was ruthless and sentimental, wily and indecisive, noble and niggardly, all at the same time. His sorcerers, in snakeskin cloaks and wooden masks, consulted their oracles—the notes of the whippoorwill? the entrails of the owl?—and reported that no Englishman would ever kill him. That was enough for him. He sent a canoe up Mount Hope Bay to warn his English friend Hugh Cole to fly before it was too late. It was a favor that might have cost him the war. Then he let the war begin, though it is said he threw himself weeping to the ground as he gave the command.

It was a superstition that the side which shed first blood would lose. On Sunday, June 20, 1675, while the settlers of nearby Swansea were at meeting, the Indians shot some of their cattle. This did not count as bloodshed, perhaps, but was enough to drive them from their scattered thatch roofs to the shelter of their garrison house. Philip ransacked their farmsteads without hindrance. On Wednes-

day a lad named John Salisbury, emerging from the garrison to
salvage his geese, found their necks wrung and a band of Indians
searching his father's keeping-room for rum. He fired into the band
and wounded one Indian. First blood was thus shed by the English.
Next day the Indians returned. They murdered the boy, and his
father with him.

The frightened settlers sent a messenger to Plymouth for help. A
troop of thirty-six under Captain Matthew Fuller (not the surgeon who had physicked King Alexander) reached Swansea on
the twenty-eighth. Benjamin Church was second in command.
Weighted down by their heavy buff coats, their breastplates, swords,
carbines, and pistols, they had taken four days to march from the
Old Colony. Behind the infantry lumbered the pack train. The
troops' ration was biscuit, dried fish, pork, oil, raisins, sugar, peas,
wine, and rum. Another "army" arrived from Boston, under command of General Cudworth. It was equipped with hunting dogs.
One-third of each troop were armed with fourteen-foot pikes, and
two-thirds with matchlock muskets so long that they required a
forked rest for the barrel. It took fifty-six separate motions to fire a
matchlock.

By the time the two details converged at Swansea, six Englishmen had been tomahawked in the village. The troops killed six
Indians in revenge. Marching down the Kickemuit River, 176 strong,
to besiege Mount Hope, they found eight more flayed heads on poles,
and the torn leaves of a Bible scattered blasphemously on the ground
below. It did not reassure them to see an eclipse that night, with a
shadow on the moon in the shape of a human scalp, nor to learn
that Indians had discovered the practice of impalement.

Although General Cudworth of the Massachusetts militia was
ranking officer, this was a Plymouth war. Command devolved on
Captain Fuller, but he excused himself from action as being "ancient
and heavy." He sent Lieutenant Church ahead with half of the army
to attack Mount Hope frontally, and set the other half to building a
fort in case Philip should attack *him*.

Church did not believe in static warfare. He fought as the Indians did themselves. He had heard one of them say, "The English always keep in a heap together, so it is as easy to hit them as to hit a house." Church's troop of Englishmen crept down to Mount Hope, sometimes waist deep in the swamp and sometimes on their bellies in the grass, but always deployed at a distance from one another.

They found the hill deserted. Philip was too wily to let himself be trapped on a peninusla. He had shipped the squaws and papooses across Narragansett Bay to shelter with his allies on that side of the water. The cornfields, unhoed, were choked with weeds. Church and his men trampled down a thousand acres of cropland. The Boston mastiffs brought in half a dozen of Philip's pigs that had been left behind in the evacuation. A Dutch soldier of fortune named Cornelius, who served with the Boston troop, came across Philip's cap; how *it* was left behind is not clear.

Church decided that there was only one direction Philip could have taken: eastward across Mount Hope Bay to the kingdom of his sister-in-law Weetamoe. He ferried across to Aquidneck and wheeled left to the straits which divide it from Pocasset. On the far side he caught sight of the enemy, lurking in the bushes at the top of the hill. Church was a humorist as well as a soldier and a diplomat. In his *Entertaining History of King Philip's War* he writes:

> The Indians had a fort on the opposite side of the river, and showed themselves, and acted all manner of mockery to aggravate the English, they being at more than a common gunshot off. At one time one made his appearance, and turned his backside in defiance as usual; but someone having an uncommonly long gun fired upon him and put an end to his mimicry.

He lashed some logs together into a raft and led a detail of seventeen men across the strait. On the far side he took cover under the fence in John Almy's peasefield. There were more Indians on the hill than he had thought: three hundred of them, it turned out afterward. The Battle of the Peasefield lasted six hours. The English

advanced as far as a well on the far side of the field, but were driven
back by a rain of bullets from the stumps and boulders above them.
At last their ammunition gave out, and they retreated to the shore.
By luck a Quaker sloop from the Island came sailing through the
strait just in time to rescue them. Two by two, she took them off in
a canoe, but not before Church, under fire, made his way alone
once more across the peasefield to retrieve his hat and cutlass, which
he had left behind at the well.

A few days later, with some reluctant reinforcement from Captain
Fuller, he made another assault on the hill. This time he had better
luck. The Indians fled before him. At the Pocasset cedar swamp, in
the kingdom of the ex-Queen Weetamoe, the first of the royal family
fell: Philip's young brother, Suconewhew, who had studied at Harvard.

Church drove the Indians northward toward the Taunton River,
where an English fort commanded the ford. He hoped to trap them
between two fires, but Philip outflanked the fort by crossing the
river above it on a raft at low tide. He escaped to the open west with
his dogs and his black horse. His army was almost intact.

He was now outside the borders of the Plymouth Colony. Except
for a skeleton guard over the prisoners taken in the Pocasset cedar
swamp, the armies of Plymouth and Massachusetts, which had taken
the field on June 24, disbanded on July 19. The campaign had been
short. Church got back to his farm in Awashonks's kingdom in time
for the fall harvest.

The strategists of the two colonies saw that Philip's escape meant
that the war might spread westward toward the Hudson, and that
he might return with reinforcements to attack them again. On July 15
they forced a treaty on the Narragansetts, who were still sheltering
the Wampanoag women and children. It promised them immunity
and set a bounty of two yards of cloth, worth five shillings the yard,
for each Wampanoag scalp they brought in, four yards for each live
Wampanoag, forty for Philip's scalp, and eighty for Philip alive.
Trusting to the treaty, 150 Narragansetts trudged into Plymouth to

put themselves under the colony's protection. No Wampanoag scalps were ever delivered, but for three months the Narragansetts were at least neutralized.

Philip himself was 120 miles to the northwest. From a camp on the Hudson among the Mohawks, at what is now Schaghticoke, New York, he directed the summer campaign. Though there is no record that he appeared in battle himself, all the western reaches of the English colonies were terrorized by the lightning raids of his warriors. On August 4 they besieged Brookfield. In September they burned Deerfield and attacked Hadley and Northfield. On the eighteenth they killed ninety Englishmen guarding a provision train from Deerfield to Hadley. On the twenty-eighth, at Northampton, they scalped Praisever Turner and Unzakaby Shakespeare when they ventured too far from the garrison house in search of firewood. On October 5 they burned thirty-two houses in Springfield, and on the ninth, with a troop of eight hundred, they attacked Hatfield, but were repulsed.

Clad in the wamus, a slipover buckskin hunting jacket, and shod with noiseless moccasins, they shot flaming arrows into the settlers' thatched roofs. They pushed firewagons against the log walls, edging them forward at the ends of lashed poles from as far away as seventy yards. That distance was about the effective range of the colonists' muskets. When the Indians broke through, they had no mercy.

Luck was not always on Philip's side. Sometimes a providential rain extinguished the firebrands. The settlers' own muskets, if the range was close enough, accounted for many of the enemy. At the attack on Hadley, says legend, a bearded stranger emerged from Parson Russell's attic, rallied the defenders, and vanished as mysteriously as he had appeared. They thought he was an angel. Long afterward they learned that he was William Goffe, one of the Roundhead judges who had condemned Charles I to the ax in 1649. He was hiding now in the new world from the long-armed vengeance of Charles II.

In one battle Captain Samuel Mosely, commanding sixty English

against three hundred Indians, plucked off his periwig and stuffed
it in his breeches for greater freedom of action. A chronicler says:

> As soon as the Indians saw that, they fell a Howling and Yelling
> most hideously. One of them called out in terror,
> "Umh! umh! Me no stay more fight Engismon. Engismon got two
> Hed. If me cut off un Hed he got noder, a put on beder as dis,"
> with suchlike words in broken English, and away they all fled and
> could not be overtaken, nor seen any more afterwards.

The Indians were merciless to the men they captured, but never
mistreated the women. At Northfield they hung up two Englishmen
on chains, with hooks under their jaws. The colonists, whose status
as God's chosen exempted them from conscience, were no less cruel.
At Springfield they ordered an old squaw "to be torn in pieces by
dogs, and she was so dealt withal." At Natick they massacred 126
Indians, including a squaw whom Increase Mather describes as
"an old piece of venom."

Cruelest of all were the Indians who fought for the English. In
Boston once, the Puritans were in the long process of executing an
Indian prisoner by hoisting him to the gallows with a rope at his
neck, and letting him down again three or four times to prolong
his departure. Another Indian, a friend of his, stepped forward,
drove a knife into him, and sucked out his heart-blood. He explained
to the spectators, "Me stronger as I was before. Me be so strong as
me and he too. He be very strong man fore he die."

The Indians bore torture bravely. Major Talcott of Connecticut
once let his own Indians execute a Wampanoag whom they had captured. They cut off his fingers and toes one by one, slicing each
knuckle-joint and then breaking the bone. At last they broke his legs.

"How do you like the war?" they asked him.

"I like it very well," the victim said. "I find it as sweet as the
Englishmen do their sugar."

The war was no longer local. It was known that the Narragansetts
had a great fort in the swamp west of what is now Kingston, Rhode
Island. Hospitality was sacred to them. Besides the Wampanoag
women and children whom they already sheltered, and in spite of

the bounty offered by the July treaty, they gave refuge to Philip's wounded and the aged who could not keep up with his fast-moving campaign. There was a chance that Philip might himself be in the camp, for he had not been seen since his escape at Pocasset. Spies reported that Weetamoe, his sister-in-law, was surely there, with her current husband. The fact that the Narragansetts had not surrendered her was excuse enough for the English to attack them. As one colonist put it, "If she be but taken, her lands will more than pay for all the charges we have been at in this unhappy war."

Canonchet, the Narragansett sachem, was summoned to Boston. On October 18 he signed a second treaty, agreeing to give Weetamoe up within ten days. The Governor of Plymouth, Josiah Winslow (he was the son of Massasoit's friend Edward), gave him a silver-trimmed coat as a reward. The ten days passed, but Weetamoe was not delivered. The ultimatum having expired, Plymouth sold off the 150 Narragansetts who had surrendered in July. They were shipped to Cadiz, Spain, as slaves—"sent off by the Treasurer," in the politer words of the official record. They averaged two shillings and twopence a head.

On November 2 the United Colonies of Plymouth, Massachusetts Bay, and Connecticut declared war on the Narragansetts. (The peaceful Quakers of the Island and the Baptists of Providence, separated from each other by Mount Hope itself, took no part in the hostilities.) They mustered an army 1000 strong, under the command of Governor Winslow. There were 158 from Plymouth, 527 from Massachusetts Bay, and 315 from Connecticut, not counting teamsters, servants, and "volunteers." Winslow offered Benjamin Church the command of a company. Church, who had no taste for the classic warfare which was the only kind the Governor understood, declined. But he promised, as he puts it, to "wait upon him through the expedition as a Reformado," which means what is now called a guerrilla.

The three contingents were to make contact at Richard Smith's garrison house, which still stands, greatly altered, near Wickford on the west shore of Narragansett Bay. Church got there by sloop several days before they arrived overland. He had captured eighteen Indians by the time the regulars marched in.

The regulars were uniformed in leather jerkins and breeches and wore Monmouth caps on their heads. Their arms were a four-foot musket and a bandolier which held a pound of powder, twenty bullets, and two fathom-length of match. They had no tents; each night of the march down from Providence they had slept under blankets on the frozen ground. But they had taken forty-seven prisoners themselves. Captain Nathaniel Davenport of the 5th Massachusetts Company bought them in for his own account as slaves at the bargain price of £80 in silver for the lot.

The Narragansett fortress, which was under Canonchet's command, covered a four-acre rise in the middle of the trackless swamp, eighteen miles inland from the garrison house. The English might not have found it at all if Peter Freeman, one of Church's Indian prisoners, had not guided them. It was hidden from sight, even on a clear day, by a jungle of cedars. On December 19, 1675, the day of the assault, it was snowing hard, and there was a two-foot fall by afternoon. That was almost the shortest day of the year, with the sun setting by four o'clock. The fort had been designed by an Indian engineer called Stonewall John, with the help of Joshua Tift, a renegade white man. Inside it, three thousand Indians were crowded into five hundred wigwams. Their winter provisions, in tubs hollowed out of sawn-off butternut trunks, were stacked against the walls to deaden the English bullets. The fort was even equipped with a forge for the repair of ordnance. Around its perimeter a sixteen-foot abatis of felled trees, with the branches forward, was backed by a stockade of logs. The only bridge between the fort and the tussocks of the swamp was a single log, with the inner end set between four-foot palisades with loopholes in them.

The attack began at two in the afternoon, while the squaws were preparing dinner inside the fort. As fast as the English ventured onto the log, the Indians shot them from the loopholes, and they toppled into the icy stream. Six captains went down. Among them was Davenport, who had just paid £80 for his slaves.

Away from the stream, the stagnant swamp was frozen over. Church, who had been stationed on solid ground with the Governor's staff, saw his chance. With thirty men, he crossed the ice and broke into the fort from the flank, through the tangle of the abatis. It was a feat which, under heavy armor, would have been impossible in a thaw and was almost a miracle now in the twilight and the snow. In his own modest words,

> He encouraged his company and ran right on, till he was struck with three bullets; one in his thigh, which was near cut off as it glanced on the joint of his hip-bone; another through the gatherings of his breeches and drawers with a small flesh wound; a third pierced his pocket and wounded a pair of mittens he had borrowed of Capt. Prentice, which, being wrapped together, had the misfortune of having many holes cut through them with a single bullet.

His troop poured through the breach behind him. After a hopeless hand-to-hand fight, the Indians fled through the dark across the ice into the fastness of the swamp. "They run, they run!" someone shouted over the tumult. A few squaws strapped their papooses to their backs and plodded away through the drifts. They had no time nor strength to carry anything else into the blizzard. Most were left behind, cowering in the wigwams.

The regulars prepared to fire the camp. Church tried to dissuade them, if only because the English would need the shelter and provision for themselves. Since he was only a Reformado, no one listened. In the darkness and terror, it was easier to burn the wigwams than to spare them. He dragged himself back to Governor Winslow, also titled General, to plead against the burning.

> The general [his story goes on] moved toward the fort, designing to ride in himself and bring in the whole army; but just as he was entering it one of his captains met him, and asked whither he was going. He told him, "Into the fort." The captain laid hold of his horse and told him his life was worth a hundred of theirs, and that he should not expose himself. The general answered that he supposed the brunt was over, and that Mr. Church had informed him the fort was taken, and he was of the mind that it was most practicable for him and his army to shelter themselves therein. The captain replied

in a great heat that Church lied, and told the general that if he moved another step toward the fort he would shoot his horse under him.

Then bristled up another gentleman, a certain doctor, and opposed Mr. Church's advice, and said that if it were complied with, it would kill more men than the enemy had killed. And looking upon Mr. Church, and seeing the blood flow apace from his wounds, told him that if he gave such advice as that was, he should bleed to death like a dog before he would endeavor to stanch his blood.

They prevailed against Mr. Church's advice. Burning up all the houses and provisions in the fort, the army returned that night [to Smith's garrison house] in the storm and cold. And I suppose that everyone who is acquainted with that night's march deeply laments the miseries that attended them, especially the wounded and dying men. Some of the enemy that were then in the fort have since informed us that near a third of all the Indians belonging to the Narragansett country were killed by the English or by the cold of that night; that they fled out of their fort so hastily that they carried nothing with them; and that if the English had kept in the fort, the Indians would certainly have been necessitated either to surrender themselves or to have perished by hunger and the severity of the season.

As it was, 207 of the colonial militia were killed that day or died that night, jolting through the blizzard to the garrison house on sapling stretchers slung from the muskets of their comrades. The Indians lost perhaps 500 fighting men. Another 500 women, children, and invalids, in spite of Church's effort to spare them, were burned to death. Only a few survived. Cotton Mather exulted:

> We have heard of two and twenty Indian captains slain, all of them brought down to Hell in one day. When they came to see the ashes of their friends, mingled with the ashes of their fort, and the Bodies of so many of their Country terribly *Barbikew'd,* where the English had been doing a good day's work, they Howl'd, they Roar'd, they Stamp'd, they Tore their hair; and though they did not swear (for they know not how) yet they Curs'd, and were the pictures of so many *Devils* in Desperation.

And his father Increase exclaimed, "So let all thine enemies perish, O Lord!"

III

After the victory, the colonies again foolishly disbanded their army. Queen Weetamoe escaped from the swamp. King Philip, after all, had not been in it but in his camp on the Hudson. Canonchet led the surviving Narragansetts westward to join him. There was no doubt now which side he was on. On the way across the Nipmuck country he joined forces with Philip's field commander Anawon, whom Church describes as "a great surly old fellow." For four months, while Church recovered from his wounds at home, the two tribes harried the English settlements almost without hindrance.

On February 2, 1676, they plundered and burned Lancaster, halfway from Boston to the Connecticut River. Among their prisoners was Mrs. Joseph Rowlandson, the minister's wife. The warrior who captured her was a Narragansett named Monoco, alias One-eyed John. He gave her as lady's maid to Queen Weetamoe.

This insatiate squaw sachem, the widow of Philip's brother, Alexander, had five husbands in her lifetime. Alexander had been her second. After his death she had remarried thrice. She never forgot that she was a queen in her own right. Her fourth husband, Petononowet, had been a commoner, and pro-English besides. She had discarded this unworthy consort. She was now married to Quinnapin, her fifth. Although he was better born than Petononowet, she refused to eat from the same bowl with him. Mrs. Rowlandson has left a vivid description of her mistress:

> A severe and proud dame she was, bestowing every day on dressing herself near as much time as any of the gentry of the land, powdering her hair and painting her face, going with her necklaces, with jewels in her ears and bracelets upon her hands. When she had dressed herself, her work was to make girdles of wampum and beads.

Cotton Mather said of her, "She was next unto Philip in respect to the mischief that hath been done and the blood that hath been shed in this warr."

Both ladies, the Indian Queen and the English captive, must have been a burden in the field. Weetamoe had a furious temper. She slapped Mrs. Rowlandson's face if she complained of the weight of her pack-load. When the captive refused to give up her apron to make a breech-clout for Philip's nine-year-old son (who was getting old enough to need one), she took after her with a cudgel. As for Mrs. Rowlandson herself, she must have been a nuisance of a different kind to the braves. She behaved herself among them, says a chronicler, with so much majestic gravity that, in their rude manner, they seemed to show her great respect.

The Mohawks of the Hudson had given Philip no help. When he attacked three of their men in the woods near the Schaghticoke camp, hoping the English would be blamed, one of them recovered and accused him instead. The angry Mohawks set upon him, and he just escaped with his life. He fled eastward, desperately short of provisions. At what is now South Vernon, Vermont, Weetamoe and the few survivors of the swamp fight met him on March 8, 1676.

For Mrs. Rowlandson, at least, life now became easier. Philip commissioned her to make him a shirt. When she brought it to him, says she,

> . . . he bade me come in and sit down, and asked whether I would smoke (a usual compliment now among Saints and Sinners), but this no way suited me. For though I had formerly used Tobacco, yet I had left it ever since I was taken. It seems to be a bait the Devil lays to make men lose their precious time; I remember with shame how formerly, when I had taken two or three pipes, I was presently ready for another, such a bewitching thing it is. But I thank God he has now given me power over it; surely there are many who might be better employed than to lie sucking a stinking Tobacco-pipe.

Though she declined King Philip's tobacco, she accepted the shilling which he gave her in its place, and spent it on a slab of horsemeat. When she made a shirt and cap for his boy, he was so pleased that he asked her to dinner and made his wife bake her a pancake the size of two fingers, rolled of parched wheat and fried in bear's grease. It was a generous reward, for the destitute camp had to subsist on acorns, artichokes, lily roots, skunks, snakes, birchbark, and even the feet of horses, besides the dependable but monotonous groundnuts. There was not enough money to buy anything better, with corn selling at two shillings a pint. Philip once had to unstring his wampum cloak and use it to buy provisions from some friendly Mohawks.

Under such circumstances, Mrs. Rowlandson gambled that he would be glad to be rid of her for a reasonable price. She asked him if he would ransom her to Parson Rowlandson for £20, which was ten times the going price for Indian slaves. "He answered Nux," she relates, "which did rejoice my spirit."

In spite of its sound, "Nux" meant yes. Along with her appeal for the ransom, Philip sent this message to Plymouth:

> . . . . You know and we know your heart great sorrowful with crying for your lost many many hundred men and all your house and all your land and woman, child and cattle as all your thing that you have lost and on your backside stand. . . .

To this defiance he let Mrs. Rowlandson add a plea to her husband for three pounds of tobacco, besides the ransom money. Later in the spring the English negotiators arrived at Philip's camp, near what is now Worcester, Massachusetts, with sashes at their waists and ribbons on their shoulders as flags of truce. They brought the £20 to Philip in silver, but only one pound of tobacco to Mrs. Rowlandson, who did not need it anyway. She sold it to Philip for 9 shillings, rather than smoke it herself.

The redemption was preceded by a four-pair quadrille in which Weetamoe and Quinnapin joined, besides Philip and his wife Nanuskooke.

> The king my master [Mrs. Rowlandson writes, meaning Quinnapin] was dressed in his holland shirt, with great laces sewn at the ends of it; he had six silver buttons; his white stockings, his garters hung round with shillings, and had girdles with wampum upon his head and shoulders. Weetamoe had a Kersey coat covered with girdles of wampum from the loins upward. Her arms from her elbows to her hands were covered with bracelets; there were handfuls of

necklaces about her neck and several sorts of jewels in her ears. She had fine red stockings and white shoes; her hair powdered that was always before black. And all the dancers were after the same manner. There were two others singing and knocking on a kettle for their music. They kept hopping up and down one after another, with a kettle of water in their midst, standing upon some embers to drink of when they were dry. They held on till it was almost night, throwing out wampum to the standers-by. . . .

The water in the kettle was "strong water." Quinnapin, whom someone else has described as "a young lusty sachem and a very rogue," drank too much of it. He politely offered some to Mrs. Rowlandson, but she, having abjured tobacco, was not likely to succumb to alcohol. He was the first Indian she saw drunk all the time she was a prisoner. At last Weetamoe broke out of the formation, and he after her, around the wigwam, with his money jingling at his knees. But she escaped him, so he pounced on one of his two other wives.

"Through the Lord's mercy," writes the captive, "we were no more troubled that night."

Philip, however, came up and took her by the hand. "In two weeks," he told her, "you will be your own mistress. When did you wash yourself last?"

"Not this month," she confessed.

The king himself fetched her some water and a looking-glass. He ordered Nanuskooke to feed her; the squaw boiled her a mess of beans and meat, with a cake of groundnuts.

"I was wonderfully revived," writes Mrs. Rowlandson, "by this favor showed me. Psalms 106:46.—*He made them also to be pitied of all those that carried them captives.*"

In the Nipmuck country in the valley of the Connecticut, Philip's spring campaign promised well. At a war council in Northfield, Canonchet and he decided to strike still farther east, into the heart of the colonies. This time Philip took the field himself. Astride the black horse, he leaped the fences of the English rather than waste time in opening the gates. He burned Medfield, just outside Boston.

After the attack, a Praying Indian still loyal to his race, named James the Printer (he had helped Apostle Eliot with the Bay Psalm Book), posted this defiance on the bridge across the Charles:

> Know by this paper that the Indians whom thou hast provoked to wrath and anger will war these 21 years, if you will. There are many Indians yett. We come three hundred at this time. You must consider that the Indians lose nothing but their lives, while you must lose your fair houses and cattle.

Philip raided Bridgewater, Scituate, and Rehoboth once, and Marlborough and Sudbury twice. At Marlborough the squaws scalped and mutilated two Englishmen. At Sudbury he annihilated a whole company under Captain Wadsworth, and prevented reinforcements from reaching them by setting fire to the windward meadows. He burned eighty houses in Providence, and would have burned the remaining twenty, except for the pleas of the aged Roger Williams, who had been his father's friend. He killed no one in the village but a man named Wright, described as being "of a singular and sordid humour." The braves disemboweled him and stuffed his Bible in his belly. Philip even struck at Plymouth itself, and burned Clark's garrison house only two miles from town. Yet he gave orders to spare the village of Taunton, for it was there that Leonard, the friendly blacksmith, had his forge.

In April, Canonchet was captured by the English. They taunted him with his broken promise to deliver the Wampanoag scalps. "I shall not give up a Wampanoag or the paring of a Wampanoag's nail," he told them.

When they sentenced him to be shot, he said, "I like it well. I shall die before my heart is soft, or I have said anything unworthy of myself."

The English divided the privilege of his execution among three tribes in their service. A Pequot shot him, a Mohegan quartered him, and a Niantic burned his corpse. His head was sent to Connecticut "as a token of love and affection."

Worst of all for Philip, Church's wounds were healing. Governor Winslow offered to put him in command of sixty men as soon as he should be well enough to take the field. Church answered that he would need three hundred, half of whom must be friendly Indians. He knew that he could never win without Indians, and added that if the English intended to defeat Philip they must make a business out of war as he did. The governor answered that the colony could not afford so large a force and would not recruit Indians in any case.

While they argued, Philip struck again. On May 11, astride his black horse, he burned sixteen more houses in Plymouth. Governor Winslow, outraged and frightened by this second raid on the capital, yielded to Church. He offered him a captain's commission, the command of 60 Englishmen and 140 Indians (if they could be found), and the right, which Church demanded, to grant clemency to any of the enemy except Philip himself. It was Church's very softhearted-ness which had so far slowed up his promotion.

> On that day [says the *Entertaining History*] Mr. Church, being at present still disabled from any particular service in the war, with tents [bandages?] in his wounds, and so lame as not able to mount his horse without two men's assistance, began to think of some other employ. But no sooner took a tool to cut a small stick but he cut off the top of his forefinger, and the next to it half off; upon which he smilingly said it was needless to leave the war, where he could lose blood as well or better; and so resolved to go to war again.

His first task was to recruit his 140 Indians. The obvious source was Queen Awashonks, if only because she was his neighbor. He knew better than to approach her directly, but arranged a meeting through her son Peter and Honest George, the courtier who, with the late Sassamon, had invited him to her dance before the war began. The parley was set for the beach at Sakonnet Point in her kingdom. Church arrived by sea, and was rowed ashore from his sloop to meet the Queen. Her troops, fully armed, stood sullenly behind her on the dunes. Church carried nothing with him except a twist of tobacco and a calabash full of strong water. He describes the meeting thus:

Mr. Church pulled out his calabash, and asked Awashonks whether she had forgotten how to drink *okape*, which is their name for rum. Drinking to her, he perceived that she watched him very diligently, to see whether he swallowed any of the rum. He offered her the shell, but she desired him to drink again first. He then told her there was no poison in it, and, pouring some into the palm of his hand, sipped it up. And took the shell and drank to her again, and drank a good swig, which indeed was no more than he needed. Then they all standing up, he said to Awashonks, "You won't drink for fear there should be poison in it," and handed it to a little ill-looking fellow, who catched it readily enough, and as greedily would have swallowed the liquor when he had it at his mouth. But Mr. Church catched him by the throat and took it from him, asking whether he intended to swallow shell and all? and then handed it to Awashonks. She ventured to take a hearty dram, and passed it among her attendants. The shell being emptied, he pulled out his tobacco, and having distributed it, they began to talk. . . .

The result of this parley was that her chief captain stood up and said to Church with a bow, "Sir, if you will please to accept of me and my men, and will head us, we will fight for you, and will help you to Philip's head before the Indian corn be ripe."

Church understood swamp warfare as well as Philip himself, and the Indian character a little better. Awashonks's men were as good as bloodhounds at following a trail. They led the force, skimming the tussocks as lightly as the enemy ahead of them. The English came ponderously behind, for fear of being mired. A whistle from Church was the signal of danger; every man dropped to the ground when he heard it.

He tracked Philip to the Bridgewater swamp, between Plymouth and Mount Hope. They made contact on Sunday, July 20, 1676. In the action he captured or killed 173 Indians. Among the captives were Philip's wife and son: the lusterless Nanuskooke, so dim beside the lusty Weetamoe and the coquettish Awashonks; and the princeling whose very name is unknown. Philip's uncle Akkompoin was killed. Philip just missed death himself, crossing a treetrunk with his hair loosened for disguise. Church recognized him, but an instant too late to bring the musket to his shoulder. The king escaped again.

"It must be as bitter as death to him," Mather gloated, "to lose his wife and only son, for the Indians are marvelously fond and affectionate toward their children."

Church sent 153 prisoners into Bridgewater pound that afternoon. Being well treated with victuals and drink, he says, they had a merry night, and the prisoners laughed as loud as the soldiers, not having been so well treated for a long time before.

It was not his long retreat that broke Philip's spirit "so that he never joyed after," nor Canonchet's death, nor even the capture of his wife and son, but the knowledge that many of his own tribe had deserted to the English. Even before Bridgewater, three hundred of them had begged Governor Leverett of Massachusetts Bay to intercede with Plymouth for pardon. They seem to have thought that the Puritans would be more lenient than the Pilgrims.

> We have been destroyed by your souldiers [they wrote him] but still we remember it now to sit still. Do you consider it again. We do earnestly entreat that it may be so, by Jesus Christ. O let it be so! Amen, Amen. . . .

If Leverett did plead for them, he was unsuccessful. Plymouth spared their lives but sold them into slavery at the new low price of £1 apiece, or 7 bushels of corn in trade.

Church's own magnanimity was repaid. At Bridgewater he captured Lightfoot and Littleyes, two of Philip's men who had threatened to kill him the night of Awashonks's dance. Instead of hanging them, as his own Indians urged, he spared them. He even made Lightfoot a sergeant. It was not Englishmen's fashion, he said, to seek revenge; they should have the same quarter as other prisoners. He would go up to a likely-looking prisoner, clap him on the back and say, "Come, come; you look wild and surly, but that means nothing. My best soldiers, a little while ago, were as wild and surly as you are now. By the time you've been with me a day or two you'll love me too, and be as brisk as any of them."

It was true. He sent a file of them on Philip's track, with Lightfoot in command, and bade them quit themselves like men. Away they scampered on the trail, like so many horses. Three days later they caught Philip at breakfast in Swansea, where the war had started. But he escaped again, leaving the kettles boiling on the campfire and the meat roasting on the wooden spits. On August 6 Weetamoe was drowned, trying to float a raft to her kingdom of Pocasset. The tide washed her naked old body ashore, and the English added her head to the row of poles at Plymouth. Philip fled through the salt meadows toward Mount Hope as if he must, like her, go home to die.

Even then he would not surrender. With his own tomahawk he killed one of his braves for suggesting peace. Church could afford to wait, for Philip could not escape. A Connecticut troop blocked him on the west, the armies of Massachusetts Bay and Plymouth on the east and north, and the sea itself on the south.

Church had sent his wife Alice to stay with the Quakers on the Island for safety during the campaign. He deserved a visit with her. After breaking contact with Philip he made his leisurely way overland to the Island, across the kingdom of the dead Weetamoe. En route he beat up the cedar swamp where he had fought the year before, and took supper with John Almy, overlooking the peasefield where he had so nearly lost his life. His wife fainted with surprise when he walked into her lodging.

The Indian whom Philip had slain for talking peace left a brother named Alderman. He was a subject of Queen Awashonks. On the morning of August 11, Alderman stole down the two miles from Philip's camp at Mount Hope to the Ferry. He signaled over to the Island that he had news. (The abutment of the Mount Hope Bridge now rests on the sandspit where he stood.) Church, summoned by messenger from eight miles down Aquidneck Island, left his wife only a few minutes after he had revived her. The vindictive Alderman paddled across the Ferry to tell him that Philip and Anawon, with 180 braves, were encamped on an upland rise above the miry swamp at the foot of Mount Hope. It was a spot which

Church knew well; he could see it from where he stood. His wife must be content with a short visit, said he, when such game was ahead. Having collected what men he could in one afternoon—eighteen Englishmen and twenty-two Indians—he paddled across to the mainland in the darkness.

It was a summer of drought. On Mount Hope a little corn had sprouted from the ears which he had trampled down the summer before, but its leaves were curling on the prostrate stalks. For coolness, Philip slept out that night on the flat top of the forty-foot rock called his throne. It faces the east. Anawon lay beside him. Their bed was a heap of the barren cornstalks.

Philip slept badly that night. He waked out of a nightmare to tell Anawon that he dreamed Church had caught him. Then he turned back to his uneasy sleep.

At dawn on the twelfth, Church deployed his men in pairs, an Englishman and an Indian in each, to close in below the camp. As the swollen sun was rising over Pocasset, he sent a pair of scouts up the hill. At their first shot, the camp became alive. Philip leaped from the bed with nothing on but his breech-clout and stockings. He seized his gun and slung his shotbag and powderhorn over his shoulder. Only a few yards away, through the morning drizzle, he saw Church's scouts. He rolled down the west face of the hill like a hogshead. By a miracle, he broke no bones and did not even lose his gun. When he struck the grass, he got to his feet and ran dizzily westward through the brush. He ducked into the swamp for shelter, and halted twenty yards from the gun muzzles of a pair of Church's beaters.

The Englishman was Caleb Cook; the Indian was Alderman. On the crest of the hill, Anawon shouted the war-cry "Iootash! Iootash!" to rally the braves. (The word meant "Stand fast!") He was too late. Cook's gun misfired because of the dampness; but Alderman's, which had two barrels, sent one bullet through Philip's heart and another two inches above it. The king fell on his face in the mud, with his gun under him. The oracles were proved right:

it was not an Englishman who killed him. But as Cotton Mather put it, the English had *prayed* that bullet through his heart.

Church did not relax his ambush at the news, but Anawon had seen the death from the hilltop. He guided the fifty survivors—all that were left of the Wampanoag tribe—through the trap over the very path the English had made when they set it. Soon the sun had dried the dew; it was now too late to track him.

Church called his company together on the ledge where Philip and Anawon had slept. When he told them Philip was dead, the whole army, he says, gave three loud huzzas. His Indians pulled the body from the mud by its heels and dragged it before him. He knew it was Philip's from the scarred hand. ". . . And a doleful great dirty naked beast he looked like," says the *Entertaining History.*

He ordered his Indian executioner to behead the corpse. The headsman, as he raised his ax, laughed and said, "He's been a very great man, and made many a man afraid of him; but so big as he is, I'll now chop his arse for him."

When Cotton Mather heard the news of Philip's death, he exclaimed from the pulpit, "God hath sent us the head of Leviathan for a feast." The head actually was sent to Plymouth and set on a pole. It stayed there for twenty-five years. The body was quartered, and a piece hung on each of four trees. Church gave the scarred hand to Alderman as a reward. For months thereafter he exhibited it in a pail of rum "to such gentlemen as would bestow gratuities on him."

Anawon, who had escaped with the remnant of the tribe, had vowed never to be taken alive. It seemed hardly worth pursuing him, now that Philip was dead. Captain Church had surely earned a rest. He went back to his wife on the Island. Two weeks later word reached him that Anawon had begun to raid the long-suffering settlements of Rehoboth and Swansea. He learned through a deserter that the old chief was kenneled at the base of a steep rock a few miles above Mount Hope. It was surrounded on all sides but one by the dismal Rehoboth swamp. Its only entrance was across a felled tree, screened by birch bushes, and down a steep crevice in the rock to a platform. Only one man could pass at a time.

Church found the hiding-place without trouble. He asked Caleb Cook, who had missed his chance of glory on the morning of Philip's death, whether he would follow him down the ravine that very night.

"Sir," Cook answered, "I am never afraid of going anywhere when you are with me."

Church, with Cook and the deserter beside him, waited on the edge of the swamp until dark, when Anawon would have stacked his guns for the night. By luck, he caught a brave returning from the swamp after a tryst with a young squaw. He held the two of them for decoys. When the moon had risen, he forced the brave to sound the wolf call which was the password of the camp. An answering howl came back from the rock. He could hear someone pounding corn in a mortar at the foot of it. The noise covered the scraping of Church's clumsy boots. With his hatchet in one hand, he pushed the squaw and her lover ahead of him as a screen, and then crashed down the fissure himself, clutching at the bushes on the side with the other hand to steady himself. Cook and the deserter tumbled down the puddingstone behind him.

Anawon and his young son, who had been asleep by the campfire, started up. When they saw Church, the boy whipped his blanket over his head and shrunk up into a heap. Anawon cried out, "Howoh!" which meant, "They've caught me!"

Church stationed Cook in front of the stack of guns. With the deserter translating for him, he ordered Anawon's fifty men to toss their tomahawks alongside, and they obeyed. He turned to Anawon.

"What have you got for supper, Captain?" he asked through the interpreter. "I've come to eat with you."

"Taubut," Anawon answered in his deep voice (the word meant "Welcome"). "I have cow-beef and horse-beef."

Church chose cow-beef. It was soon got ready by the squaws.

King Philip, by Paul Revere

Melinda Mitchell, descendant of King Philip's sister Amie

Benjamin Church, by Paul Revere

The Battle of the Peasefield

The Great Swamp Fight

The death of King Philip

Ship *General Jackson,* teak-built and copper-bottomed, was originally the *San José Indiano,*
a prize to the *Yankee.* Used by James deWolf in the carrying trade and whale fishery, she
was sold in 1846 to the United States government for use against Mexico, and was junked
about 1850 on a Florida reef, being incombustible. This picture shows her entering Trieste
under full sail, a dangerous piece of bravado by Captain Joel Abbot

Diagram of a slaver's half-deck, reproduced in Commodore Andrew H. Foote's *Africa and
the American Flag* (1854) from an English engraving of 1808. The tight pack is less
typical of the early days of the trade than of the later

Brigantine *Macdonough*, 300 tons, built in 1814 by Caleb Carr for James deWolf. She took ne prizes, but all were recaptured by the enemy or surrendered on the declaration of ace. Driven ashore in the gale of 1815, she was floated off and sold to George deWolf, ho transferred her to foreign registry under the name *Enriques*. Chased by HMS *Forrest*, e was lost on a reef off Matanzas in 1817 with a full cargo of slaves

Vigilant versus *Valkyrie II*, 1893. *Vigilant*, named for Collector Ellery's revenue cutter, was e first Herreshoff yacht to defend the *America*'s Cup

Sea-captains carousing at Surinam, painted by John Greenwood in 1757–58, not many years after Simeon Potter's stop there

Baranov's fort at Sitka. Ships, left to right: *Juno, Russisloff, Maria, Yermak*

The silver flagon brought from
Oyapoc by Simeon Potter

Site of the original town alarm post

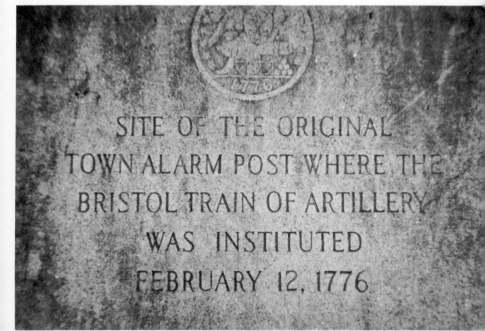

SITE OF THE ORIGINAL
TOWN ALARM POST WHERE THE
BRISTOL TRAIN OF ARTILLERY
WAS INSTITUTED
FEBRUARY 12, 1776

With the corn they had just been grinding, Church seasoned the supper—and Anawon's too—from the bag of salt which he always carried.

He had been on his feet for sixty hours. After supper he ordered Cook to stand watch while he rested. But he could not sleep. After lying some time beside Anawon he opened his eyes. Cook was fast asleep, and so were all the Indians except Anawon himself.

For an hour the two soldiers stared at each other in silence. Church spoke only a few words of Algonquin, and supposed that Anawon spoke no English. At last Anawon stood up with a groan, throwing off his blanket. With nothing on but his breech-clout, he walked out of sight around a corner of the rock. Church, supposing he went to ease himself in private, let him go, but took care just the same to lift a gun from the stack and shelter himself behind Anawon's son in case of a trap.

Then by the moonlight he saw the old warrior returning with a deerskin pack in his hands. Church stood up, grasping the gun. Anawon dropped to his knees before him.

"Great Captain," he said in plain English, "you have killed Philip and conquered his country. I and my company are the last that war against the English. The war is ended by your means; therefore these things belong to you."

He opened the pack. It held Philip's regalia. He draped the wampum stole on Church's neck. Its fringe reached the ground at the captain's boots. He laid the red cloak on Church's shoulder, the breastplate on his chest, the fillet on his head. He offered him two hornfuls of glazed powder and a red blanket.

The two men sat down to smoke while the others still snored. A curious sight they made to the moon: the naked old Indian and the young Englishman decked in his victim's regalia. They talked the night through. Church let Anawon boast of the victories he had won for Massasoit in the old days, against the Narragansetts. Old soldiers are seldom so patient with each other.

Church sent Anawon and his troops to Plymouth under guard, with the promise that their lives would be spared. But the Governor was not so lenient. When Church got there himself, he found Anawon's head on a pole. Beside it was that of Tispaquin, the Black Sachem, who had married Philip's sister Amie. He was the last straggler of the royal family to be captured.

Only Nanuskooke and her son were left alive. They had lain in Plymouth jail for a month. John Eliot, the old Apostle, asked the General Court to set them free, now that the war was over. Church agreed with him. He reminded the Governor that he had given him the right to pardon any Indian except Philip himself. Most of the colony, however, were for executing the two prisoners before the boy could grow up to avenge his father.

In the end, their fate, like most vexed questions, was referred to the clergy. The two parsons to whom the verdict was left—Arnold of Marshfield and Cotton of Plymouth—gave this decision:

> The question being propounded to us by our honoured rulers, whether Philip's son be a child of death! Our answer hereunto is that we do acknowledge that rule (Deuteronomy 24:16) to be morall and therefore perpetually binding, viz., that in a particular act of wickedness, though capitall, the crime of the parent doth not render his child a subject to punishment by the civill magistrate; yet, upon serious consideration, we humbly conceive that the children of notorious traitors, rebells and murtherers, especially of such as have bin principall leaders and actors in such horrid villainies, and that against a whole nation, yea, the whole Israel of God, may be involved in the guilt of their parents, and may, *salve republica,* be adjudged to death, as to us seems evident by the scripture instances of Saul, Achan, Haman, the children of whom were cut off by the sword of Justice for the transgressions of their parents, although concerning some of those children it be manifest that they were not capable of being co-actors therein.
>
> > Samuel Arnold
> > John Cotton

Sept. 7, 1676

However, the General Court tempered justice with mercy, and made a little money for the colony besides. It ordered them sold into slavery in Bermuda. On March 20, 1677, Parson Cotton wrote casually to his brother, "Philip's boy goes now to be sold."

Nanuskooke and he are never heard of again. A century and a half later the orator Edward Everett flung Cotton Mather's exultation back at him. "An Indian princess," he declaimed, "sold from the cool breezes of Mount Hope, from the wild freedom of a New England forest, to gasp under the lash, beneath the blazing sun of the tropics! Bitter as death? Aye, bitter as Hell! . . ."

IV

The Plymouth colonists moved fast to take over King Philip's land. They petitioned King Charles II to award them Mount Hope as the spoils of war. But they did not get it without a struggle. In London, an impoverished court playwright named John Crowne put in a claim for it. He had done nothing to deserve a reward except to write a bedroom comedy called *Sir Courtly Nice*. It was not a very good one, nor spicy enough to suit the Merry Monarch. But Crowne's father had lost *his* lands in Nova Scotia to the French, and he was willing to accept in place of them any disposable real estate that came in His Majesty's way.

Charles was an ungrateful monarch at best, and a little afraid of his cranky Bible-spouting subjects overseas. He left John Crowne unrequited. He sold Philip's seven thousand acres to the Plymouth colony in 1679 for an annual quit-rent of seven beaver skins, to be delivered at Windsor each Saint John's Day. There is no record that the rent was ever paid.

The General Court of Plymouth turned over the land for £1100 to four Boston investors named Byfield, Walley, Oliver, and Burton. The colony's agent, William Ingraham, broke a twig from the nearest bush and a clod from the ground. He handed them to Walley, who represented the syndicate. On September 24, 1680, title was thus transferred. The first town meeting, on September 1 of the next year, named the settlement Bristol, after the great slaving port of England.

In the fourteen months King Philip's War had lasted, half the English settlements in the Plymouth and Massachusetts Bay colonies had been attacked. It had cost them 600 men—a tenth of their fighting force—1000 houses, and £100,000. The sale of 500 Indian slaves and of Philip's land did not nearly pay for it, but the colonies asked for no help from England. Church complained that his troops were paid only four-and-sixpence apiece for the final campaign, with no more bonus for Philip's head than the 30 shillings which ordinary ones brought. He did get his choice of acreage when the four proprietors divided the land into farmsteads, but he had to pay for it. He built a farmhouse for himself in the shadow of Mount Hope, and a town house on the harbor for his son, the huge stone chimney of which, until a few years ago, stood at the foot of Constitution Street.

He could never rest for long. Promoted to colonel, he fought on through the wars of King William and Queen Anne. In 1691 the Puritans absorbed the Pilgrims; Plymouth colony, and Bristol with it, became part of Massachusetts. In 1705, when he was sixty-six, he led a regiment on the Nova Scotia front against the French, though admitting he was "ancient and unwieldy." At last he had to quit fighting. Forty years after he had killed Philip, he dictated his *Entertaining History* to his son. The lapse of time had not dulled his temper or his wit. Writing in the third person, he complained that:

> For his Colonel's pay there were two shillings and fourpence yet due him. As for his Captains' pay and his man Jack, he has received nothing as yet. Also, after he came home, some ill-minded persons did endeavor to have taken away his life. But His Excellency the Governor, the Honorable Council and House of Representatives saw fit to clear him and give thanks for his good service done.

In 1709 he deeded two hundred acres in what is now Fall River to the Indians who had served under him. In 1717 he crossed from Bristol to visit his sister Mrs. Irish in Fall River, which had been part of Weetamoe's old kingdom. Like the lands of Awashonks and Philip, it had long since belonged to the English.

"I have not long to live," he told his sister solemnly when they parted, "but I hope to meet you soon in Heaven."

Riding homeward, he had not gone half a mile before his horse stumbled and threw him over its head. Colonel Church, "being exceeding fat and heavy," fell with such force that a vessel was broken and blood gushed from his mouth like a torrent.

Most of the surviving Wampanoags were sold into slavery. At the war's end, when the supply was plentiful, their price averaged 32 shillings in silver, or, in barter, 12 bushels of corn or 100 pounds of wool. By 1750, when the paper currency had depreciated and the supply was low—for the Indians did not propagate well in captivity —an occasional one brought up to £50. They were intractable; the colonists were more than a little afraid of them, and often traded them for Negroes from Virginia or the West Indies. In 1774 only sixteen purebreds were left in town. By 1785, out of a population of twelve hundred, there were only two.

When none of their own race offered, the red slaves married the black slaves. Their high cheekbones, straight black hair, and fine nostrils used to be seen, not many years ago, on a few copper-dusky faces in town. The mixture of black and red was called the "mustee" breed —the word may derive from *mestizo*—and Negroes who could claim Wampanoag blood were proud to do so.

King Philip's War was soon forgotten. A century later, in the Revolution, the British War Office issued a guide for troops sent overseas to the rebellious colonies. Its author confused the long-dead Wampanoag chief with the Spanish kings of the same name.

"Bristol," he wrote, "is remarkable for King Philip of Spain having a palace nearby and being killed in it."

We shall never know what Benjamin Church looked like, nor King Philip either. Paul Revere engraved portraits of them both, but at the time of his famous ride Philip had been dead ninety-nine years and Church fifty-seven. His portrait of Philip looks as if it had been drawn to frighten children. When he came to Church, he did not even invent. He copied a likeness, frame and all, of the English poet Charles Churchill. The process of engraving reversed the original. Revere added a powder-horn at the neck, but that was all. It is easier to believe that Benjamin Church looked like his Bristol descendants of today; they are bluff, straight, and ruddy, with an occasional aquiline nose and jet-black eye which hint a drop of Wampanoag blood.

In 1878 Miss Melinda Mitchell of North Abington, Massachusetts, fifth in descent from Amie and Tispaquin, had her portrait engraved beside King Philip's Spring on Mount Hope. It is remarkable not for its beauty but because it is the only surviving likeness of the royal line of Massasoit.

Mount Hope itself has never been divided. Most of it is too steep for cultivation. Its owners have been men who could afford not to cultivate it, such as Proprietor Byfield, Isaac Royall the Tory, Governor Bradford, Captain Jim deWolf, and R. F. Haffenreffer the brewer. Captain Jim, who married Governor Bradford's daughter, built an octagonal summerhouse on the summit where Philip slept his last night; but so many lovers carved their names on its posts that it fell down many years ago. In the 1890s his grandson Willy B. set up a summer resort on the east slope, with a dock for steamers, a dance hall, a bar, a shed for clambakes, and a row of cottages with fireplaces of white quartz. The resort failed, and so did its promoter. R. F. Haffenreffer set up an Indian museum on the turntable of the merry-go-round, and the Army is now setting up a radar station on the site of Captain Jim's summerhouse. The ownership of Mount Hope has always been the criterion of wealth. As Ben Mott the blind man used to say, "If Mount Hope was for sale for one cent, and you didn't have the cent, you couldn't buy it. So there."

Philip's quartz throne still rears up from the eastern shore; his cold spring still flows. His only relics are the lock of his musket, preserved in Boston, and his iron kettle in Rehoboth. In 1913 a group of Bristol boys dug up a Wampanoag burial mound in Warren. They found, among wampum and arrowheads and flawless human teeth, a copper necklace which may have been Winslow's gift to Massasoit, and a soapstone pipe, shaped like a manikin, which may have been Philip's. Guarding them, in the museum on Mount Hope, was ranged the world's largest collection of cigar-store Indians: two hundred of them, more warriors than stood by Philip on the morning he was shot. But in 1957 even they were sold at auction in New York. They brought a hundred thousand dollars.

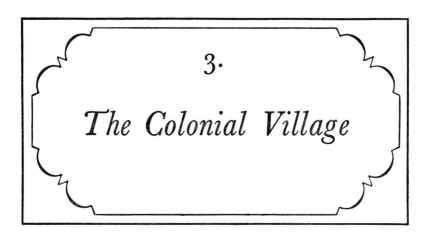

3.

The Colonial Village

EVEN in Philip's lifetime the twin peninsula had divided Providence, to the north, from Rhode Island, or Aquidneck, to the south; hence the longest name for the smallest state: Rhode Island and Providence Plantations. It was part of Plymouth Colony from his death until 1691, when Massachusetts absorbed Plymouth, and Bristol with it. In 1747 Massachusetts ceded the town to Rhode Island, where, by the logic of geography, it belongs. For the first time a Rhode Islander could travel between his two capitals, Providence and Newport, without passing through alien territory.

The four Boston proprietors who bought the peninsula were alike only in having nosed out the bargain. John Walley was a vigorous merchant who, within four years of the purchase, was in command of a detachment against the French in Canada. Nathaniel Oliver never even moved to the settlement, but sold his share within a year to a mariner named Nathan Hayman (he may have been Jewish), "a man of much enterprise and shrewdness." Stephen Burton was an Oxford graduate who wrote a beautiful hand, but was unable to endure much work, says Professor Munro, "because of a disorder in the head." Nathaniel Byfield was the richest and most powerful of the four. He acquired title to Hog Island, which Richard Smith had bought from King Philip, by seizing Smith and threatening him with death. He had evaded the draft in the war by quoting Scripture.* Later, on one of his voyages to London, an observer wrote:

> His age makes him impatient of the fatigues of application. His frugality makes him impatient of coach-hire, fees to officers and door-keepers and other expenses, so that I believe he now heartily wishes himself back in his own government at Poppysquash,

and an American contemporary says:

> The character of Colonel Byfield was neither so elevated as to command the veneration of the people, nor so low as to incur their contempt,

which is about as faint praise as ever damned a man.

The syndicate laid out a town through King Philip's woods a good deal as modern speculators develop a tract of land. The Royal Surveyor, Sir Christopher Wren, is said to have drawn the plat. The streets were not to follow the meanderings of cows, like Boston's, but to cross each other in spacious squares, like Philadelphia's. They were platted wide—from four to six rods. Four ran lengthwise of the bigger lobster claw, and nine crosswise, down to the water's edge and even into the harbor as far as ship-channel. You still see the water at the foot of every block as you walk along Hope Street, and the open-end streets, like so many funnels, draw the salt air up to the center of town. The proprietors kept the best tracts in their own hands, but offered a houselot and ten acres of backland free to each of the first sixty settlers. Byfield chose Mount Hope for himself, but soon traded it for Poppasquash. They allotted land for a Congregational meetinghouse, a cemetery, a town hall, a market, a school, and a common. They ordered mazzard cherry trees from England to line the future streets. The seven thousand acres remaining they held for sale to late-comers.

They did not have to wait long for settlers. Like most men who get something for nothing, the first sixty were malcontents. They bore

---

* Deuteronomy 24:4: "When a man hath taken a new wife, he shall not go out to war, neither shall he be charged with any business; but he shall be free at home one year, and shall cheer up his wife which he hath taken."

names like Hezekiah Wardwell and Mahershalalhashbaz Bourn.
The Walker family moved over from Aquidneck because they could
not get along with Anne Hutchinson, the awesome Quakeress of
Newport. (Few people could.) Obadiah Papilion, a Huguenot privateer, migrated from Boston. William Throop came from Barnstable
on Cape Cod; he was the grandson of Adrian Scrope (in England
the name is still pronounced Scroop). Adrian was, like Goffe of
Hadley, one of the judges who had sent Charles I to the block. Even
though William had changed his name, it was not safe for him to
stay too long in one place. He was a cobbler, and the only man
among the sixty who owned an oxcart. The others walked through
the woods to the new settlement or rode there on horseback.

John Saffin migrated from Plymouth to escape from his wife—she
was his third. He had no sooner received his allotment than he began
to spread slanders against the proprietors. They forced him to re-
tract, on pain of deportation back to Mrs. Saffin.

But in spite of contentions, the empty lots filled up fast. The settlers
exterminated the foxes and wolves, as King Philip had promised to
do but failed. They cut the nine streets to the generous plan of the
proprietors. The boulders of puddingstone, which made plowing diffi-
cult, were dug out of the earth, heaved onto sledges, and laid up dry
as boundary-walls or heaped into the harbor to form docks. For its
first quarter-century Bristol, except on the Sabbath, was as noisy as a
logging camp. The trees which were felled to clear the fields were
split into timber for ships and houses, and for firewood. The stumps
were grubbed out and dumped into the harbor. The single cavernous
chimney of a house would devour forty cords in a winter. One cold
morning Proprietor Byfield found his cow lying among the warm
ashes of his fireplace; during the night she had butted through the
door to get warm.

The proprietors agreed to build their own houses two stories high,
with two rooms to a floor, but they let the settlers build with a single
keeping room at the ground story and a roof sloped from a full ceil-
ing at second floor front down to a low woodshed at the back—what

was called a camelopard roof, from the old name for a giraffe—so that their houses looked two stories high, at least from the front. The stone fireplace, big enough to stand up in, filled one end of the keeping room. The other walls were laid up of logs chinked with a mortar of sand and oyster-shell lime, or, later, of clapboards nailed to a skeleton of posts and girts. Inside, the walls were stuffed with eel grass and faced with lapped oak boards to keep out the cold. The windows, until glass could be imported from England, were filled with oiled paper. They were fitted with sliding inside shutters, not only for warmth but for protection against the still-dreaded Wampanoags. The roofs were thatched with marsh grass, and later, when iron nails were made at the Taunton forge, with rived shingles.

The colonists were poor men. They grew corn, barley, tobacco, and onions. They wore leather or homespun jackets and canvas breeches, overall cloaks with collars to turn up in the cold, square-toed boots, and stiff-brimmed peaked sombreros of felt. They shaved with mussel shells. Their wives wore skirts and bodices, with a kerchief over the head for out-of-doors. There was no glass and little metal. Cups were made of gourds or horn, and spoons of oyster shell or pewter. The women spun flax, and dyed it, depending on the color, with imported indigo from the "blue-pot" in the corner of the keeping room, or with local walnut hulls, sassafras, goldenrod, or iris petals. Shirts and stockings were so laborious to make that they were handed down as heirlooms. Important personages like the proprietors, the clergy, and the royal tax-collector shaved their heads close, keeping them warm in the daytime with horsehair wigs, and at night with stocking-caps. Humbler folk wore their hair short and made their wives trim it around the edge of a bowl.

Their drinks were tea or rum, both imported through Boston. They had no white flour. They baked johnnycakes of white meal and salt, rolling them on a board for lightness and flavor, and Indian pudding of yellow meal and molasses. An armory of utensils hung from the crane or nested on the hearth. They ate venison, salt codfish, pork, clam pies, succotash, and pumpkins—which they called pompions. They had parties at weddings, house-raisings, sheep-shearings, cornhuskings and "infairs"—when a bride and groom moved in together. They celebrated Thanksgiving and Guy Fawkes Day, but not Christmas. They died of dropsy and childbed fever and black jaundice and consumptions and of falling off yardarms and of being crushed by trees; of "throat distemper," which was probably diphtheria, and smallpox, and what the old town clerks vaguely called "weakness." At their funerals each pallbearer received a mourning ring inscribed with the mottoes of immortality. They believed in the mottoes, too. They knew not only that there was a life after the grave, but also that it began with the cradle. Their hardships, including even the Indians, were a punishment for the sin of the Garden of Eden; but the same hardships made Paradise more blissful and more sure, and robbed death of its terrors. When Deacon Bosworth lay on his deathbed his wife held a glass of wine to his lips. He waved it off with the murmur, "I am going where I shall have better."

For the first four years this deacon held services in his house, which still stands beside Silver Creek. The worshipers had to cross the creek on steppingstones at low tide, and wait for the next ebb to get back, so the meeting had no excuse for being short. Everyone was a Congregationalist—it would be fifty years before a missionary arrived from the Church of England. The colonists paid tithes to the church and taxes to the village, but nothing, except customs duties, to the royal collectors. Except for their discomforts, they were better off than their fellow Englishmen at home.

By 1684 the necessary meetinghouse was built, at the taxpayers' expense. It stood where the Court House now stands, on the west edge of the Common. There was a little park of elms in front of it, with rings in the bark for the tethering of horses. The building was a cube of unpainted clapboard with a pyramid roof. It was framed, like a ship, with heavy cambered timbers. From a belfry in the center the bellrope hung down to the aisle. The floor was honeycombed with box pews; a gallery for Negro and Indian slaves hung above it. On those early Sabbaths the wagons started first from the outlying farmsteads to the meetinghouse, with the children aboard, warming their feet, in winter, on hot bricks wrapped in cotton. The oldest boy, afoot, drove the ox. Husband and wife—or goodman and gossip, as they were often called—followed on horseback, she leaning forward from the pillion to shelter her face in his many-caped greatcoat.

At church the family settled into their square pew. Its seats hinged so they could face the pulpit or the choir at the turns in the service. The meetinghouse had no chimney. When it was cold, the women lighted footstoves. In the robing room the minister doffed his three-cornered hat and adjusted his powdered wig. Over his coat and black velvet smallclothes he draped the black robe of his office, with white bands at the throat. The congregation stood when he entered. The clerk, standing before the pulpit, slowly "lined out" the hymn. The bull fiddle under the choir-loft at the opposite end scraped out the tune. The congregation turned about to face the music, with squeaking of hinges, and sang the hymn line by line. After the prayers, they stood again as the parson mounted the wineglass pulpit for his sermon. The children always feared—or hoped—that the sounding-board would fall on his head before his hourglass ran out of sand. Below him stood the tithing man with a long black staff in his hand, ready to rap whisperers and drive dogs out of church.

Cotton Mather, as a compliment, assigned the learned Reverend Samuel Lee to Bristol. He called him "the light of both Englands." Perhaps he was biased, for he was in love with Lee's daughter and later married her. Parson Lee was a rich man. He wrote twelve books and owned several thousand, including a section on witchcraft and astrology. He built "an elegant mansion-house" on the water side of Thames Street. It was two full stories high, like the proprietors' houses, with a gambrel roof. The stair risers were only four inches high. It had a leanto besides. (In Bristolese, this word is pronounced "linta.")

The English of the learned was still the gnarled and Gothic language of Elizabeth's time. It is hard to believe that Parson Lee's congregation of farmers understood his sermons, one of which begins like this:

> Let the world rage in storms of contradiction, and, like him in
> Laertius, affirm snow to be black, or assert the sun shines not when

I see it, or a cordial comforts not when I feel it, or that a troubled conscience is but a melancholy fancy, when the terrors of the Lord drink up the spirits of men. These should be sent to Anticyra to purge with hellebore for madness.

When the morning service was done, the men dropped in to Shear-jashub Bourn's tavern, only two blocks down street, for their nooning. They drank flips or gin slings in the taproom, while the women fed cold pasties to the children in the church park. After dinner, the second service lasted all afternoon.

In spite of his eloquence, Parson Lee was unpopular with the pioneers. As one observer wrote, "He conceived a most insuperable dislike to America, which was heartily reciprocated by the people."

He stayed in Bristol only till 1691, when William and Mary, the new sovereigns, relaxed the ban on dissenters in the home country. In that year Cotton Mather began his crusade against the witches of Salem. Parson Lee, perhaps as a rebuke to his son-in-law, burned his collection on the supernatural and set sail for England. He was captured by a French privateer off St. Malô, and thrown into prison. He died there, without ever seeing England again. In after years his fine mansion became a boarding house for sailors, called, for no known reason, "The Old Bay State."

II

The New England colonists traveled by sea, for the roads on land were few and often impassable. Bristol's first shipyard was the one which Deacon Woodbury built at the head of the harbor. His first vessel, ordered by Proprietor Byfield, was a sloop named *Bristol Merchant*. The deacon ordered her mahogany from a Scotch dealer in Dutch Guiana, named Mackintosh. When he failed to pay for it, the Scot came north to collect. Having collected his bill, he married Byfield's daughter and stayed for the rest of his life. As early as 1686 Colonel Byfield was shipping horses and onions back to the Guianas, where Mackintosh knew the market, aboard the *Bristol Merchant*.

The onions which he exported were the prized Bristol Reds; the horses were Narragansett pacers, a small-boned breed famous for

steady gait. The pacer did not rack from side to side as the trotter did
—in fact, the purebreds could not trot at all. Comfort in the saddle
was important when there were no roads and therefore no carriages.
One lady, in sidesaddle, rode a pacer 190 miles in five days without
discomfort. Even after a few passable roads were cut, pacers were
never broken to harness. They were too valuable to have their legs
stiffened by pulling a chaise. On clear ground a good pacer could
run a mile in just over two minutes. (There was no such ground in
Bristol, but twice a year races were held on the hard beaches of
Newport and Narragansett. The prize was always a silver tankard,
and sportsmen came to watch from all over New England.) The
breed was so well suited to hacking over the sugar plantations of the
West Indies that it was exported to the French and Spanish planters
in great numbers. As a result, it died out at home. By 1800 there was
only a single pacer left in all Rhode Island.

The bead currency of the Indians was soon replaced by the colony's
paper money, but this tender was continually running out of control
and being exchanged for new issues at a fraction of face value. In
1756, for instance, the fare across the ferry to Aquidneck Island was
five shillings in "old tenor"; in 1767 it had dropped to sixpence in new.
The new issue in turn depreciated; by the Revolution it was com-
monly called "rag money" and stood at about a tenth of sterling.
Alluding to the colony's habit of issuing unlimited notes, a visiting
Irish parson wrote:

> Rhode Islanders are perhaps the only people on earth who have hit
> on the art of enriching themselves by running in debt. There are
> more lawsuits in a year than the County of Derry has in twenty.

The most contentious and ornery Bristolian in the colonial century,
if not in the town's whole history, was Captain Simeon Potter. He
was born in 1720 at the southeast corner of Hope Street and Church
Street, which was then called Queen Street, and catercornered from
where Saint Michael's Episcopal Church was later built.

He shipped to sea early as a cooper aboard the *Bristol Merchant*.
His job was to repair the staves and shooks of the casks in the hold.

He did well in trade to the sugar islands, setting out with a few pacers hobbled on deck and ropes of onions stowed in the hold, and returning with molasses—to be distilled to rum—and mahogany planking.

In 1744, when he was twenty-four, he held a captain's license, signed by Nathaniel Hubbard, His Majesty's agent for Bristol. That year, on a round of the Caribbean, he put in at the islands of Guadeloupe and signed on a young clerk named Mark Antony deWolf. In spite of his outlandish name, and of having been born on a French island, Mark was a Yankee. His grandparents had emigrated to Guadeloupe from Lyme, Connecticut, where there are still deWolfs above ground and below. He was just what the illiterate Potter needed, for he spoke and wrote all the languages of the Main, as well as his native English. He went back to Bristol with Potter that summer.

Potter had nine sisters. The one who happened to answer the door when the two young men walked up from the harbor was Abigail. She pretended to bar the door to them, but her brother pushed up her arm.

"Let us pass, Abby," he told her, "or you shan't have Mark. I'll give him to one of your sisters."

Abby Potter and Mark Antony deWolf were married that August in the new Episcopal church across the corner. They were both eighteen.

Within two weeks of the wedding, King George's War broke out. As usual in the eighteenth century, France and Spain were the enemies. Potter had no love for George II, but he saw a chance to make money from the war. He had saved enough to buy a quarter-share in a Newport privateer named the *Prince Charles of Lorraine*.

A war was always a good excuse for an honest merchant to turn privateersman. Under a good-conduct bond of £1500 sterling, Potter, on September 8, 1744, was granted a commission to "set upon by force of arms and to subdue, seize and take the Men of War, ships and other vessels whatsoever, together with the goods, monies and merchandize belonging to the Kings of Spain and France." The ship was registered in Newport, and the commission was signed by the Royal Governor of Rhode Island.

The *Prince Charles* was a ninety-ton sloop mounting ten carriage-guns and manned by an overflow crew of eighty. She carried provisions for a six-month cruise. According to her outfitting return, Potter was captain, and deWolf, his brother-in-law, was clerk. Most of the crew were Bristol boys. The cook, Jeffrey Potter, was an Indian slave of the captain's with no surname of his own but the right to use his owner's. The privateersmen, who were nothing but legalized pirates, wore the traditional pirate uniform: heelless shoes, loose knee breeches, broad belts, open shirts, red kerchiefs at the throat, and knitted cap-sox. Each man's hair was plaited in a pigtail.

A shot from the heavily armed French merchant ships would send the frail *Prince Charles* to the bottom, but she made up in speed and ease of handling what she lacked in armor. Potter and deWolf knew the trade routes of the Indies and the South American bulge as well as any of the enemy. They put out of Newport on the day they received the commission.

Two months after weighing anchor, they raided the Jesuit mission of Oyapoc, at the mouth of the river of the same name which divided the French colony of Guiana from the Portuguese colony of Brazil. French Guiana was an empty land of marsh and jungle; even now it has no more than thirty thousand inhabitants, half of whom live in the capital city of Cayenne.

Two relics of their raid survive. One is the account which Father Fauque, the missionary at Oyapoc, wrote back to Father de la Neuville, his superior at the headquarters of the Society of Jesus in Paris. The other is a silver flagon, clearly sacred to the wine of the Holy Sacrament, and engraved with the d'Orvilliers coat-of-arms.

Though the Jesuits were the aristocracy of the Church, Father Fauque's name is a bourgeois one. He can hardly have been entitled to bear arms. He was a frail and zealous young priest when he first had braved Guiana in 1727. He had written confidently back to Paris that he would persuade the natives to wear clothes: "*Nous metterons d'abord des jupes à toutes les femmes.*"

This laudable attempt had failed, but Father Fauque and his fellow missionaries had at least built a straw-roofed church in honor of Saint Joseph and erected a large cross on the river-bank. He wrote that:

> The missionary passes his life in obscurity, amid the woods. God is the only witness to his loneliness, his sufferings, his sweat and his exhaustion.

When Simeon Potter and Mark Antony deWolf sailed from Rhode Island he had already spent seventeen years among the still-naked Bilibis in a raucous landscape peopled by scorpions, crab-spiders, boa constrictors, howler monkeys, trumpet birds, and vampire bats. His mission in Guiana was an outpost of Heaven, and of France. Here, somewhat shortened, is the letter which describes how the Bristol buccaneers destroyed his life's work:

22 December, 1744

My reverend Father:

The peace of the Lord be with you. I wish to share with you the greatest joy I have ever experienced, by suffering something for the glory of God.

Scarcely had war between France and England been declared than the English were sent out from North America to raven the islands to the leeward of Cayenne. They hoped to capture our vessels, pillage our dwellings, and in particular, to destroy a *senau* which had recently grounded near the river Maroni. [*Senau*, English "snow," was a two-master with boom mainsail.]

Having gone too far south, and their water giving out, they sailed up to Oyapoc to obtain some. We should have been warned of their approach, either by our Indians, who often put out to hunt and fish, or by the French guard which our Governor had posted on a hill at the mouth of the river. But the Indians, being seized by the English, told them of our little mission of Oyapoc (of which they had never heard); and the sentinels who should have protected us actually guided the pirates, and thus we fell into their hands.

Their chief was Simeon Potter, fitted out to cruise under a commission from Willems Guéene [William Greene], Governor of Rodelan, and commanding the vessel *Prince Charles of Lor-*

raine. He cast anchor on the 27th of October and began taking in water. On the 28th his longboat, returning to the ship, saw a canoeful of our Indians. The English pursued them, frightened them by a volley of musketry, seized them and carried them aboard. The next day, having seen a fire on shore at night, they came ashore and seized the two sentinels. These young men had time to come and inform us; but one of them, a traitor to his country, persuaded the other not to do so.

Having thus learned all about the post of Oyapoc, the pirates determined to surprise it. They arrived a little after the moon had set. Guided by the two young Frenchmen, they landed a hundred yards from our fort. Our sentry challenged them, but they made no reply, from which he knew that they were enemies. Everyone woke up, but the English were inside before anyone could collect his thoughts. I, who was living outside the fort, was roused by the first cry of the sentry. I saw them file by in great haste, and immediately ran to rouse our Fathers.

So unexpected a surprise in the middle of a dark night, the weakness of the garrison, which comprised only ten or twelve men, the frightful shouts of a multitude which we supposed more numerous than it really was, the vivid and terrible fire which they kept up with their guns and pistols—all this induced each of us, by an impulse he could not master, to hide in the surrounding woods. Our commander, however, fired, and wounded the English captain in the left arm. He was a young man about thirty years old. [Father Fauque is wrong: Potter was only twenty-four.] What is singular, this captain was the only one wounded on either side.

For myself, I remained in my house, which was about a hundred yards from the fort. I resolved to go first to the church to consume the consecrated wafer, and afterwards to carry spiritual aid to the French, supposing some of them had been wounded. I thought, from hearing so much gunfire, that they had met some resistance. I went outdoors to execute the first of these projects, when a Negro servant, who, through goodness and loyalty (rare qualities among the slaves), had remained with me, warned me that they would not fail to fire at me in the first heat of the contest. I yielded to his reasoning, and decided to wait for daybreak before showing myself.

You can easily imagine, my reverend Father, what a variety of emotions agitated me that night. The air ceaselessly resounded with shouts and cries, and with the discharge of guns and pistols. I heard the doors and windows of the houses opened, and the furniture thrown crashing out through them. I could distinguish the noise they made in the church, and feared lest the Holy Sacrament be profaned. I would have given a thousand lives to prevent this sacrilege. I inwardly addressed myself to Jesus Christ, and earnestly prayed Him to guard His adorable Sacrament from the profanation which I feared.

My Negro advised me to take flight, but I could not do so. I told him that now he was his own master, and added that if he had any mortal sin on his conscience, it would be best for him to confess it, since he was not sure they might not kill him. This address made an impression on him, so that he remained steadfastly beside me.

As soon as day dawned, I crept through the underbrush to the church. As I entered the sacristy, which I found open, tears filled my eyes when I saw the cupboard for the vestments and linen, where I also kept the chalice and the sacred vessels, broken open and shattered. The altar was half uncovered, and the cloths thrown together in a heap. Examining the tabernacle, I found they had not noticed the little piece of cotton which I had stuffed in the keyhole to keep out the ants. Placing my hand on the door, I saw that it was untouched. Overcome with wonder and joy, I took the key which these heretics had held in their very hands. I opened the door and partook of the Sacrament, uncertain whether I should ever again have that blessing. For what has a man of God not to fear from pirates, and English pirates at that!

Now I myself had to surrender, so I came with a sailor to the fort. When we entered, all their faces expressed the greatest joy at having captured a priest.

The first pirate who approached me was Captain Potter himself. He was a man of slight stature, not differing in any way from the others in dress. His wounded left arm hung in a sling. His right hand held a saber, and there were two pistols in his belt. As he was acquainted with some words of French, he told me that I was very welcome and had nothing to fear, as no one would attempt my life.

At last dinnertime came. I was invited to eat, but had no appetite. I knew that our soldiers and the two other missionary Fathers were in the depths of the forest without food or proper clothing. However, I had to accept the repeated invitations, which seemed to be sincere. Scarcely had the meal begun when the first plunder taken from my house was brought in. It was natural that I should be moved; and indeed, I showed my emotion. As an excuse for himself, the captain said to me through his interpreter [Mark Antony deWolf, his brother-in-law] that the King of France had first declared war against the King of England, and had already taken, pillaged and burned an English post named Camp near Cape Breton, and that several children had been smothered in the flames.

I answered that, without entering into the quarrels of kings, I was surprised he should have come to attack Oyapoc, which was not worth the trouble. He answered that he himself regretted having come there, as the delay might make him miss two richly laden merchantmen which he had heard were sailing from Cayenne. [As the crow flies, Cayenne, the capital, was seventy-five miles northwest of Oyapoc.] I then prayed him to accept a reasonable ransom for my church, myself, my Negro and everything I owned. But he refused. He demanded that I treat with him for the fort and all its dependencies. This was not a fit proposal to make to a priest.

Well, said he spitefully, since you do not wish to consider it, we must continue our looting, and make reprisals for all the French have done against us.

They continued therefore to carry out our furniture and clothing with a disorder that amazed me. What gave me the deepest pain was to see the sacred vessels in their profane and sacrilegious hands. I reproached them for so criminal a profanation, and did not forget to remind them of Belshazzar's Feast. I must say, my reverend Father, that many were inclined to return the sacred vessels to me, but greed and avarice prevailed. That same day all the silver was packed up and carried aboard the sloop.

Captain Potter, more sympathetic than the rest, told me he would willingly return me all he could, but that he had no control over the others; that since all the crew had shares in the booty, he, as captain, could not dispose of any but his own, but that he would do all he could to persuade the others. . . .

During the whole year here, the sun sets at six o'clock. At this hour the English drums began beating. The pirates assembled on the square, and posted their sentries on all sides. The rest of the crew spent the night in eating and drinking. As soon as it was day, the pillage began again. Each man carried to the fort whatever happened to fall into his hands, and threw it down in a pile. One arrived wearing an old cassock, another in a woman's petticoat, a third with the crown of a bonnet on his head. Those who guarded the booty searched in the heap of clothes. When they found anything that suited their fancy, such as a peruke, a laced hat, or a dress, they put it on and made three or four turns through the room with great satisfaction, after which they resumed their own fantastic rags. They were like a band of monkeys or savages who have never left the depths of the forest. A parasol or mirror—any showy article, no matter how small—excited their admiration. This did not surprise me when they told me they had scarcely any communication with Europe, and that Rodelan is a kind of little republic which does not pay any tribute to the King of England, which elects its own governor every year, and which has not even any silver money, but only paper for daily commerce.

In the evening the lieutenant asked me about the houses of the other Frenchmen along the river, and afterward took ten of his crew, with his clerk as interpreter, and the treacherous French sentinel as guide, to pillage them. But they found nothing, for the colonists had hidden all their property, especially their Negroes, who excited the greed of the English above all else. So they vented their anger by burning the houses.

I was now told that I must go aboard the *Prince Charles of Lorraine*, as Captain Potter wished to speak with me. I was obliged to obey. The second lieutenant, taking hold of his tongue with one hand and pretending to cut it off with the other, made me understand I must take care what I said. At about three in the afternoon we embarked in a canoe. The ship was not more than three leagues off, but it took us eight hours to reach her, because of the carelessness of the English rowers, who were constantly drinking. When I first saw her hull by the moonlight, she seemed to be entirely out of water. In fact she had run aground in only three feet. This alarmed me, for they had impressed my Negro as pilot and I feared they might revenge his carelessness on me.

As soon as our canoe reached the ship, a young man ran down the ladder. He kissed my hand and told me, in murderous French, that he was an Irishman and a Catholic. He even made the sign of the Cross, though indifferently well, and added, through the interpreter, that in right of his rating as second gunner, he had a berth which he wished to give up to me; and that if anyone showed me the least disrespect, he knew how to avenge it. This introduction, though made by a man who seemed to be very drunk, could not help comforting me. He gave me his hand to help me up the rope ladder.

Scarcely had I climbed aboard when I met my Negro. I asked him why he had run the ship aground. He told me it was the fault of Captain Potter, who stubbornly held his course in midstream, though he had told him repeatedly that the channel ran close to shore. At the same time, Captain Potter appeared on the quarterdeck and told me, very coldly, to go below to the cabin. After this he continued to devote himself to working the vessel. My Irishman, however, did not leave me. Sitting at the door, he renewed his assurance that he was a Catholic, that he wished to confess before I left the ship, and that he had once received the Sacrament. In all his talk he mingled invectives against the English, so that they made him leave me, and threatened him with the lash if he spoke to me again. He took this hard, swearing and blustering that he would speak to me in spite of them.

He had hardly left me when another came, as drunk as he and an Irishman too. He was the ship's surgeon. He addressed me with two Latin words: *"Pater, misereor."* I answered him in Latin, but soon found he knew no others. As he was no better acquainted with French than I with English, we could hold no conversation together. It grew late, and I had not slept for two nights. Yet I did not know where to obtain a little repose. The ship was careened over so far that I could hardly stand upright. I wanted to lie down in one of the three berths, but did not dare, for fear someone would make me leave it. Our storekeeper had also been captured. He and I sat together, leaning on the seachests. Captain Potter was at last touched by our unhappy faces, and told us we might lodge in the berth at the foot of his cabin. He even added politely that he would like to have given us one apiece, but that his ship was too small for him to do so. We accepted his offer, and disposed ourselves on a pile of rags as best we could.

Being awake half the night in spite of my drowsiness, I perceived that the *Prince Charles* had begun to move. Insensibly, she floated. To prevent her from settling down again, Captain Potter drove two yardarms into the mud, one on each side, to hold her hull in equilibrium. As soon as day came, when one must take nourishment, I met a new torment, for the ship's water was so foul I could not swallow it. Even the Indians and Negroes, who are far from fastidious, preferred to drink the water of the river, muddy and brackish as it was. I advised Captain Potter, therefore, to send to the spring near our fort, which I myself used. He did not answer, thinking that I planned to lead him into an ambush. But at last, after questioning the treacherous Frenchman and the slaves, he sent his longboat to fetch water from it, with my own Negro in charge. It made many trips during that day and the succeeding, so we had the pleasure of good water. Many of the English, however, scarcely tasted it, preferring the rum and wine which they had on deck at will. But I should say in defense of Captain Potter that he was entirely sober. He expressed pain at the excesses of his crew, to whom, according to the custom of pirates, he was obliged to allow full liberty.

On Sunday morning I expected to see some religious service, for till now there had been no sign of Christianity among them. But everything went on as usual. Captain Potter, however, took out of his chest a book of devotions, and I noticed that during the day he occasionally looked at it. He even told me that some day he hoped to give up the business of privateering, for God might give him treasures today that he would lose tomorrow, and that he was well aware he could take nothing out of this world. I confess to you, my reverend Father, that I was astonished to hear such sentiments from the lips of a Huguenot from Rodelan, for everyone knows how far that part of the world is removed from the kingdom of God. On that very day the boats which ferried pillage from the mission brought out five of my Indians. I told Captain Potter that since Indians were free among us in Guiana, he should not take them prisoner. But he answered that this kind of people were used for slaves in Rodelan, and that he would take them thither in spite of me.

On Tuesday morning he took me ashore. The pirates spent the next morning in making up packages, in destroying what furniture was left and in tearing off the locks and hinges, especially those which were made of brass. At noon they set fire to all of our huts, which were soon reduced to ashes, being made of straw as is the custom here. I begged them to spare the church, and this they promised. But they burned it notwithstanding. When

I complained, they told me the wind had carried sparks to the roof and set it afire in spite of them. With this answer I had to be content, leaving to God the time and manner of avenging this insult to His house. For myself, seeing the flames rise to the clouds, I recited the Seventy-sixth Psalm: "O God, the heathen are come into thine inheritance."

The wind having freshened, and our settlement being completely destroyed, the *Prince Charles*, with myself aboard as prisoner, sailed westward all night, and approached Cayenne the next morning. We cast anchor seven miles offshore. Toward three in the afternoon there was a great commotion on board. It was caused by the departure of the boatswain who, in command of only nine men, including the clerk, set off in a longboat to raid the outskirts of the capital. You must know, my reverend Father, that in time of peace Rodelan trades to this place, principally to import horses for the sugar plantations.

But by Monday the longboat had not returned, and I ventured to hope it had been captured by the garrison of Cayenne.

"What do you think of your boatswain's longboat?" I asked Captain Potter.

"I think it is captured," he said. "So much the worse for him if he gets into trouble. I know that Cayenne is not an Oyapoc. His energy and stubbornness have probably led to his capture. I have great esteem for him, and needed him badly. But my light anchor will not hold, and I must leave for Surinam without him. I can bear the loss of ten men and still have enough left for my cruise."

He told me that, far from fearing an attack from the capital, he desired it, and would capture any Frenchman who dared approach us. He had a privateer's full complement of arms: sabers, pistols, guns, pikes, grenades, balls filled with bitumen and sulphur, grapeshot—nothing was lacking.

With this, he gave orders to work the ship. I took him aside and told him that while my views were not official, he could send me in a boat to Cayenne under a white flag, with any proposals he chose, and leave it to our Governor, M. le Commandant d'Orvilliers, to accept or reject them. He followed my advice, and asked me to write the letter myself, at his dictation. This I did, adding on my own account that part of the terms should be the return of my church silver of Oyapoc for its value in specie.

He then put me, with our storekeeper, into a small and leaky boat, rowed by five of his crew.

After rowing upstream through a night of horror—one of the masts fell on the storekeeper, almost crushing him—we approached Cayenne in the morning under our white flag. A detachment was sent to the landing to receive us with presented arms, as is the custom. All the ramparts which front the roadstead were crowded with people. It was a comforting spectacle, my reverend Father, to see all Cayenne coming to welcome me. Even the slaves pressed around me. A large crowd followed me into the church, where I at once repaired to give thanks to God for the great blessings He had bestowed on me, and for which I beg you also, my reverend Father, to give thanks.

Captain Potter's prophecy had come true. The boatswain and his Englishmen, after having pillaged some of our dwellings, were encountered by a company of French and entirely defeated. Three were killed on the spot, and the other seven made prisoners.

M. d'Orvilliers was in retirement due to the death of his wife. As soon as he had heard my report, he ordered the five Englishmen who had accompanied me to be confined in the guardhouse. He then arranged to return them to the *Prince Charles* with the seven survivors of the boatswain's crew. He was willing to release them, I flatter myself, in order to ransom me. On the following night they departed in their longboat with all the tackle and provisions they needed. They shouted several times "Houra" and "God Save the King"—to which we replied as vigorously "Vive le Roi." The *Prince Charles* disappeared toward Surinam the next morning.

I pray that she arrives safely, for I have written to the governor of Surinam for his help in recovering the sacred vessels of my church which are aboard her, on the conditions agreed upon with Captain Potter when we parted. But if I should not succeed in recovering them, I trust that you, reverend Father, will supply my need by sending me from Paris a complete church service to replace the one I have lost.

You see, my reverend Father, a very long letter—perhaps a little too long. I should esteem myself happy if it affords you any pleasure, for I had no other object in writing it.

I am, with respect, in the unity of our holy sacrifices, etc.,

Elzéar Fauque

The *Prince Charles of Lorraine* headed northwest from Cayenne, with the trade winds behind her, to the neutral waters of Surinam, or Dutch Guiana. On the two-hundred-mile voyage Potter and his brother-in-law counted the loot of Oyapoc. By the ship's articles, half of it, after deducting the duties and the 50 per cent due to the Crown, belonged to the owners, and half to the crew. As part owner Potter drew one eighth, and as captain another. He had taken seven Indians, three Negroes, twenty large spoons, nine ladles, two swords, two watches, two bags of gold, four cannon, and sixty small arms, as well as beef, flour, ammunition, and miscellaneous rings, buckles, candlesticks, and church plate. The silver flagon was among the booty.

He reached the mouth of the Surinam River on December 10, with only a single hogshead of water left, and no firewood in the galley. Although the Dutch were neutral, their sympathies were with the French. From Paramaribo, the capital, Mauricius, the Dutch Governor, sent orders refusing to supply him or let him land. For a time he had to beg water from British ships in the offing. At last he was allowed to anchor at the river's mouth and draw stores, provided he stayed twenty miles downstream from the city and kept his crew aboard. The grounding at Oyapoc had started the ship's hull, but the current was too swift to let him careen her; he could only heel her over against the bank and bout-top her as best he could. After twenty-three days, during which four of his crew jumped ship, the Governor ordered him out of Dutch waters altogether.

The night before he sailed, Captain Potter invited some Dutch and British sea-captains aboard the *Prince Charles* for dinner.

After plenty of rum for all hands, he ordered his crew to heap the Oyapoc loot on deck, except for the specie and the church plate. He even made the crew bring up their own hammocks, clothing, and other loose property to the value of forty pieces of eight. (The piece of eight, or Spanish milled dollar, contained $1.07 in present-day silver. It traded for 6 shillings sterling or £6 in Rhode Island paper.) Then he auctioned everything off to his guests.

At dawn on January 5 he weighed for the British colony of Bar-

bados, where twenty-four more of his crew deserted. He reached
Bristol with a depleted and mutinous company on the afternoon of
April 24, 1745. A letter from Mauricius to His Majesty's Court of
Vice-Admiralty at Newport was awaiting him, complaining, in the
name of Their High Mightinesses the Lords the States General of the
Dutch Republic that he had "affronted the Republic's flag" and violated the neutrality of Holland by selling the Oyapoc loot to Dutch-
men. Before the same court, the crew brought action of replevin
against him. Jeffrey, the Indian cook, deposed that between Surinam
and Barbados

> . . . the men demanded that Captain Potter would share the
> money according to the articles; to which Captain Potter answered
> that he would share none until his return, for all the men were in-
> debted to the owners more than that amounted to, and swore at them
> and Damn'd them, threatening them with his drawn sword at their
> Breasts, which treatment obliged them to hold their Peace; and when
> the ship arrived at Barbados . . . supply'd the men only with Rum
> and Sugar for their drinking; and further this deponent saith that
> Captain Potter refused to let the men have their share, and his ill
> treatment of them by cheating them had occasioned 24 to leave the
> vessel, whose shares Captain Potter retained in his own hands.

Potter was described in court as "tall and slim, with a long sharp
nose, in light-colored longclothes with his hair tied behind, looking
more like a shoreman than a seaman." Ben Munro, the boatswain of
the *Prince Charles,* has handed down to his descendants the word
that he was "bent at the waist, so his nose was always forrard of his
feet." Potter won the suit. He stamped the Oyapoc silver with his
own initials and forgot to return it to Father Fauque.

He was proud. Hubbard, the King's agent, complimented him on
the appearance of the *Prince Charles* as she lay alongside the Pump
Lane wharf.

"You deserve a larger ship, Captain Potter. If you ask the Governor for one, Admiralty will provide it."

"When I want a larger ship," Potter told him, "I'll not ask the King
for one; I'll build her myself."

For two years more the *Prince Charles* cruised in company with the *Queen of Hungary* out of Newport. They took four prizes in 1746. The next summer she captured the French brig *Greyhound* by herself, but broke up the following winter in a snowstorm off the Sakonnet shore. In the spring of 1748 the war with France was ended by the peace of Aix-la-Chapelle.

In 1754 Louis XV expelled the Jesuits from Guiana. Father Fauque probably returned to France. His mission was not rebuilt. In 1777 a French official named Malouet, on a tour of inspection in the colony, describes the site:

> Ascending the river, we passed the abandoned post of the Jesuits. No trace of cultivation is left. The forest has taken possession of the plowed land. The only sign of civilization that remains is a worm-eaten cross at the crown of the river-bank.

III

Although Potter was still a young man when the *Prince Charles* foundered, he never went to sea again. He invested his spoils in shipping and real estate. He expended his energy in advancing the fortunes of his deWolf brother-in-law and nephews, and in litigation with almost everyone else. When the Seven Years War spread to America in 1756, he outfitted the fifty-ton privateer sloop *Rhoba,* forty hands and six guns, and placed Mark Antony in command. On a three-week cruise in Bermuda waters, she took a French snow, from Martinique for Bordeaux, with a cargo of sugar, coffee, indigo, ivory, and logwood. After the war, he put Mark's oldest son Charles in command of the hundred-ton slaveship *Phoebe* and later of the sloop *Hopestill,* which was named for his own father. He owned eleven slaves, including twin pickaninnies named Simeon and Hannah, in honor of himself and his wife. Bristol having been ceded to Rhode Island, he bought a farm in Swansea, over the Massachusetts line, and thereafter divided his time between the two towns according to their respective tax rates and the demands of his lawsuits. He built a ropewalk in Bristol and spent the profits from it on lawyers' fees. He kept an aged man named Matthew Watson in debtors' prison for four years. When one of his deWolf nephews asked him how to make money, he roared, "Money? Why, I'd plow the sea to porridge to make money."

His most famous fight was with his own rector, the Reverend John Usher of Saint Michael's Episcopal Church. Usher, who was maintained by the Society for the Propagation of the Gospel in London, led as hard a life in Bristol as did Father Fauque in Oyapoc. He wrote his sermons before his huge chimney, his face toasted and his back frozen—for the cold seeped through the cracks of his settle, making icicles in his inkwell. Wrapped in a cloak and shod in moss-stuffed moccasins, he preached to a shivering handful of crown officials and the few sentimentalists who were homesick for the Church of England. Those of his congregation who owned slaves would not let him baptize them, for the slaves, both Indians and Negro, had a superstition that baptism would make them free. His salary was only £60 sterling (the Congregational minister got £100), out of which he had to maintain all the widows in his parish. The population of the village had not yet reached a thousand, almost all of whom were Congregationalists. Its isolation is described in one of Usher's reports to London:

> The town extends a mile in length and a quarter-mile in breadth. The farmers live at a greater distance, 3 or 4 miles off. The next church (in Newport) is 13 miles off, but hard to get there because of a troublesome ferry that must be crossed and of the deep snows which often fall in these parts, and render all travel exacting and difficult.

Although Potter was a churchwarden of Saint Michael's, he had no more mercy on Mr. Usher than on Father Fauque. Here, in part, is Usher's report on Potter's assault in 1761, the year when the pastor was seventy-three and the privateersman only forty-one:

> He is one that has arisen from nothing, being bred a Cooper only; but by following the Seas he became the captain of a Privateer, and by his undaunted courage acquired some interest in the world; and since, by Trading, is become a rich Merchant, though a loose vicious prophane scut as he had been all along. Notwithstanding he has an

agreeable wife, he has by report for some years back kept a criminal conversation with a young woman, one of my parish. . . . After many general hints from the Pulpit . . . I told her what reason I had to suggest she was guilty of the notorious sin of Adultery. . . .

Upon this she told the man immediately what I had said unto her, upon which the said man, Simeon Potter by name, attack't me in the street with bad and prophane language, as I was passing by his house, which stands upon the street near my Church. He first pushed and then struck, with his fist doubled, on the bone of my left cheek, and drew blood; and likewise sprain'd the thumb of my left hand, which is painful and useless to me still. One of my sons, being providentially near, rescued me by engaging him. I have bro't an action of £2000 damages, and this same man that so shamefully abus'd me hath brou't action of £10,000 against my son, who interpos'd and rescued me out of his violent hands.

Sir, please to excuse the blunders of this letter. I am hardly myself, for I never struck nor threaten'd, neither was I ever struck since I was a man, and now to meet with this is almost too hard for me in my old age.

The parson won a verdict of £500 "in our currency" for assault and battery, but since Rhode Island paper had dropped to £6.10 to the silver dollar, the damages were less than $100 in hard money. Potter's frivolous countersuit was thrown out by the royal magistrate in Newport, but he appealed to London. There the award against him was confirmed on condition that Usher come to England in person to collect it. He could not afford the voyage, so Potter never paid.

Potter moved out to Swansea until the popular indignation subsided, and then back to Bristol as if nothing had happened. He gave Saint Michael's a new bell, with a French inscription on it. Where could he have got it except at Father Fauque's mission in Oyapoc? After Usher died, he became the stanchest friend of his son and successor, the Reverend John Usher, Jr., the very man he had sued for £10,000; and during the Revolution, when Church-of-England worship was suspended, he hid the Saint Michael's silver in the same locked sea-chest with his own.

He was the first Bristol sea-captain to engage in transporting slaves from Africa to the southern colonies and the sugar islands. While he never made a slave voyage himself, and did not achieve the later success of his deWolf nephews, his investments in the traffic were considerable. The invoice of his slaver *King George* in 1764 amounted to £18,000 of "rag money," and his grasp of the business is shown by the instructions he sent to William Earle, her captain:

> Make yr. Cheaf Trade with the Blacks and Little or none with the white people if possible to be avoided. Worter yr. Rum as much as possible and sell as much by the short mesuer as you can. Order them in the Bots to worter thear Rum likewise, as the proof will Rise by the Rum standing in ye Son.

In 1772 Potter took part in the first American action against the Crown. Standing in the stern sheets of his own eight-oared whaleboat, with a crew of twelve Bristol boys, he rowed with muffled oars fifteen miles up Narragansett Bay to join a band of Providence rebels in burning His Majesty's grounded revenue-schooner *Gaspee*. He was never brought to trial.

The Revolution broke out more suddenly than most people believe. Although Rhode Island declared her independence in May of 1776, two months before the other colonies, the event passed unnoticed, and Benjamin Franklin could write in the same year, "I have never heard from any person, drunk or sober, the least wish for a separation."

Except for the burning of the *Gaspee*, there was no violence in Rhode Island until 1775. In that year, the last of his life, the Reverend John Usher preached a sermon from Romans 13: "The powers that be are ordained of God." (Most Episcopalians, unlike Potter, were Tories.) Parson Burt answered on the next Sunday from *his* pulpit that this text was "a damnable doctrine, which none but fools will believe." Then the battle of sermons became real warfare.

Bristol suffered more from the Revolution than any other New England seaport except Boston and Newport. On October 7, 1775, a squadron of fifteen sail, including a bomb-brig, approached the town from the royal garrison at Newport. It was led by Captain Sir James Wallace, aboard the twenty-gun frigate *Rose*. After saluting the vil-

lage with a carronade, he bawled through his trumpet an order that
the leading citizens come aboard. Nobody obeyed: an epidemic of
dysentery was raging in town, and most of those who were well
enough to move had fled behind Mount Hope. Wallace fired on the
town as night fell. The bomb-brig threw up "carcasses," which were
oval vessels filled with combustibles and bound with iron hoops. One
ball ripped open three hogsheads of rum in Potter's distillery. Another whistled over the bed of Benjamin Smith's imbecile son and
lodged in the fireplace. William Bradford, who shared the title of
leading citizen with Potter—he was Lieutenant-Governor of the
colony-state, and Potter commanded its militia—climbed over the
fence into his garden; a charge of grapeshot splintered the fence-
board an instant after he had let go of it.

At the height of the bombardment Potter strode out alone to the
wharfhead and signaled for a truce. Wallace ordered him to row
out to the flagship, where he demanded thirty fat cattle and two
hundred sheep as the price of a cease-fire. (The Tories later claimed
that Wallace had bought and already paid for them, but that the
farmers had failed to deliver.) Potter bargained with him. He beat
the price down to forty sheep, with no cattle at all. The animals were
delivered aboard at dawn the next day, their owners to be repaid by
the town. The squadron sailed back to Newport, and Bristol was at
peace again for a while. No one was killed in the bombardment; in
fact, Captain Wallace seems to have fired high on purpose. But the
next morning, which was Sunday, Parson Burt did not appear in
meeting. They found his body lying face down in "Mammy" Waldron's cornfield. The old man had died of fright. As Potter was the
day's hero, Parson Burt was its martyr.

When formal war broke out the next year, Sir Henry Clinton, the
British commander in America, acted promptly to bottle up Narragansett Bay. In December 1776 he dispatched to Newport a force
of more than five thousand men. This garrison was under command
of General Richard Prescott, and later, after Prescott had been captured in his nightshirt by rebel raiders, of Major General Sir Robert
Pigot. It is surprising to find that it included three regiments of Tory

Americans: the Prince of Wales Volunteers, the King's American Regiment, and the Loyal New Englanders. The British garrison was supported by a flotilla under Sir Peter Parker, strong enough to blockade the bay and to harry the commerce of the colonies farther north. Since Rhode Island, or Aquidneck, on which Newport lies, is separated from the mainland only by the mile-wide channel of Bristol Ferry, both sides set up batteries across from—and just out of reach of—each other. The American force on the Bristol side was a regiment of 300 under Colonel Nathaniel Cary, and a company of artillery under Captain Nathaniel Pearse. His Majesty's frigate *Emerald* blockaded the mouth of Bristol harbor. No Bristol vessel slipped past her during the occupation, but Bristol men served aboard the privateer *Oliver Cromwell* of Salem. Among other adventurers, two of her crew were sons of Mark Antony deWolf.* She was later captured off Saint Vincent by the British, but the brothers were never seen again.

For almost two years the royal forces faced the rebels across the ferry, with only a rare and ineffectual exchange of fire. Many Rhode Islanders enlisted in Washington's armies. The state recruited a regiment of slaves, whose pay was divided between their owners and themselves; in addition, the owners received a bonus of $180 and the slaves were promised their freedom in three years. An inconclusive battle was fought on the Island, almost within sight of the Bristol batteries, but it does not appear that the Bristol regiment took part in it. Major Frederic Mackenzie of the Royal Welsh Fusiliers drew in his diary a map of the situation at the south end of Bristol as it remained throughout the blockade. British and American redoubts face each other across the ferry, almost where the abutments of the Mount Hope Bridge now stand. The *Emerald* is anchored offshore, and the eighteen-pound American battery is far left, on Poppasquash.

On Sunday, May 25, 1778, five hundred British troops, mainly of the 22nd Regiment of Foot, with Hessian mercenaries for reinforcement,

---

* One of them, Samuel deWolf, died of fever and was "heft overboard," says the family Bible, the next day.

were ferried up from the Island to destroy some American ketches which were building in the Kickemuit River, at Warren. They landed on the Neck, between the two villages, under command of Lieutenant Colonel Campbell of the 22nd. One detail marched west to dismantle the eighteen-pound redoubt on Poppasquash. The main force turned up to Warren, where it blew up the ketches, killing seven Americans, and burned the Baptist church. The two groups then rejoined and marched down to Bristol.

The English wore lobsterback coats with many pleats, buff facings, and a profusion of white lace striped in red and white. They had cocked hats on their heads and smallclothes (knee breeches) on their legs. They had buckles at their shoes and knees. Their hair was clubbed and tied behind with a ribbon. They carried "Brown Bess," the standard musket of the British Army. The Hessian auxiliaries, who were part of the Bunau Regiment, wore huge fur busbys (though it was a warm day), black belts at their waists, and gaping boots in which to carry their plunder.

Colonel Cary, the Rhode Island commander, ordered his three hundred militiamen to retire westward to the Back Road, out of range of the British advance. Colonel Campbell met no resistance. The few Tories in town had set up a cask of punch for his troops' refreshment at what is now the corner of Hope and Bradford Streets. Campbell kicked it into the road. Hezekiah Usher, the pompous lawyer son of the Reverend John, tried to intercede for the town.

"Sir," he told Campbell, "I am a friend of the King."

"The very man I want," said the colonel. "Fall in."

Simeon Potter was absent in Swansea that day, but the British burned his house, along with Mark Antony deWolf's and thirty others. Saint Michael's Church was empty; Campbell, suspecting that arms were stored inside, set fire to it.* Did Potter, when he heard

---

* Caesar Walker, the colored sexton, had fled to Fox Hill. When they told him the church was gone, he answered, "Why, they can't have burned her. I've got the key right in my pocket."

When Governor Bradford's house was fired, his slave Nero had just sat down to dinner. He fled to the East Burying Ground with a skillet still in his hand, and finished his pork chops on a tombstone.

that his French bell had gone down in the flames, remember that "by mistake" he had burned Father Fauque's church in Oyapoc, thirty-four years before?

To avoid the rebel fire, Campbell formed a rear platoon of sixty prisoners and marched down the length of Ferry Road to a waiting sloop. Except for some sniping from behind stone walls, Colonel Cary did not molest him. After spiking the twenty-four pounder in the redoubt above the Point, he carried them across the Ferry and marched them to Newport. His only casualty was a diminutive Hessian drummer. His drum was so big, and the day so warm, that he could not keep up with the troops. Besides, he was tipsy. When he had fallen far enough behind, a group of women headed him off with pitchforks and kitchen knives. They retrieved his plunder from his boots and marched him back to town as a prisoner of war. In the end he was exchanged by Governor Bradford for the sixty Americans.

That summer a storm destroyed all the crops and most of the cattle in the village. For fear of another attack, most of the inhabitants fled to Massachusetts. In September, Lafayette, in titular command of two thousand Americans, arrived to set up a line of defense across the Neck. His command post was the high ground still called Fort Hill, across the road from Deacon Joseph Reynolds', and he planned to billet with the deacon. Lafayette, though a Major General of the Continental forces, was a kind of one-man army. He rode down alone to the deacon's, without epaulets and without announcing his name. In 1778 he was only twenty years old. Mrs. Reynolds, who had expected a whole retinue of venerable officers, supposed he was an equerry. She fed him, but warned him not to eat too much before General the Marquis de Lafayette arrived.

"Madam," said Lafayette, "*I* am the marquis."

He did not stay long in Bristol. That winter was the coldest in the town's history. The harbor froze solid for six weeks, and wood soared to twenty dollars a cord. British sentries at Newport froze to death at their posts. There was not much danger that Pigot would attack, but Lafayette retreated to Swansea, out of range of the British fleet. A map still exists on which Bristol is marked, in his handwriting, *"position abandonnée."* In Swansea he must often have dined with Simeon Potter.

Although Potter, by being absent on the day Bristol was burned, had been unable to prove his courage a second time, he became a hero all over again when he got the Assembly to reduce the town's tax assessment as one way to relieve the distress of the blockade. And then, when the future looked bleakest, the blockade was suddenly lifted. On October 25, 1779, the British, threatened by the arrival of the French fleet, abandoned Newport. Two or three of the Bristol Tories went with them, leaving their property to confiscation. Among the emigrants were Hubbard, the royal tax-collector, and William Vassall, who had bought Poppasquash from the heirs of Proprietor Byfield. It is not unlikely that Potter was among the crowd which stoned Vassall's coach as it rounded Poppasquash corner on his way to exile, for he was an ardent rebel and loved to repeat these lines:

> The man that's called a Tory
> To plague is all my glory.
> How righteous is the cause
> To keep the Congress laws.
> To fight against the king
> Bright Liberty will bring.
> Lord North and England's king,
> I hope that they will swing.
> Of this opinion I
> Resolve to live and die.

IV

The seaborne commerce of Rhode Island, including the slave trade, was paralyzed for the duration of the Revolution. Before and even during the British occupation, Newport, with a population of nine thousand, was one of the largest towns in America, and, except perhaps for Charleston, the most civilized. Its trade fled for safety to Providence, which was only half the size, and never returned. Bristol, with a population of only twelve hundred, recovered as soon as the British withdrawal moved the theater of hostilities to the southern states. Potter, who now bore the title of Colonel, built himself a new house on the harbor front. The Tory estates were sold off to pay the wages of the Continental troops. Governor Bradford, who was on the state committee to arrange the sale, himself bought in, at £11 sterling an acre, the confiscated farm of the Tory Isaac Royall. It included Mount Hope.

Washington passed through Bristol on March 15, 1781. The reporter who covered his visit says that

> The inhabitants, clad in their best apparel, stood upon either side of Hope St., being divided according to their sexes. As the General passed, they showed their respects by strewing his path with evergreens, pussy willows, etc., accompanied by the highest marks of civility.

That was a famous occasion, and Potter must have witnessed it. For years afterward Widow Burt, the relict of the parson who had died of fright in the bombardment, made each pupil in her Dame School learn and recite this quatrain:

> In fourteen hundred ninety-two
> Columbus sailed the ocean blue.
> In seventeen hundred eighty-one
> I saw General Washington.

He returned in 1793, as President, to spend a week with Governor Bradford, but it is recorded that Bradford did not present Potter to him, even though he was Potter's lawyer and his daughter Nancy had married Potter's nephew James deWolf. Professor Munro suggests that Potter's long absences in Swansea were due in part to the fact that the respectable Governor disapproved of him. One imagines Potter angling for the introduction too, and jealously watching from the Back Road as the President and the Governor, dressed alike in civilian smallclothes of black velvet, with powdered hair tied up in queues, paced the Mount Hope orchard arm in arm.

In spite of two wives and at least one mistress, Potter had no children. It must have galled him to see his sister Abby deWolf with fifteen. He lavished his churlish affection on her sons. As the slave trade revived, he launched the younger nephews in it, as he had already launched Charles. Under his guidance they turned the town into a smuggler's paradise. Simeon Potter became a sort of Satan Emeritus of the village.

He was not so loyal to the "Congress laws" as he pretended. Under an act signed by President Washington in 1794, it became a federal crime to import slaves into any state whose own statutes excluded them, or to carry them between foreign ports. All the states did exclude slaves except Georgia; and there was little money to be made by trading there, for the state was only partially settled, and the few Georgia planters were all poor men. The richest slave-buyers were the Spanish sugar-planters of Cuba. Potter advised his nephew Jim deWolf, in a letter which still survives, to import his slaves openly to Savannah, pretend to sell them to a Georgian, and then carry them to Cuba, where they would bring a high price. There was no law against importing slaves to Georgia, nor in exporting them from any state; but in case the question was raised, he advised fitting the slave ship with a false bottom—known to the trade as a "sug" bottom. His letter ends:

> You may depend this evades the Congres law, you gitten the act and peruse it, youl find it so. This is my advise you can take or leave as you please, but it must be kept a Profound Seckret.
>
> Yr. friend
S. Potter

The brothers evidently followed his advice, for in June 1797 the sloop *Sally*, Captain Isaac Manchester, landed 149 slaves from Anamabo at Savannah. She belonged to William and James deWolf.

Potter devoted his latter years to accumulating more land and to prosecuting his numerous lawsuits. He was elected moderator of the Bristol Town Meeting, but declined to serve, perhaps suspecting a trap. When he stalked out of Town Hall, the tax-collector followed him with a bill in his hand. He had paid no taxes in Bristol since the Revolution, and the collector found he had paid none in Swansea either. But Rhode Islanders—or Bristolians, at least—have always admired independence. He was elected to the state Senate in the following year, though he refused to attend the sessions and finally had to be subpoenaed into taking his seat.

War or peace, his avarice never slackened. In 1798, when he was nearing fourscore, he was swindled by an itinerant schoolteacher named Darby, who convinced him there was treasure buried in Bristol. Potter was eager to believe him and followed him night after night, in a ring with other believers, all chanting those two old songs "Nine Pots of Gold" and "Captain Kidd's Treasure." One can almost see his long nose twitching and his eyes aglint in the lantern-light at the thought of getting gold for nothing. In the end, the treasure turned out to be mica, for sale at a dollar an ounce. Darby evaded the law but was run out of town, in a coat of tar and feathers, by his victims.

Colonel Potter seems to have relished litigation for its own sake. In 1801, when he was over fourscore, he brought suit against one Charles Dudley, a Tory, for debts which he claimed had been incurred as long before as 1775. Dudley had long since left town, but Potter discovered some property he had abandoned—four tons of hay, a chaise, some harness, and a roasting-jack—and had Governor Bradford attach them. Bradford's disapproval of his client did not extend to declining a case; for if lawyers insisted that their clients be respectable, they would starve.

When Jim deWolf, his nephew, ran for the Assembly in 1802, on the Jeffersonian ticket, Potter did what he could to elect him. From Swansea he sent word to all his debtors, like this letter to Thomas Swan:

> You no I have been yr. friend, and have now a favor to ask of you: to vote for my Friend James deWolf as I no he will also be yr. Friend. Much depends on how you act in this affair, and not be led away by that bully Wardwell [Captain Sam Wardwell, the Federalist candidate]. Thus youl oblige me and Ill oblige you.
>
> Yr. friend,
S. Potter

At the end of his life he softened. Though he seldom went to services, which, since the British had burned Saint Michael's, were held in the keeping rooms of the faithful, he remained on the vestry. In the hatred of everything British which followed the Revolution, Saint Michael's almost passed out of existence—but Potter guarded its communion silver. Though he could hardly write, he gave the village three hundred dollars to found a public library and name it in his honor. He presented the Encyclopædia Britannica besides, in twenty volumes, two of which contained engravings. Dues at the Potter Library were twenty-five cents a year. If two subscribers wanted the same book, an auction was held, and the book went to the highest bidder. The length of time it might be kept out depended on its weight; a thick volume of sermons might last the whole winter, what with the scarcity of candles and the short hours of daylight.

He may have repented the sacrileges of his youth. Father Fauque and the Reverend John Usher could have told him that his childlessness was a punishment for his sins.

In 1805 he abandoned Swansea for good. On February 20, 1806, he died at his house on Bristol harbor, envied and unloved. His deWolf nephews bore him to the graveyard at the southeast corner of the Common. He had watched the little hamlet, scarcely conquered from the Indians, grow into a seaport with a population of two thousand and a commerce far out of proportion to its size.

Suspicious of tax-gatherers to the last, he left no will. The court appointed his sister Alithea Oldridge and his nephew William deWolf to act as administrators. They found he had left a quarter-million dollars and nine farms. They had to pay out most of the money to settle his pending lawsuits, but they found a letter directing that his real estate be divided among his nine sisters—not equally, but in proportion to his opinion of each. The best farm went to his sister Abigail deWolf. It adjoined the land of Governor Bradford, and Captain Potter thus posthumously achieved respectability himself. The flagon he had stolen fifty-eight years before in French Guiana descended to her son John. It has descended from him to a later John deWolf, himself a vestryman of Saint Michael's.

4.

The Slave Trade

AT THE end of the Revolution, American shipping revived quickly. The richest years of the New England seaports lasted from the peace treaty of 1784 to the election of Jackson in 1828. For half a century any port with adventurous merchants and a channel of twenty feet could harvest all the oceans of the world. During these years the fortunes of Boston and Providence were made in the China trade, those of Salem in the East Indies, and those of New Bedford and Nantucket in the whale fishery. Bristol, almost alone among the seaports, owed its wealth in this golden age to the slave trade and privateering—which is only a politer name for piracy—and soon became poor again when the two professions were at last outlawed.

Simeon Potter had dabbled in both, but what wealth he left was in farmland. Mark Antony deWolf, the clerk whom he married to his sister Abigail, never made a fortune himself, but he sired a generation which did. Although "Wolf" is a translation of the French *loup,* his curious name has nothing to do with the islands of Guadeloupe where his brother-in-law found him. There is record of an Abraham deWolf who in 1661 cornered the market for salt in New Amsterdam, before it became New York, and of a Balthasar deWolf who, at the end of the seventeenth century, was haled to court in Lyme, Connecticut, for smoking in public. As soon as he had paid his fine he lit up his pipe again, right in the courtroom. Some historians think the family is Swedish, some Russian, some German, and some Jewish. Another school, pointing to Abraham, claims it is Dutch, and that the "de" is not the French prefix of nobility at all but the Dutch word for "the"; so that the surname properly means "the wolf." It suits more than one of the family.

Some of its members have signed themselves Dwolf and even Dolph. The earliest spelling was d'Wolf. The actor deWolf Hopper stabilized the present orthography because, he said, it looked impressive on a billboard. In the presidency of Hayes, Bishop Mark Antony DeWolfe Howe—the present writer's grandfather—added the capital D and the final "e" for tone. In Benjamin Harrison's, the poetess Theodora Goujaud deWolf Colt hired heraldic experts to trace the origin of the name, and their fee was small for the delight they gave her. They reported that in 1369 King Charles "the Wise" of France, while hunting in the forest, was attacked by a she-wolf. One of his courtiers, at the risk of his own life, killed the beast. Charles ennobled him on the spot, with the title of deWolf, though it isn't clear why he didn't give the critter her French name. For good measure, the experts threw in a coat of arms with this impressive legend:

> *Or,* three wolves' heads erased sable, borne on the crest of an imperial double-headed eagle, sable-beaked. *Or,* a coronet of Baron of the Empire. Crest: out of a ducal coronet a demi-wolf *gules,* holding in dexter paw a fleur-de-lys *or.* Motto: Vincit Qui Patitur—He Conquers Who Endures.

No one could ask for more.

Even the non-deWolfs of Bristol are proud of the family. The old lady who did their sewing told me proudly, "They was handsome, dashing and reckless, but for morals something fierce."

And an aged Negress, so long ago that she may herself have been a slave, peeked through the counting-room window when two of Mark Antony's sons divided the profits of a voyage to the Slave Coast, weighing out gold dust, Spanish doubloons, and Portuguese Joes on a green baize table.

"Them was famous times," she sighed. "I looked through the window and seen them heap it up."

In 1956 a hundred and forty-six of Mark Antony's descendants gathered at the family's remaining mansion on the Fourth of July. The old seamstress was right: they *was* handsome—most of them dark and slim, with Roman noses and periwinkle eyes, but a few fair-haired. Their morals were invisible. Their other great houses have vanished, but no one was ashamed, and some hardly knew, that they had all been built from the profits of the slave trade, of privateering, smuggling, and piracy. The deWolfs had even outlived their arrogance. Only lately a Portuguese laundress was overheard to say of her employer, "She's *sweet*. Her name is deWolf, but she speaks to me."

The face of Abigail Potter deWolf, potato-brown and wise with many motherhoods, gazes down the centuries beneath her mob-cap. Mark Antony's nose almost meets his chin; he suggests a benevolent Mr. Punch. But he was a hard man, as sea-captains had to be: when one of his crew failed to answer the muster on sailing day, he had him bound in chains and carried aboard by the Bristol constable. Mark Antony stayed with the sea long after Simeon Potter had left it—had to, for he was perpetually in debt to support his growing family. On his voyages he carried a folio Bible in his sea chest; when he reached home, he would enter on the blank leaves at the back the names and birthdays of his children. One entry reads:

> Monday morning
> 25 minutes after 2 o'clock
> Decr. 19th 1762 william was
> Born.

He owned a share in Potter's privateer *Ranger* in 1777 and in the eighteen-ton sloop *Speedwell* in 1779, but they never got past the British blockade; in the thirty-ton sloop *Molly* in 1783, and a schooner of the same name in 1785, when he was fifty-nine. His vessels were all small, and he never owned them outright. It is possible that Potter gave him the shares in lieu of wages, for after the British burned his house in 1778 he seems to have had no money of his own at all. By then he was too old for the rigors of the sea. When age forced him ashore, he moved out to Swansea with Potter, since he had no home of his own. He would walk the ten miles to Bristol to sell a pailful of huckleberries. He would stop in for a meal with one of his daughters, and get her to sew up his straw hat. He became so shiftless that he once traded a good milker for a copy of Scott's *Commentaries on the Bible*. He turned his eyes to the hereafter. On the eve of the French Revolution he wrote to his son John, in Paris on the family slave business:

> I would advise you to make all despatch possible from that savadge country, as the world is in great commotion. We no not what difficulties may turn up; we hear there's sivel war in France, for independence. We are all passing through this life to a world of spirits. God grant we may all be ready at that hour.

His sons revered him even so. One old account-book of his son Jim's lists "a scarlet coat for my honor'd father M. A. deWolf." At last they raised $150 to build him a house on the Neck, across from Lafayette's old camp, and there, in 1793, he died insolvent. The Town Clerk's diagnosis of his last illness was "a nervous fever."

Between voyages he had sired fifteen children. Thirty-two of his immediate descendants, during New England's golden age, are listed on the Treasury records as owners or masters, or both, of sailing ships. Three of his daughters died at birth; the four who lived married husbands as poor as himself. Three of his sons died at sea, but five survived. All of his children, even the girls, had a little salt water in their blood. His daughter Nancy Kinnicutt, for instance, long after she had moved out West, did not forget the language of the sea. She wrote one of her brothers this exhortation:

> Eternity's vast ocean lies before us; be ready; give thy mind sea-room; keep it wide of earth, that rock of souls. Weigh anchor; spread thy sails; call every wind. Improve each breath of the spirit's eye, thy great Pole Star. Make the land of life, and look to Jesus. His countenance dispels the gloom of death, and guides thee through the darksome reef to everlasting day.

The five surviving brothers, for various lengths of time, engaged in the slave trade. The wealth they amassed depended on their acumen and the toughness of their conscience. Levi, the youngest, quit the trade in disgust after a single voyage, and spent the rest of his life with his Bible and his onion sets. The upland where he knelt in prayer each day has become Juniper Hill, the most beautiful of cemeteries.* His brothers, with affectionate contempt, called him "Quakerish." John, after several lucrative years in the traffic, became a farmer too, the best in the state, and the scribe and counselor of his brothers. His passport describes him as "34 years of age, with dark complexion, blue eyes, slim make and 5′10″ tall." That is almost a composite picture of the brothers, except for the homely Levi.

Charles, the eldest, was the most avaricious. He once invited Parson Wight of the Congregational church down to his counting-house.

"Parson," he told him, "I've always wanted to roll in gold." He lay down among the canvas sacks and wallowed, while the impecunious man of God looked on.

William was one of the few chubby deWolfs. Under his short curls, his smile is genial; but his kindliness did not keep him out of the trade in human flesh. After amassing a competence from the quarter-deck, he retired as owner of a dozen slavers and became the head of the company which insured Bristol vessels against shipwreck, piracy, and the penalties of the law.

James, who became the richest of the five, was the handsomest, with florid cheeks, a blunt nose, gray eyes, an upper lip as sheer as a carpenter's plane, and big capable sailor's hands. At fifteen he shipped aboard a privateer belonging to John Brown of Providence. The ship ran the Newport blockade, but Jim was captured by the British off Bermuda and imprisoned. He escaped, and they caught him again. At twenty-five he served aboard Brown's slaver *Providence*, with a share in her profits. At twenty-six he owned his own: the brig *Little Watt*. That year—1790—he came ashore to marry sharp-tongued,

---

* A vandal has scratched on the slate of Elkanah Waldron, "To Hell with death if you can die here," and Little Scamp has a headstone of his own between the Codman sisters, under a giant elm. His paws are carved in relief on its top, as if he were climbing up it from below.

button-nosed Nancy Bradford, the daughter of Washington's honored friend. She brought him as much money as he had made himself, and a respectability which was beyond the reach of his immigrant father or his low-born disreputable uncle Potter. James had the touch of Midas. As early as 1799 he contracted to build for the infant Navy, at a shipyard in neighboring Warren, the 624-ton ship-of-war *General Greene*. By 1800, next to the Brown brothers of Providence, he was probably the richest man in the state. His partnership with his own brothers was modeled on that of the Browns—James and Josey, Nick and Mosey, as Providence called them—and just as Moses Brown, even before the others, abandoned the slave trade for conscience' sake, the deWolfs had a maverick in the person of the Quakerish Levi. If John had the intellect of the family, and Charles its meanness, and William its gentleness, and James its comeliness, what piety the deWolfs inherit comes from Levi and the girls. In 1814, when Congress imposed a direct tax to prosecute the war with England, the brothers' possessions were valued as follows:

Levi	$ 7,500
John	18,800
Charles	25,500
William	43,500
James	91,500

II

Slave labor was never profitable in Rhode Island. As early as 1708 Governor Cranston wrote of

> the general dislike our planters have of them [slaves], by reason of their turbulent and unruly tempers. The inclination of our people in general is to employ white servants before negroes.

In 1784, when most families of substance had bought or inherited one or two slaves, the Bristol stock was only 73, or 5 per cent in a population of 1195. Oddly enough, none belonged to the deWolfs, though Widow Burt the schoolmistress, poor as she was, owned four. In the same year, Parson Wight's census reports 122 white bondservants and 25 free Negroes, besides two surviving Indians. Though there were 600,000 slaves in the whole country, fewer than 900 were owned in the state. Byfield kept ten bonded whites and one slave.

The carrying trade was a different matter. Its history runs from 1619, when a Dutch ship sold six Africans in Virginia, to 1820, when it became a hanging crime. The first native American traders of record are two elders of Boston who in 1645 imported a pair of slaves aboard the ship *Rainbow*, only to be forced by the horrified governor to ship them home again. The first Rhode Islander was one Edwin Carter of Newport: in 1700 he sailed for Africa with two sloops in company, and returned with full cargoes.

By a treaty with Spain in 1713 called the Assiento, Great Britain was granted a monoply on supplying slaves for the Spanish colonies of the Western Hemisphere, and bound herself to ship at least 4800 a year. This treaty, under successive names, lasted through the colonial century; most of its beneficiaries were English merchants, but those of the American colonies profited from it as well. Most New England seaports shunned the traffic, but the little colony of Rhode Island, and especially the ports of Bristol and Newport, became the chief suppliers of the great consumers to the south. In 1770 a hundred and fifty Rhode Island vessels, outnumbering those of all the other colonies together, engaged in the slave trade, and thirty distilleries manfactured the rum which was its currency. Since the early registers are lost, it is unknown which of the slavers hailed from Bristol. The first dealer on record is Simeon Potter, for whose account Captain Charles deWolf, in 1775, sold a few slaves in Jamaica for £42/6 from an unnamed vessel. But Potter was a casual trader; the first recorded voyage from Bristol to Africa for the specific purpose of buying slaves was made by Shearjashub Bourn's tiny schooner *Nancy*, of twenty tons. She cleared September 24, 1789, with John deWolf in command.

An act of 1774 prohibited the importation of slaves to the colony, but excepted those brought from the West Indies in Rhode Island bottoms. Another, in 1784, granted freedom after ten years of servitude to any slaves imported thereafter. In 1787, after the Revolution, the Assembly forbade all participation in the foreign slave trade,

under a penalty of £100 per slave and £1000 per ship. Even then,
as the *Nancy*'s voyage shows, the law was not enforced.

The framers of the Constitution would have abolished the trade
altogether, except that Georgia and South Carolina threatened to
secede if they did. To keep the two states in the Union, the document
contains this compromise:

> The importation of such Persons as any of the States now existing
> shall think proper to admit shall not be prohibited by the Congress
> prior to the Year one thousand eight hundred and eight,

in which the only consolation for the trade's opponents was the fact
that slaves were described as Persons, and that the legislatures of
every state except Georgia had in fact forbidden their importation.

Yet the trade had always been a little disreputable, even when it
was legal. After the act of 1787, merchants at least became less inclined to boast of it, and John Brown of Providence wrote apologet-
ically to his Quaker brother Moses in that year:

> I have it in mind to fit the ship *General Washington* to the East
> Indies, in which case I shall not be any more concerned in the
> Guinea trade.

By 1788 enough of the former colonies had ratified the Constitution to form a new nation. Although Rhode Island had declared her
independence two months before the rest of them, now, contrary as
always, she refused, for almost two years after President Washington's election, to join the Union. It was only when Congress threatened to lay tariffs against her shipping that she yielded. The Assembly wrote the President in 1789, "We are induced to hope that we
shall not be altogether considered as foreigners," but when he
would not relent, they capitulated. In 1790, last of the thirteen
original states, Rhode Island ratified.

The following year Washington appointed his old friend William
Ellery as Collector of the Port for the Newport district, which included Bristol. Ellery had signed the Declaration of Independence.
Like the other signers, he had done so at the risk of his life. He was a
straight-gazing patriot, scholarly, energetic, and incorruptible. Now

sixty-three, he wore his hair to the shoulder in the new-fashioned way, and mounted steel-rimmed spectacles on his nose. He had nothing against the village of Bristol—in fact, he had lived there in his youth. Widow Burt was his sister. His own father had dealt in slaves, while the trade was still legal. But he was sworn to protect the government's revenue, nine-tenths of which was derived from tonnage and import duties at the seaports. He regarded smuggling, and especially the smuggling of slaves, as nothing short of treason.

Except for foreign envoys, the Cabinet, and the Supreme Judiciary, Collectors of the Port held the most honored and lucrative posts in the President's gift. There were twenty-two collection districts in Massachusetts (which still included Maine), one in New Hampshire, four in Connecticut, and two—Providence and Newport—in Rhode Island. Ellery's district promised to give more trouble than any of the rest. He had no doubt that the deWolf brothers of Bristol—Charles, William, John, and James—with the help of their uncle Simeon Potter, were violating both state and federal law, and defrauding the Treasury of customs duties, by fitting ships to Africa for the slave trade and selling their human freight in Havana, far out of his reach, or, still worse, in the southern ports of the United States.

But this was not the only illicit conduct charged to them. Since a slaver's insurance covered mortality only in excess of 20 per cent, it was a natural temptation to throw a sick slave overboard rather than let him infect the others. In 1791 the federal grand jury, in its first session for Rhode Island, returned an indictment of murder against James deWolf for jettisoning a female slave who had caught the smallpox on the Middle Passage aboard a bark of which he was master. The ship registers are missing for the years from 1786 to 1791, so we do not know the name of the vessel or her owner. We do not know which citizen was brave enough to prefer the charge against Captain Jim, but Collector Ellery would be a good guess. The faded indictment, still buried in the files of the Department of Justice, charges that

> . . . James deWolf, not having the fear of God before his eyes, but being moved and seduced by the instigation of the Devil . . .

did feloniously, willfully and of his malice aforethought, with his hands clinch and seize in and upon the body of said Negro woman . . . and did push, cast and throw her from out of said vessel into the Sea and waters of the Ocean, whereby and whereupon she then and there instantly sank, drowned and died.

Though President Washington, through Attorney General Jay, issued a capias for Captain Jim's arrest, and though Bristol is almost within sight of Newport, the federal marshal, for the next four years, reported semi-annually to the court that "he could not by me be found," until, in 1795, a more lenient district attorney nol-prossed the case.

A story was long extant in town that the young captain of the deWolf slaver *Sukey*, had thrown several slaves overboard, and, when they clung to the taffrail, had cut off their hands at the wrist. There may be some truth in this tale, though Captain Jim was a humane man, for the broad-minded John Brown wrote to a friend, just before the election of 1802:

> I wish it may properly be introduced to Mr. James deWolf that it already begins to be talked of in our streets that if he don't conduct himself within the bounds of reason, the statement of his murdering his negroes in the smallpox to preserve the other part of his cargo in his passage from Africa will be echoed through the papers of the various states. . . . I assure you that his going a deputy will, in my opinion, cause great clamor against the town as being in favor of the Guinea Trade directly in the face of the law.

Eighteen hundred and eight was a long way in the future, but the public conscience gradually awoke. An act of 1794 forbade Americans to carry slaves between foreign countries, or into or out of any state whose own statutes prohibited the trade. This was the law which Potter taught Captain Jim to evade, and it soon covered all the states, for even Georgia outlawed the business. The penalty was a hundred dollars per slave and forfeiture of the ship. Another law, in 1800, added two years in prison and fined the crew of a slaver a hundred dollars a head. This act did not pass without the opposition of the New England shipowners. During the debate the reformed John Brown, by then a Congressman, exclaimed on the floor of the House,

"Why should we see Great Britain getting all the slave-trade to themselves? Why may not our own country be enriched by that lucrative traffic?"

It was one thing to enact laws and another to enforce them. The infant government had no navy. The Bristol captains, who knew Narragansett Bay like the inside of their own pockets, could slip past Newport by any of three channels under cover of darkness or fog, and then stand for Africa, where there were no consuls to prevent their loading slaves, and thence to the sugar islands, which were only too willing to receive their black cargoes.

In July of 1799 the schooner *Lucy*, in ballast, tied up at the deWolf warehouse. She was a trim vessel of sixty-six tons with two masts and the figurehead of a woman. She had been built only two years before at Norwich, Connecticut. Charles Collins, a brother-in-law of James deWolf (his wife had been Lydia Bradford, a sister of Nancy's), was her master. Collins, a politician with impudent hazel eyes and full cheeks like a chipmunk's, was an old hand at evading the law. In 1791, at Halifax, before he was twenty, he had been fined for smuggling flour, and had written a letter home, which Ellery had seen, in which he said of the British judges who sentenced him, "May the great God curse the bunch of them."

Charles deWolf was the *Lucy's* owner. William and James had posted her good-conduct bond for $1500. Most of the village, directly or indirectly, had some stake in her. She had not lain a week at the wharf before Collector Ellery, in Newport, libeled her as a suspected slaver. The United States District Court at Providence condemned her to be sold for the benefit of the government. Ellery ordered his local surveyor at Bristol, Samuel Bosworth, to attend the auction and bid on her for the Treasury. She was a brisk sailer, as slavers had to be, and would make a fine revenue cutter for Narragansett Bay.

It was an unpalatable assignment for Bosworth, for he depended on the deWolfs for his fees, and even for his livelihood. So did many of his fellow townsmen—the seamen and coopers and chandlers who made their living from the outlaw trade. Collins and the deWolfs urged him to defy Ellery's order, so that they could bid the *Lucy* in themselves, without competition. John Brown himself rode down from Providence to dissuade him. But Bosworth, grandson of the deacon who had built the first house in town and led the first prayers, was not a man to shirk his duty. He asked Ellery to let him off, but when the order was repeated he prepared to attend the sale and bid for the *Lucy* against her owners.

He reached the wharf a little before ten on the morning of July 25. A good crowd was waiting for the "vandoo" to begin, though no one except the government or the deWolfs themselves could afford to buy the vessel. As the unwilling surveyor passed the corner of Thames Street and Pump Lane, Collins, standing in a doorway, waved his hat. Instantly eight men dressed as Indians, with faces blacked, ran out from the crowd. They seized Bosworth and hustled him into a skiff that lay tied to the piling of the wharf. He called to Russell Warren, the housewright, who was in plain sight through the open door of his shop. Warren did not hear him. Captain Aaron Usher bustled to help him, but was too late. The agent of the United States government was rowed off from the wharf in silence, down the harbor and around Ferry Point, and dumped ashore at the base of Mount Hope, two miles afoot, and through the woods at that, from the *Lucy*. The federal marshal postponed the sale as long as he dared. Collins and the deWolfs had not forgotten that it takes two to make an auction. They let themselves be outbid by a Cuban captain in their own employ. The *Lucy* resumed her trade under the flag of Spain, and the Treasury was enriched by a paltry $738.

To most New Englanders, Jefferson was a dangerous radical, if not the Devil incarnate. Potter and the two seafaring deWolf brothers, Charles and James, were almost the only men of substance in New England who supported his new Republican party against the Federalists. (William and John did not commit themselves.) They even organized a Tammany Society in the village, with free beer supplied by Captain Jim. Two years after the affair of the *Lucy*, when Jefferson succeeded John Adams, they took their revenge on Ellery. They persuaded Jefferson to set up an independent revenue district for Bristol and Warren, with a collector of its own. The man whom Jefferson appointed was Charles Collins, captain of the convicted slaver. Surveyor Bosworth wrote bravely to Albert Gallatin, the Secretary of the Treasury, that Collins was even then part owner of the slavers *Armstadt* and *Minerva,* and Ellery himself protested to Jefferson: if erecting the unnecessary collectorship at Bristol was an insult to him, handing it to Collins was a disgrace to the country. The protests did them no good, for Jefferson knew the value of rich friends in a hostile state, and his apparent innocence was the greatest part of his acumen. The deWolfs did not dare have Bosworth dismissed as surveyor, but he was never promoted. He stayed on as a subordinate for the rest of his life. Like many officeholders since, he had learned the penalties of independence, and complained no more. The Senate confirmed Collins. On the day he swore to uphold the Constitution, the *Minerva* landed a hundred and fifty slaves at Havana.

Soon after his appointment, Ellery wrote resignedly to a friend:

> The slave traders, as if determined to set Congress at naught, are driving on their trade Jehu-like. Not less than eight or ten vessels have sailed or are about sailing from Bristol to Africa. But forsooth most of them, like deWolf's vessels, claim they go for elephants' teeth and gold-dust. I expect that the houses of some of the Great Folks will be adorned with ivory, and their horses shod with gold. Some suspect and hope that the slave act will be repealed at the next session of Congress. I can see that this open defiance of law will be as likely to effect it as the late exploit of the Indians was to procure a collector of customs for the district of Bristol. *Quos Deus vult perdere, prius dementat.*

Collins continued as collector for Bristol twenty years, issuing clearances to any vessels he chose, without control by Ellery. Ellery's only advantage was his command of the revenue cutter *Vigilant,* but he could not use her against the Bristol traders without clear proof they had violated the law, which was always hard to get.

In 1802, with Potter's help and over Brown's protest, James deWolf was elected to the legislature, defeating the Federalist Sam Wardwell. Wardwell dealt in slaves too, but had not been accused of drowning them. Not long after the election, Captain Jim passed

Wardwell's pigpen on Thames Street. Wardwell was leaning over the fence, admiring his stock. When Captain Jim was rash enough to taunt him with his defeat, Wardwell swung around, grasped him by the breeches, and threw him into the sty, shouting, "deWolf, you're the *hoggiest* hog of them all."

Everybody deplored the slave trade; Jefferson himself exclaimed, "I tremble for my country when I think of the Negro and reflect that God is just." But most people still tolerated it. Neither Bishop Griswold at St. Michael's nor Parson Wight up street denounced it from his pulpit. Griswold, in fact, inherited a plantationful of slaves in Cuba. This saintly giant who strode from his house to his church bellowing a hymn and fully vested, who was so humble that he blacked the boots of his students and carried the slops downstairs to spare his own servants the chore, was offered a good price for his slaves by Charles deWolf's son George. He declined to sell them, or even liberate them—not because he condoned slavery, but because, as he sensibly put it, the plantation could not be run without them.

III

Barring shipwreck, confiscation, and disease, which were covered by insurance,* the operation of the deWolf partnership was almost foolproof. There was a deWolf at each corner and on every leg of the triangle. Molasses from the deWolf plantations in Cuba reached Bristol in deWolf bottoms, was turned into rum at the deWolf distillery, and exported with other trade goods, again in deWolf ships, to the slave coast of Africa. There the cargoes were exchanged for slaves,

---

* Modern businessmen would welcome the simplicity of the policies. Here is one which Major William deWolf of the Bristol Insurance Company issued to his brother Charles:

"Q. What premium will the Cy. ask for a Risk of $9000 on ship *Constantia* and her cargo from this port to, in and from Mozambique or any other port or ports of Africa, to the Havanna or Rio de la Plata in So. America, or both, including natural mortality exceeding 20 pr. Centum and Illicit Trade, and also every other kind of Risk, whether contemplated at the time of this insurance or not? On ship and outfits $5000; on Cargo, valued at $140 each, $4000. Chas. deWolf.

"A. The Company will take this Risque @ 15 pr. Cent. William deWolf.

"Agreed. Charles deWolf."

and the new freight brought back for sale at the starting point in Cuba. Captain Jim's distillery on Thames Street converted 300 gallons of molasses every day into 250 gallons of rum. The cost of distillation was 10 cents a gallon. He paid the Treasury an import duty of 5 cents, but received a rebate of 3 cents, called a drawback, when he exported it as rum. The casks, stamped with his mark, $_{DW}^{J}$, would unload from his own ship at his own wharf, pass Bosworth's inspection, and be hauled by his own oxen. As long as they stood on the wharf they were surrounded by boys of the town, clustered like flies about the oozing sweetness and dipping slivers of shingle into the bunghole or scraping the leaky rims.

(This operation was called "labbing 'lasses"; Bosworth did not molest it. From the name came a rhyme the boys sang on Babbitt's wharf next door:

> Mister Babbitt,
> Lemme labbit.)

After the rum was distilled, it was stowed in hogsheads, along with other trade goods, aboard the same vessel or another of the deWolf fleet. It retailed at 35 cents a gallon, but had cost Captain Jim much less. It was stowed in the bilge. The six-foot space below the main deck was packed with the more perishable cargo. On one African voyage the three-hundred-ton ship *Ann* took aboard:

184	hogsheads, 26 tierces and 33 barrels new rum	28	doz. silk hats
16	boxes claret	2043	lbs. ham
6	pipes molasses	80	hogsheads salt
2	pipes gin	5	chaldrons coal
8	pipes brandy	3	casks porter
1	case cambrics	6	cases India goods
10	hogsheads tobacco	2	boxes calicoes
620	hogsheads codfish	17000	staves
20	firkins butter	1200	pieces nankeens
110	bars iron	1	bale muslins
100	" American steel	30M	boards
20	pots and kettles		Ships stores for the voyage

The *Sukey*, on a voyage of 1802, carried such items as twenty bolts of scarlet broadcloth; a case of lute-strings; two gross of men's hats in red, green, and white, embroidered with tinsel lace; three thousand yellow-handled knives; and miscellaneous necklaces, rings, muskets, snuff, and segars. There was little demand for specie on the Slave Coast, and none for paper money. Except for the rum, most of the outward cargoes for the slave-trade were bought from wholesalers like Samuel Parkman of Boston—a grandfather of the great historian.

Any boy in town with a heart for the sea and a strong stomach could get a job aboard. Each was allowed a "venture" of his own—a few bunches of red Bristol onions, or a dozen knives from Pardon Handy's ship chandlery. He would trade them in Africa or Havana for whatever trifles might please his wife or his girl. The ship would return with such souvenirs as parrots, birds of paradise, ring-tailed monkeys, cases of oranges and bananas—or if a sailor had no girl, he might turn his venture into Havana segars for himself. Captain Walter Dalton of the brig *Olive Branch* brought back a leopard. It was just a playful kitten when it landed, and almost white; as it grew older its coat blossomed with beautiful black spots on a tawny ground. On shore, Dalton kept it in a cage next to the fireplace. But once it broke out, and Mrs. Dalton found it with its paws on the edge of her baby's cradle, its pink tongue lolling out between sharp white teeth. That was the end of leopards for *her*. But the captain was a thrifty man; instead of executing his pet, he sold it to the circus which visited Bristol every Fourth of July.

Most of the men in town would be involved in the fitting-out. Before weighing anchor, Captain Job Almy of the *Sukey* settled accounts with Jabez Chase for a medicine chest, with Ben Tilley for cordage from his ropewalk, with the pious Levi deWolf for onions at 2 cents a bunch, with sailmakers, carpenters, calkers, painters, ship chandlers, and innkeepers. He paid Quackey Babbitt, a servant of the wharf-owner, $3.20 for sawing firewood, and Russell Warren the house-wright (he was later the architect of all the deWolf mansions) $6.07

for scrap iron. Besides his chest of small arms, he carried, for defense against pirates, two carronades lashed amidships and a "chaser" of brass at the stern. The *Sukey* was a seventy-foot topsail schooner— the most weatherly rig and profitable burthen for the slave trade. At 1½ tons per foot of length, and at $25 a ton, she must have cost Captain Jim under $3000 to build, but her cargo, and the wages of her crew, brought his investment up to $15,000. (A vessel's tonnage in those days had nothing to do with displacement. It was a measurement of volume: length by beam by depth of hull. One ton was the equivalent of ninety-five cubic feet.) Wages ran from $8 a month to Elkanah Waldron, boy, up to $30 for Captain Almy.

At the customhouse, Collins signed her bill of health:

> To all the faithful of CHRIST to whom these presents may come.
> Whereas it is pious and just to bear witness to the Truth, lest Error and Deceit overthrow it; and
> Whereas the schooner *Sukey* of Bristol, of which Job Almy, under GOD, is Master, and now ready to depart from the PORT of Bristol, and, if GOD pleases, to sail for the Coast of Africa and other places beyond the Sea with twelve Men, including the master of said Schooner;
> We therefore to you all, by the Tenor of these Presents, do make known, that (Praise be to GOD the MOST HIGH AND GOOD) no Plague or any dangerous or contagious Disease at present exists in the said port of Bristol.

His fee for this document was $5.46, and Nathaniel Ingraham's, for pilotage to the open sea at Newport, was $6.00.

The outward voyage of the slaver would be spent in cutting the planks which would form the slave deck on the return. The planks were listed on the manifest as lumber for repairs to the ship herself, or as merchandise for sale abroad. They were not fitted in place, however, until the outward cargo was sold in Africa and the slaves ready to load, for the possession of slave decks in place was *prima facie* evidence against the ship.

Having crossed the Atlantic, the slaver would put in to refit at one of the stations on the western shoulder of Africa—Goree, or the

Cape Verdes, or the Los Islands—or, until Britain outlawed the trade in her colonies, at Sierra Leone. The captain laid in bananas, horse-beans, rice, palm wine, farina, and a few live goats, on which to feed his expected cargo. (Slaves were fed twice a day at sea, in lots of ten at a time. The starchy diet was spiced with slabber-sauce, made of flour, water, palm oil, and pepper.) He checked his wooden spoons against the carpenter's chart of lading. Iron spoons, which the slaves might use as weapons, were not carried. The blacksmith checked his thumbscrews, used to punish obstinate slaves, and his iron jaw-openers (called *speculum oris*), for forcible feeding. The quartermaster refilled his 150-gallon water butts. Then the ship stood down the Gulf of Guinea, past the Grain Coast, the Ivory Coast, and the Gold Coast, to the Slave Coast and the Bight of Benin, where her cargo awaited her. The trip across the gulf was fifteen hundred miles.

The shoreline of the Gulf of Guinea is always green, for there are no seasons at the equator. The wind blows from the south. One Bristol skipper wrote home that the temperature at Saint Paul de Loanda reached 120 degrees in December. There is no tide. Long rollers break far out from the flat beaches, so that ships of any draft had to moor offshore and send longboats in for the bargaining. At times the harmattan wind blows yellow dust five hundred miles out to sea. Shallow rivers, feeding the twisted stilted roots of the mangroves, wind down from the jungle. Along their banks, hidden from the open sea, were the beehive-roofed straw huts of the vendors, called palaver-houses, where the bargaining took place. Beside them stood the stockades, called barracoons, where the slaves were fattened and oiled for sale.

The slaves came from many different tribes in the interior: the round-headed chestnut Fulas and the flat-nosed dark Mandingos. Bound together with thongs and forked sticks they had been driven from the interior in long files called kaffles.

The religion of the Mandingos combined Mohammedanism with voodoo. They venerated the Mumbo-jumbo, a straw fetish with a man

hidden inside it. Quarrels between husband and wife were referred
to the Mumbo-jumbo, who always decided in favor of the husband.
About their necks they wore charms called grisgris, written on paper
by the marabouts, who sold them for high prices to protect the
wearer. They believed that an eclipse was caused by a cat putting its
paws between the moon and the earth; and they sacrificed chickens
to read the future in the entrails. The Fulas were more advanced.
They were thrifty and neat. Many of them spoke Arabic and they
were excellent cooks. The tribes all feared the sea, except for the
sturdy Krus from what was later to become Liberia. The Krus often
bought their freedom by manning the slaver's longboats.

A slave might have been doomed to servitude by his king in punishment for a crime, or captured in a tribal war and sold to the dealers
by his captor, or simply kidnapped. The kings themselves avoided the
coast. The King of Benin was so shy of foreigners, to say nothing of
the sea, that he lived invisible in his great tent, only displaying a foot
through the flap from time to time to show his subjects that he was
still alive. The King of Dahomey, at his capital village of Abomey,
lived in a straw palace lined with the skulls of twenty generations of
tribal enemies. Among the sovereigns of the Slave Coast were King
Ephraim of Cambo, King Mammee of Yallaba, King Holiday of
Bonny, King Quaco Dooah of Ashantee, and King Vinegar of Rio
Bassa. The latter is said to have sold seventy thousand of his subjects
in the years from 1808 to 1813. There was King Boatswain of Shebar,
who was seven feet tall. None failed to collect his tax—called the
coomey—from every white trader who did business in his territory.
Liberia itself, the colony of liberated slaves, was bought in 1820 from
a syndicate of monarchs named Peter, Long Peter, George, Zoda,
Governor, and Jimmy. The price was six muskets, two casks of tobacco, a box of soap, four umbrellas, four hats, eight pairs of shoes,
three mirrors, three canes, miscellaneous crockery and dry goods, and
a barrel each of powder, beads, nails, and rum.

Nominally the country was in Portuguese hands; one of the titles
of the King of Portugal was Lord of Guinea. In crumbling castles

such as Ambriz and Saint Paul de Loanda a show of government
was maintained by the Portuguese proconsuls. But the power lay in
the dealers, or "factors," as they were more politely called, who
bought slaves from the native kings and resold them at a profit to the
white ship-captains. To satisfy the demands of the Cuban canefields
and the Carolina cotton plantations, the factors were not above starting a jungle war by offering two rival kings the same price for whatever captives each might take from the other.

The factors were of many races. DaSouza, known to the coast as
Cha-cha, was a Brazilian mulatto. Madame Ferreira, who perhaps
did not trade directly in slaves, but maintained herself handsomely
by provisioning those who did, was Portuguese. Henry Brotherton
was English. Charles Slocum, who peddled slaves offshore in a bum-
boat, was a Yankee. When George deWolf's ship *Eliza* was condemned by the British Admiralty court at Sierra Leone in 1804,
Slocum had the enterprise to buy her in and send her back to Bristol
for resale to deWolf.

Don Pedro Blanco was a Spaniard from Malaga, Thomas Jourdain
was French, Blas Covado a Mexican, and N. P. Biering of the Los
Islands a Dane. The cynical Theodore Canot, known to the trade as
Mongo Gunpowder ("mongo" is the Mandingo word for "king")
claimed to be an Italian. When on the search for inventory, in the
jungle, he wore a cruising dress of red flannel shirt, Panama hat, and
white duck leggins. Canot thus describes the persuasion of rum in the
trade:

> Next day the King made his appearance in all the paraphernalia
> of African court dress. A few fathoms of check girded his loins, while
> a blue shirt and red waistcoat were surmounted by a dragoon's cap
> with brass ornaments. We proceeded to formal business. His Majesty
> called a palaver of his chiefs and headmen, before whom I announced
> my terms. Very soon, several young folks were brought for sale who,
> I am sure, never dreamed, at rising from last night's sleep, that they
> were destined for Cuban slavery. My merchandise revived the mem-
> ory of pecadillos that had long been forgotten, and sentences that
> were forgiven. Jealous husbands, when they tasted my rum, suddenly

remembered their wives' infidelities, and sold their better halves for liquor in which to forget them. I became a magician, unroofing the village and baring its crime and wickedness to the eye of justice. Law became profitable, and virtue had never reached so high a price.

The Africans took their rum straight; the factors and their clients, more prudent, diluted theirs with water or lime-juice. New England shipped more rum to the coast than other parts of the country, to the point where a "rum vessel" became the word for a New England slaver.

Nobody on the coast, except the slaves themselves, wanted the trade to end. For fifteen hundred miles, from the Gambia to Cape Palmas, the country was a continuous slave market, interrupted only, after 1786, by the free British colony of Sierra Leone, and, after 1820, by the republic of Liberia. European countries maintained trading posts, called "factories," where their citizens could store the slaves they had bought, under guard, while awaiting shipment to market: the Dutch at Almena, the Danes at Accra, the Prussians at Fredericksburg, the British at Annamaboe and Cape Coast Castle, and the French at Fort St. Louis and Goree. There were no factories for the use of Americans, but, on the other hand, there were no American consuls to enforce the laws against the trade.

The Bristol captain had to be a shrewd trader as well as a good sailor. Since he might be absent a year or more, the owners gave him great latitude. As soon as his ship anchored, he stacked his trade-goods on deck for the inspection of the factors. As tween-decks was cleared of the outward cargo, the carpenter set up the planking he had cut on the voyage, riveted the leg-irons to it, stretched netting along the gunwales to keep the expected cargo from jumping overboard, and erected a barricade at the quarterdeck to prevent their invading the cabin. Since tween-decks was never more than six feet high, the planking, which was framed midway across it, left a little less than three feet headroom for each layer. Ideal lading was 16 inches by 5 feet 6 inches by 2 feet 10 inches per head. A tight pack was to the captain's interest, for he was entitled to buy for his own account 5 per cent of the total cargo carried, and ship them without paying freight.

After showing the factor his wares and giving him a "dash," or bribe—perhaps a bottle of rum or a musket—the captain rowed ashore with him to open negotiations in the palaver-house. They could take a long time, for the captain insisted on quality and bought the goods a few at a time. The ship's surgeon examined every inch of a slave before passing him, for a single sick one, in the crowded conditions aboard ship, could endanger the whole cargo. Sometimes the captain had to haggle for weeks at the palaver-house, squatting on a palm mat, while his crew grew mutinous or sick aboard ship. Sometimes he would load only a few head before sailing on to the next post, and he had to weigh anchor at night, for the land breeze rose at ten and failed at two. On the *Sukey's* voyage Captain Almy had to put in at Cape Mesurado, Grand Popo, Tradetown, Picaninni Sestus, and Bassa before he had disposed of his outward cargo and loaded all of his hundred and twenty slaves. He spent five months in this coasting, which was longer than Captain Jim had allowed for the whole voyage. By the time he cleared from Bassa, twenty-two of the slaves he had bought at Cape Mesurado had died—some of smallpox, some of dysentery, and some of jumping overboard.

Through the eighteenth century, while the trade was still legal, the market on the Slave Coast was fairly stable. Prime mercantile males, good for work or breeding, cost a 120-gallon hogshead of rum plus 30 gallons "dash" to the factor—or, if bought for cash, which was rare, about $30 in gold-dust or Spanish milled dollars. The demand for slaves increased enormously with the invention of the cotton gin in 1793. Charleston exported twenty thousand pounds of cotton in 1791, twenty million in 1801, and forty million in 1803. The price of slaves in Africa rose to as much as a hundred dollars in barter. In 1796 Jeremiah Diman of Bristol writes home to his deWolf brothers-in-law that he has paid 8 Joes for slaves on the Coast and sold them for 25 Joes in Havana. (The Joe was a Portuguese gold coin worth $8.) Complicated deals were computed in a unit called the bar, a fictitious currency based originally on the worth of a pig of iron, and soon standardized at 50 cents in gold. An ounce of bullion traded for 32 bars, or $16. A musket was worth 12. Two yards of cotton cloth were worth 1, and so were 24 ounces of tobacco or 16 ounces of ivory. On the *Sukey's* voyage Captain Almy traded 120 dozen knives for one fine male. They had cost $1 a dozen at Pardon Handy's chandlery. At all times, women over twenty-five years old, and boys under four feet four inches tall, were subject to 20 per cent discount, and the victims of dysentery went even cheaper.

When the purchase was completed, the slaves were put in good humor by a parting feast. The day before embarkation their heads were shaved and the initials of their new owner—in the *Sukey's* case, JDW—were branded on their hips or thighs with an iron seal or a silver wire. The brands were just hot enough to blister the skin without burning it. On the morning of sailing day they were stripped naked and ferried through the surf by the Kru oarsmen to the slaver waiting offshore. Sad stories are told of those departures. An old Negro called Charles Coomer, who died in Bristol at the end of the last century, recalled that he had been snatched from his mother by the boatswain of a longboat when he could not have been older than three or four. Why he did not take Charles's mother too, Charles himself could not say; perhaps the slaver had no room for one more grownup, or perhaps she was too old for the market. He had long since forgotten all about her except that she ran into the surf after him, begging to be taken, and that when the boatswain shook her off she held out a piece of bread to Charles as a parting gift. When the boatswain reached Bristol he smuggled Charles ashore and sold him to Mr. Coomer for a bag of coffee.

With all cargo stowed, the ship stood westward on the second leg of her voyage. The Middle Passage, from Africa to the West Indies, lasted seven weeks in fair weather. Officers and crew slept above deck in temporary cabins called doghouses, for the slaves filled every square inch of the forecastle and wardroom, as well as the tween-decks. The males were shackled in pairs, the left ankle of one to the right ankle of the next, with a yoke-iron stapled to the planking between them. The women and children, unfettered, lay behind a screen. With ideal lading the deck-shackles were spaced so closely that the cargo, to lie down, must bend their knees and nest spoon-wise, front to back, and, to sit up, telescope themselves like the crew of a toboggan. They were wedged so tight to the boards, and left there for so long, that when they were taken on deck for air they sometimes left strips of their skin on the planking. Then the leg-irons were replaced by darbies at the wrists, the quartermaster turning his heavy bitt-key in one lock before he threw open the other. The slaves were herded up the hatchway, and the retching crew went below to swab out their quarters with vinegar. They say you could smell a slaver five miles down wind. Sometimes the clean-ing her out for another round was so expensive that she was sold in her filth at Havana for whatever she would bring, as Captain Sam Wardwell, the deWolfs' rival, sold his *Merry Quaker* in 1795.

Sometimes, in the doldrums, she ran into a week-long calm. The white crew, reduced to a gill of water each, lay panting under the deck awning, some of them crying like babies, while the cargo groaned and sweated beneath them and the dogvane above veered from side to side as the vessel rolled on the lazy swell. A tropical shower would sweep down to relieve them, but in five minutes the sun would blaze out again.

The slaver's crew was always in danger, either from malaria (it was called the "African fever") or from French or British hijackers, or from the cargo itself. Many Bristol boys laid their bones beside the sultry African rivers. In 1796 Mark Antony deWolf III, son of the Mark, Junior, who had been lost at sea on a slaving voyage, died of the fever; and in the same year his cousin Simon, Junior, whose father had been washed overboard from a privateer, cut his own throat on the Guinea coast. Once, aboard a Bristol vessel in the Bight of Benin, the slaves escaped from their shackles and drove every white man overboard except the captain. He, left alone at the hatchway, saw a huge slave bear down, ready to crash the swinging darbies on his head. He reached into his cabin, picked up a cask of gunpowder, and held a lighted match to the bung. The Negroes, thinking he was about to blow up the ship, climbed over the net and leaped into the sea. Those who could swim reached the shore; those who could not were eaten by sharks.

One of the most harrowing tales of the Middle Passage is that of the French brig *Rodeur*. Heavy with a full cargo, she sailed from Saint Paul de Loanda for Havana. Three days out the slaves, one by one, went blind from ophthalmia. Tight-packed as they were, nothing could halt the contagion. The surgeon persuaded the captain to let the whole cargo on deck at once, in the hope that fresh air would end the plague. As *Niles' Register* reports it:

> When they were so permitted, they locked themselves in each other's arms, with the shackles still on their ankles, and, to put an end to their miseries, plunged into the ocean. This, the surgeon said, was the effect of a disease called *nostalgia*, arising from a desire to revisit their native land. We say that it is as strong a symptom of a broken heart as could be imagined.

The *Rodeur* was justly punished. A passing ship found her adrift in the Sargasso Sea without a black man aboard, and with every white man blind.

Such incidents were exceptional. Generally the slaver reached Havana with less than 10 per cent mortality. At the first sight of land the danger of disease and mutiny was considered over. The water butts were opened to crew and cargo alike. The cat-o'-nine-tails was thrown overboard. The netting was dismantled. Sailors shared their biscuit and clothing with the slaves. The females were fitted out with sheets, tablecloths, spare sails, oilcloths, and even monkey-jackets from the wardrobes of all hands, and danced unshackled on the deck. The immigrants' last day aboard was one long masquerade.

Arrived at Havana, the captain had to pay a tax of five dollars a head to the Spanish customs and a bribe of eight dollars more—politely called a "douceur"—to the inspector, before he could start unloading. To lighten this overhead, he might list a dozen slaves or so as "died on voyage," besides the ones who *had* died, and smuggle them ashore at night. But in spite of the risk and expense, the lot which might have averaged fifty dollars on the Coast would generally fetch two hundred dollars in Cuba. After all deductions, the shipowner netted 25 per cent. On a voyage of the *Eliza*, Captain Sabens paid for fifty-two slaves in Africa with an outward cargo which had cost his owner $2000. Thirty-nine of them survived the Middle Passage. He sold them on the Havana market for prices ranging from $160 to $250; the whole parcel fetched $7853. When he had sold it all, he dismantled the *Eliza*'s slave-deck, loaded again with deWolf molasses, and set out on the shortest and happiest leg of his voyage. He was back in Bristol within two weeks, and made ready to start the Round Trade over again.

While the act of 1794 was enforced, no slaver dared enter an American port. But if the price at Charleston rose above that at Havana, it was not too hard to smuggle the slaves, in small boats, from Cuba to the smaller ports of Georgia and South Carolina. Captain Charles Clark of the brig *Nancy* (she was named for Mrs. James deWolf) describes the operation simply in a report to Captain Jim from Charleston on January 7, 1802.

When I wrote you before, I was bound out of the city after my cargo, which had been on the beach to the northward of Charleston. I found them all well, and much better than I expected, for the weather was very cold. They had no clothes, and no shelter except the sandhills and cedar trees, and no person to take care of them. I arrived in Charleston with them on the 14th Decr. without being troubled. I shall not make as much as I expected, for slaves was very high on the African coast, and my time being short, I was obliged to make the best bargain I could. I sailed with 70 cargo, and lost 4 of them; but they are all very good and will bring the highest price, that is, from $350 up to $500. I don't see that the Trade stops much, for they come in town 2 or 3 hundred some nights. I believe there has been landed since New Years as much as 500 slaves. They land them outside the harbor and march them in at night. 2 or 3 vessels has come in from Africa in ballast. The revenue cutter seized one brig bound from N. Orleans to Charleston. [Louisiana being still French territory, this constituted a violation.] She was cleared from N.O. by calling them passengers. They clear out from there and go into Havana "in distress," and ship from there to the U. States, or sell if the price is high. I think there will be more distressed vessels this winter than ever before. I left on the [African] Coast 14 vessels belonging to the U. States, a great part of them for Charleston.

In any event, Captain Jim never had to sell at a loss. If the market at Havana slumped, and the Revenue Marine, as the Coast Guard was then called, made it risky to smuggle into American ports, he could afford to wait. He owned three plantations in Cuba—the Mary Ann, the Mount Hope, and the Esperanza—where he could hold his stock until prices rose again, as they always did, sooner or later. Meanwhile the stock increased by breeding, and grew sugar to be converted into rum at the Bristol distillery. If quarters grew crowded, or the overseer needed ready cash, it was easy to sell off surplus on the Havana market, or to mortgage it at the bank. The slaves were transferred on printed forms, in which the price was inserted by quill. They carried the standard guarantee of health:

> *En el precio de quinientos pesos, con la calidad de bozal, alma en boca, huesos en costal, a uso de feria, sin asegurar de tachas ni enfermedades, mal de corazon, gota, coral de San Lazaro, ni otra cualquiera que pueda padecer la humana naturaleza.*
>
> (For the price of five hundred dollars, newly imported, well-mannered and hard-working, fit for daily labor, but with no guarantee against weak heart, gout, leprosy, or any other defect or ailment.)

If, on the other hand, more stock was needed quickly, Captain Jim could dispatch one of his ships direct from Cuba to Africa to buy it. Her bond was not forfeited provided it was renewed at her hailing port each two years. If there was danger of seizure under the act of 1794, he could transfer her, by a wash sale, to the name of his Cuban agent, and send her out under Spanish colors. He had only to notify Collins that she was sold to a foreigner. Collins then struck her name from American registry and canceled her bond.

The state of South Carolina had forbidden the importation of slaves as far back as 1787, for even then the population of Charleston was a dangerous three-quarters Negro. But the invention of the cotton gin promised unlimited profits from slave labor, and the year 1808 was drawing near, when Congress, regardless of the wishes of the states, might abolish the trade altogether. On December 7, 1803, South Carolina reopened her ports for the four years remaining.* The market soared, for the planters knew that their imports would soon be cut off for good. On the Slave Coast the factors knew the same thing and hurried to unload while they could. Simultaneously prices rose in Charleston and fell in Africa. To take advantage of the combination, the deWolf syndicate sent young Henry, the son of brother William, to Charleston. He opened a commission house for the family cargoes, in partnership with an established Charleston merchant named Charles Christian, at 18 Federal Street. The firm not only sold slaves, but dealt in drafts on New York, where "Gentleman Jim," the oldest son of James, stood ready to honor their paper.

Charleston was a gay city for those who could afford it. The Jockey Club held weekly races at the Washington Track. There were plays at the Charleston Theatre and balls at the Saint Cecilia Society. The Marine Hotel on Queen Street was one of the best in the country, offering beefsteak, coffee, and relishes at all hours, horses and sedan-chairs at livery, and a coach "for family use." The Charleston planters were so hungry for slaves that a cargo could usually be disposed of directly from the slaver's deck, as soon as she tied up at Gadsden's wharf. Like their rival brokers, Christian and deWolf advertised extensively in the newspapers (in 1807 twenty-two Charleston firms were engaged in the business), listing their wares under a general description such as "prime Windward coast Negroes," or by country of origin. The best grades came from Gambia on the northwest shoulder of Africa, and from Mozambique on the east coast, though the latter were rarer. Slaves from Calabar, in Nigeria, went cheapest.

In hot weather the slaves brought better prices if they were "finished"—i.e., oiled and fattened—for a few weeks before sale. Then the auction would take place at the open-air Exchange, behind

---

* In the same year, Cuba, to maintain her own supply, required that all cargos entering Havana must include slaves for sale. The trade was abolished by civilized nations in the following years: Denmark, 1802; Great Britain and the United States, 1807; Sweden, 1813; Holland, 1814; Portugal (north of the equator), 1815; Spain (north of the equator), 1817; France, 1818; Spain, 1820; Brazil, 1829; Portugal, 1830.

the post office at the foot of Broad Street, only a short barefoot walk from the wharf. The women wore blue flannel frocks called "long-shorts." The men wore blue cotton trousers. In cold weather the more humane traders gave them warm clothing and imported "Negro shoes" from Boston, at seventy cents a pair, to cover their bare feet. At auctions on the Exchange the lots were displayed on two long tables, while the partners walked through the crowd touting their wares. Henry deWolf, like his father William, was softhearted. He did his best to sell slaves by lots, without separating families, even when they might have brought more at retail.

Around the three-legged course Captain Jim shuttled as many slavers as he could buy or charter. He often carried slaves as freight for other owners, at an average rate of forty dollars per head for the Middle Passage. Compare the profits of a voyage in the years when abolition was far in the future with those of one in the four years of open port. At Savannah, in 1785, he sold a consignment which had cost him $38.50 apiece in rum; sale prices ran from $180 for prime fellows down to $4.50 for one woman, totally blind. But on July 17, 1807, 106 slaves from his brig *Three Sisters*, Captain Champlin, brought $29,090 on the Charleston block, the best grade fetching $500. Prices ran down to $100 for "one foolish boy" and $50 for "one sickly man-boy with the flux." The average was $274.43, yet they had cost him only 75 gallons of rum, or $25.25, on the African coast. The sale lasted three weeks. Purchasers settled for $2250 in cash or produce, and the rest in notes running from sixty days to six months. Christian & deWolf charged 5 per cent commission on the gross, but part of their fee, of course, remained in the family.

Even in Charleston there were runaways and hijackers. On December 31, 1807, the last day for legal importation, twelve "new" Negroes, fitted out in red flannel shirts, blue wool trousers, and red worsted caps, were lured from Captain Jim's ship *Cleopatra* at Gadsden's wharf by a seasoned slave from the up-country ricefields. Speaking their own language, he promised to get them back to Africa if they followed him. All twelve escaped. Henry posted a reward of fifty dollars a head, with five hundred dollars more for

the capture of the kidnapper. It is doubtful that they were returned
to him. More likely, the kidnapper sold them to his own master.

The horrors of the trade did not disturb the Bristol boys who
served before the mast. They were more homesick than disgusted.
They knew the Gulf of Guinea as well as they knew Massachusetts
Bay, and Havana better than Boston. Here, verbatim, is a letter
home from a seaman aboard Captain Jim's slave brig *Sally*, which
reveals a tough conscience, a sketchy education, and that disease
which the *Rodeur*'s surgeon called nostalgia:

Havaner, Jany. 17, 1804

My dear Parence:
I now take the opertunity to In form you that I am well at present,
hopeing that these lines will find you the same. I am a frade it will
not hold so long. Capt. Gladding talks of heaving the Brig out a gin
to grave her, for wee do not no when we shall git out of this durty
Howl. you may not look for us until you see us for God noes when wee
shall git out of this place. . . . I have ben gorn so much longer than
I expected I have nearly got out of Clothing and Clothing is verry
dear heaar and verry sces and tell Betsey to tell her Father if hee
sells eny more trousis such as mine wus hee will never git to Heaven
in the world hereafter. . . .
I roght 2 letters by Capt. Cartwright bound to Newbryport. I expected by Capt. Bradford or Capt. Munrow to have a letter but I
have rec. none as yet. I was glad to hear that my Father had moved
out of that old rattrap for I was a frade it would Blow down upon
them, and tell Unkle Throop I shall beware of the third time for he
cheated me once with an old gun out of 9 shilling and one Bitt and
the second time he cheated me was with an old bantum Hen that
warnt worth ninepence and charged me one and sixpence. If Unkle
Sam asks after me ask him if he dont want me to help him pitch of hay
agin? Wee all keep up a good hart. In hope to git away some time
or other. remember my love to Grand dady and grand mamma
Waldron and to all the Family and so no more at present I remain
your loveing Son un till Deth
Richard Waldron

Nor did the slaves touch at Bristol to trouble the civic conscience,
except for the happy few whom the sea-captains brought in as

servants for themselves or their employers, for under Rhode Island law they would become free after ten years' servitude, and their offspring were free from birth.

They were known as "privilege" slaves, and had been branded specially with the letter P on hip or shoulder before ever leaving Africa, to set them apart from the commercial cargo. Their masters could take credit for having saved them from the auction block. It was the purser's right to pick names for the privilege slaves. They were solemnly baptized on the long beat across the Atlantic with such names as Jack Crowbar, Bottle of Beer, Flying Jib, and Pea Soup. One cabin boy aboard Captain Jim's *Yankee* was called Jack Jibsheet, and another Cuffee Cockroach.

(Cuffee was a common name for black boys; it is a corruption of the Mandingo word *qofi*, meaning a child who is born on the sacred Mohammedan Friday. Many popular names for Negroes were imported directly from Africa. Quackey Babbitt, who sawed wood for the *Sukey*, was probably one of the Quaqua tribe from the eastern end of the Ivory Coast. Sambo is the name of another tribe. The word "pickaninny" is taken directly from a town off Cape Lahore, and "coon" itself probably derives from the factors' barracoons.)

Captain Jim kept two of the likeliest youngsters. They were captured at two different beaches on the same voyage of his brig *Lavinia:* the girl when she was caught peering from behind a mangrove at the white men, and the boy while he was playing in the sand. They were of different tribes, he perhaps a Mandingo and she a Fula. On the trip home the purser called them Pomp and Peggy. They became the pets of the voyage. When Nancy deWolf received them—they were a Christmas present from her husband in 1803— she gave them the more elegant names of Polydore and Agiway. When they came of age, she had them married in her front parlor by Bishop Griswold. Polydore made numerous voyages back to Africa as a cook—the Negroes, being small, made good sailors. He was mild and quiet, while Agiway was as cranky as her mistress. They raised a family of nine daughters whom Captain Jim, with vulgar merriment, often compared to the nine Potter sisters, his mother and his aunts. He set them up in a cottage on Goree, at the northeast end of town, where Polydore was frequently elected mayor in the annual election of the colored population. They lived out their days in importance on a monthly salary of four dollars. Captain Jim never let anyone but Agiway pleat his ruffled shirts, and Polydore's chowder was the best in town. Nothing would have persuaded them to return to Africa. Agiway claimed to have inherited the secrets of voodoo and was much feared by the other ex-slaves. But her amulets and incantations she promised never to use against the Great Folks. In the 1820s, when the abolitionists were recruiting settlers for the Negro republic of Liberia, no less a person than President Elijah Johnson visited Captain Jim to get him to release Polydore and Agiway for the colony. They listened upstairs, each with a kettle of boiling water to pour on the unwelcome liberator in case he persuaded their master to give them up. He failed. They overheard the captain, as he offered the President a glass of canary, tell him, "Lord, your Excellency, they're not my slaves; I'm theirs. If you'll take *me* to Liberia and set me free from them, I'm ready to go right now."

In their old age, when they needed sunlight, they would sit on the slanted bulkhead of their cottage, and Captain Jim's grandchildren teased them with this jingle:

> Agiway and Polydore
> Sitting on the cellar door;
> Polydore and Agiway,
> Sitting in the cellarway!
> Down fell the cellar door,
> Bump went Polydore;
> Up flew the cellarway,
> Off blew Agiway!

Besides the planters and slave-brokers from Havana and Charleston who visited Bristol in the course of business, the opportunities of the African and Caribbean trade led foreign seamen and merchants to become permanent residents. The village became almost as cosmopolitan as Newport or Salem. As Father Fauque related, there had been Irishmen in the crew of the *Prince Charles of Lorraine.* The deWolf fleet often picked up Portuguese hands in the Azores on the outward voyage. One of them was Jack deCosta, ancestor of many present Bristolians. When the daughter of John Brown of Providence married a German named Herreshoff, son of one of Frederick the Great's bodyguard, he set the young couple up on Proprietor Byfield's old Poppasquash farm, which he bought in at the sale of Tory property after the Revolution. A French merchant named Captain Daniel Morice—he had been an officer in the army of Louis XVI—fled to Bristol from Haiti. The time was 1803, when the Negro slaves revolted against the French. Captain Morice went first to Cuba, where Don Marcos, the son of Captain James deWolf, smuggled him aboard a homebound brig one night. Thereafter Captain Morice lived in Bristol as an American citizen, and his daughter, Mrs. Arselia Babbitt, beloved of all, was still alive as late as 1925.

IV

On March 2, 1807, President Jefferson signed the long-expected act which would outlaw the slave trade on the first of the following year. Captain Jim had not gone to sea since the start of the century. He was now forty-one and too old for the rigors of the slave trade, but that summer he took his favorite ship, the *Andromache,* on one last voyage to Africa. Perhaps he made it for sheer bravado, perhaps for an example to his effete sons, or perhaps for a final firsthand taste of the lucrative business he had learned so long before from his uncle Potter and John Brown.

He never dealt in slaves again. But he foresaw the depression which would follow the end of the trade. In the last week of 1807 Jefferson, harassed by the English and French depredations on our commerce which had lasted since the start of the Napoleonic wars, clamped an embargo on all American seaborne commerce. The embargo ruined many New England shipowners. Sam Wardwell, Captain Jim's enemy, was forced to move out West and take up farming. The firm of Christian & deWolf was dissolved; Henry deWolf returned to Bristol and took up farming too. The Navy had to bunk and feed the crews of the idle ships in Charleston harbor.

But the embargo hardly affected Captain Jim. He could afford to let his fleet lie idle for a while, for he foresaw the future of steam power. Long before the shipowners of Massachusetts transferred their capital ashore, he invested his slaving profits in the textile mills being built along the watercourses north of Providence. The invention of the gin promised an endless supply of clean Carolina cotton, cheaper and surer than the cotton of the Guianas; and the slaves which he himself had helped to import assured plenty of labor to grow and pick it. Steam power and Yankee ingenuity would soon provide the country with cloth, free of foreign or presidential interference.

He turned his energy to philanthropy, agriculture, and politics. He had sat in the state legislature since 1802. When the Town Council voted to build a house of industry—i.e., a poorhouse—for the village paupers, he donated the land, saying that his sons would need to make it their home when he was no longer alive to provide for them. (This grim stone building, overlooking Mill Gut, stood until 1952, but there is no record that any of the Great Folks was reduced to living in it.) Russell Warren, the carpenter-architect, built him a fine house, which he called the Mount, on a thousand acres of farmland across the Back Road from his father-in-law Governor Bradford. Warren could build a portrait in brick and clapboard as a painter does in oils. The house he had built for Levi deWolf was ascetic, John's was thriftily comfortable, William's was lavishly careless, and young George's (Charles's son) was flamboyant—all like the owners themselves. Captain Jim's was spacious and substantial; nothing was wasted and nothing stinted. It dwarfed the house of Governor Bradford, and the farmhouse which his old mother had inherited from her brother Simeon Potter. The saddle on which it stood was almost as high as Mount Hope itself. From his third-story windows Captain Jim could look over Bristol harbor and Mount Hope Bay at the same time. The *United States Gazetteer* wrote that

. . . for elegance of style, for the general splendour of its appearance, and the beauty and extensiveness of the various improvements, it will rank among the finest in our country.

It was three stories high, of clapboard, with a curved stone wall at the driveway, and a twelve-foot arched gate leading up to the sandstone steps. The rooms were lighted by astral chandeliers with opal hurricane globes, and heated by Franklin stoves set into marble mantelpieces. On the fireboard of one was a portrait of the captain's five sons on horseback. The drawing room was painted with scenes from the Cuban plantations. In the hall a tall clock chimed "Over the Water to Charlie" every hour. Each day little Agiway (and after her, her nine daughters) in her long-short, with a turban on her head, washed down the teakwood floors with tea leaves. The whole house was scented with rose petals. A score of stables, outbuildings, and barns surrounded it. On axis of the central hall, fifty yards from the house, stood the privy, raised on its own sandstone steps. Pilasters of the Scamozzi order embellished its corners. A painted statue of King Philip surmounted its peak, aiming an arrow at Mount Hope. Inside, there were six holes. The pair facing the door were a little larger, and raised a little higher, than the pairs at each side.

On the summit of Mount Hope, a hard mile distant, Captain Jim built a summerhouse, crowned with a second statue of King Philip. On Tanyard Lane, just south of his stables, he laid out a deer park; it was the only one in New England. A high fence, set on a granite wall, enclosed it, and urchins from town would walk the two miles out to the Mount to peer through the palings at the red deer grazing inside.

On March 4, 1809, the day when Madison succeeded Jefferson, the unpopular embargo was repealed. The commerce of legitimate seaports like Salem revived at once, but that of Bristol, too long rooted in the outlaw slave trade, languished still. The years from the end of the trade to the outbreak of war in 1812 were idle ones

in Bristol, which was not used to idleness. But most Bristol boys
were trained to the farm as well as to the sea, and Dicky Waldron
probably got his wish to pitch hay for his uncle Sam. The village
grew more onions than any other town in New England except
Wethersfield, Connecticut.

Farmer John deWolf's eccentric son 'Fessor wrote an idyllic poem
which describes the village during the lull:

THE SUMMER EVENING

The sun beneath the western hills
His upper edge now dips;
His last departing ray with gold
King Philip's feathers tips.

The sou'west breeze has died away,
The poplar leaves are still,
And half unground remains the grist
In Stephen Gladding's mill.

The sea is calm, and not a wave
Rolls o'er its surface fair,
And half to Prudence one may hear
Old Uncle Springer swear.

Now onion-boys with shoulder'd hoes
Come trooping into town,
And trumpets made of onion-tops
Proclaim their labor done.

Now round the crib, with necks upstretch'd
Thick swarms the gabbling train,
While Goody on the stepstone sits
And lib'ral throws the grain.

With dimpled cheek and bosom fair,
Bedeck'd with many a posy,
Now sally forth in smiling bands
The lasses plump and rosy.

Hail, Bristol, happiest village, hail!
What rich produce is thine;
Girls, geese and onions thou canst boast,
O Triad most divine!

The lasses, sheltered in bonnet and petticoat and stay, were as abject as the squaws of King Philip's time, and the lads were as restless as Simeon Potter. In the year when this poem was written, a youth was haled before the Town Council for accosting a girl at night on the Common, but when he proved she had "shown him an ankle," they lectured her instead of whipping him.

5.

The Voyage of
Norwest John

SLAVES were not the only cargo of Bristol traders. In those intervals of the Napoleonic wars when American trade with Europe was possible at all, Bristol ships loaded for Bilbao, Bordeaux, Havre, Liverpool, Amsterdam, Antwerp, Hamburg, Copenhagen, and even as far as Cronstadt, the port of St. Petersburg in Russia. But for most of the presidencies of Adams and Jefferson, and for the first half of Madison's, they were liable to seizure, if they traded with any but neutral ports, by British cruisers acting under Orders in Council or by French under the Berlin and Milan Decrees. While Jefferson's embargo lasted, they were forbidden to leave the country at all. Neutral ports grew fewer as Napoleon gradually swept the mainland of Europe. Yet in 1806, the year of his greatest power, sixty-one ships entered Bristol harbor from foreign voyages, apart from more than a hundred coasting vessels, and paid $120,000 in customs duties to Collector Collins. And before Napoleon entered Moscow, before Lewis and Clark had even crossed the American mainland, one Bristol captain became the first American, and perhaps the first non-Russian, to travel by land from the Pacific to the Baltic, across the empire of the Czars.

While Collins and the deWolf brothers were still plying the slave trade, the shipowners of Boston, Providence, and Salem had already made fortunes from China and the East Indies. The *General Washington,* which John Brown of Providence fitted for Canton in 1787, returned in 1789 with a cargo of tea, silk, china, and lacquer ware worth $150,000. Brown unimaginatively named another of his Indiamen the *George Washington,* and a third the *President Washington.* Both made the long Pacific voyage round Cape Horn and returned him profits which could not be matched by the deWolf slavers, no matter how fast they shuttled the triangular course of the Round Trade.

The deWolfs, who had become used to making two profits from Africa on a single voyage, hit on the idea of doing the same thing from Asia by trading Yankee goods for the furs of the north Pacific, and then trading the furs in China for such eminently marketable cargo as the three *Washingtons* brought back for the temptation of Rhode Island housewives. Only two Bristol sail, so far, had entered the Pacific. In 1801 the deWolfs' brig *Lavinia,* Captain Holbrook, had circled the globe only to break up in a snowstorm off Cape Cod, as she was nearing home. In that disaster five of their nephews—sons of their sisters Abigail Howe and Lydia Lee—had gone down. In 1802 Captain James Phillips's ship *Juno* reached Canton and returned with China goods, including firecrackers, worth $30,000. Phillips claimed that his profit would have doubled if he had included a trade along the northern fur-grounds, charted only four years before by George Vancouver.

The deWolf brothers determined to follow this course themselves. In 1804 James and Charles, with Charles's ambitious son George, bought the *Juno* from Phillips for $7600. Armed with eight defensive carriage-guns, she was a full-rigged ship of 206 tons—a large vessel for Bristol, though not to compare with the 950-ton *President Washington,* which could hardly have entered Bristol harbor. She had been built for Phillips in 1799 by Caleb Carr, the Warren shipwright.

James, who took the largest share, hired as her captain his nephew John deWolf II. This John should not be confused with Farmer John, nor with *his* son, 'Fessor John. His father was Simon, one of those two sons of Mark Antony who had been lost during the Revolution on a voyage to Hispaniola, and his brother was the Simon, Junior, who later cut his own throat on the Slave Coast.

The *Juno*'s new captain was born in 1779, only a month after his father sailed on his last voyage. He grew up into a fun-loving loose-jointed boy with the family periwinkle-blue eyes, a bevel-end nose, a peak of unruly black hair, and creases of mirth down his slab cheeks. He describes himself as "light and spare of person." His hands were big and square like his uncle Jim's, but his chin jutted forward, plow-shaped, like nobody else's. His education consisted of a few years at the grammar school—his uncles had had no more—where Captain Noyes, the schoolmaster, taught from the Alden Speller, the English Speaker, and Daboll's Arithmetic, mended the pupils' quills, and set exercises in trigonometry from *The Practical Navigator,* by candle-light, to such boys as were ambitious and could afford his fee. At thirteen John went to sea, starting as cabin-boy in one of his uncle Charles's slavers. He was a head too long, even then, for the bunks in the forecastle. He rose to foretopman, then boatswain, then mate; but he confessed in later years that though he had a strong stomach, and, being an orphan, had to take what was offered, he hated the slave trade almost as much as his Quakerish uncle Levi.

It was an honor, and must have been a welcome relief from the trade, for John, a bachelor of twenty-four, to take command of a clean home-town ship like the *Juno*. Her owners filled her hold with hardware, rum, tobacco, beads, dried beef, firearms, and cottons—trade goods, they guessed, which would be to the taste of North Pacific trappers. The lading cost them $27,400.

The *Juno*'s departure was a great event in town. The farmers' drays took a week to load her provisions: pork, molasses, live poultry, and long ropes of red Bristol onions. The poultry was stowed in a coop under the carpenter's bench amidships. A ram named Billy, with his ewe, was tethered to the capstan. Major William of the Bristol Insurance Company underwrote her at 30 per cent of value, which was a high rate, for the trip around the Horn was dangerous and unfamiliar. (Premiums on slave ships ran from 35 per cent for the Middle Passage down to 2½ per cent for the last leg, from Havana to Bristol.) Captain Charles and Captain Jim signed her bond. Farmer John gave his namesake $200 as a venture to spend in Canton, directing him to lay it out in a dining set of painted china (what is now called Lowestoft) at no more than $40, a tea set at $10, and the rest in Hysong tea. His wife sent $25 for a bolt of satin and a fan, with $5 more, as an afterthought, for two silk shawls. Their son 'Fessor ventured $25 for silk handkerchiefs and a bolt of nankeen suitable for trousers.

On August 13, 1804, the *Juno* put out of Bristol and stood to the east. John sailed almost to Africa in order to bypass the adverse trade winds. He met no cruisers, either French or British. He did not turn south till he had sighted the Cape Verdes. At seven knots top speed, it took him two months to cross the equator, two more to double the Horn, and two to reach the line again on the Pacific side. The ship *Mary* of Boston was in company. They were lucky to get round the Horn at all. He wrote his mother dryly:

> In those latitudes the sea is very seldom smooth, because the cessation of gales is of so short a period that the swell has not time to subside.

In a blinding storm off the desolate tip of the world the *Mary* bashed into the *Juno*'s sides with a crash that made every timber quake, and tore her copper sheathing off in sheets. By the time she reached warm water, far up the coast of Chile, her seams had sprung and the teredos had eaten into her hull. The salt-water spray had blinded the poultry. Firewood was so low that Hanson, the cook, dared not serve hot food oftener than once a week.

The Spaniards on the west coast of South America, almost unaware of the wars in Europe, did not welcome visitors. Their few settlements were sparsely manned by priests who had come to convert the Indians and by prospectors who had come to find gold for King Carlos IV. They were poor in everything but precious metals. They wore ragged trousers, straw hats, and coarse *camisas*. Fruit grew riotously along the seacoast, but they were too lazy to cultivate vegetables. They were too poor to own stockings, yet they boiled their water in kettles of silver.

The governor of Valparaiso grudgingly let John take on food, water, and firewood, but would not let him land for repairs. The *Juno* hobbled on to the little port of Coquimbo. There the commandant had to let him land, for he trained his guns on the garrison until he got permission. The *Mary* set her course northwestward toward Hawaii and Canton. John careened the *Juno* on the beach. He spent a fortnight calking her seams and repairing her spars and canvas. Then he stood to the north again, toward the fur grounds. He hugged the coast, venturing into the open sea only to take on green turtle for the galley at the Galápagos Islands.

It was April of 1805 before he reached shelter on the north coast of Vancouver's Island, in 51 degrees north, 128 degrees west, at the narrow inlet of Newettee. To get past the breakers and the cliffs, he had to hoist out his boats to tow. His longboat sank alongside; his yawl and his whaleboat were too light to pull the *Juno* by themselves. However, with the cliffs only an oar's length away, he managed to drift inside the anchorage.

The Eskimos of that coast belonged to a tribe called the Kolosh. They had plenty of sea otter, the *lutra marina* of science. The fur of this little animal, jet black with silver sheen beneath, was the most precious in the world. Sea otter were hunted on the open sea with javelin or arrow, to avoid breaking the skin. In the Chinese markets a sealskin might bring a silver dollar apiece, and a sable ten or fifteen, but a single pelt of the sea otter had once sold in Canton for a hundred, and even average skins brought twenty-five.

John was impatient to trade, but the Kolosh seemed in no hurry. While their log canoes rode in a circle about the *Juno*, they would lie on her deck by the dozen all day long, stubbornly repeating their exorbitant prices and indifferent whether he bought their pelts or not. He took care to disarm the traders before he let them aboard; but he saw that sharpshooters ashore, in case of trouble, could damage him before he had time to make sail, for the harbor of Newettee shelved so sharply that his anchors hit bottom only within gunshot of the shore. He decided not to haggle any longer with the Kolosh, but to head five hundred miles northward, where he knew the Russians had an outpost. A week later, on August 17, 1805, he reached the settlement of New Archangel on the west coast of Baranov Island. It is called Sitka now.

The vast territory of Alaska—or Alashka, as John called it—was discovered in 1741 by a Dane named Vitus Bering in the employ of the Czarina Elizabeth, daughter of Peter the Great. The Russians had never settled Alaska, but it was the preserve of a semi-official corporation, known as the Russian-American Company, which exploited Alaska much as the Hudson's Bay Company exploited Canada. It held title to the country, and paid the Czar for its monopoly from the profits of the fur trade.

Alexander Andreivich Baranov, the resident governor, was almost a czar himself. (In early life he had been a dry-goods salesman, and not a successful one, on the Russian mainland.) Eighteen years before John reached Alaska, Baranov had entered the company's employ and crossed the Bering Sea to the unexplored territory, creeping along the chain of Aleutians—they were called the Fox Islands then —to Kodiak, and finally pushing five hundred miles, in pursuit of the retreating sea otter, across the gulf to the island which is named for him. In 1802 the Kolosh had burned his fort, after massacring its garrison, but Baranov had already recaptured and rebuilt it. It stood on an island citadel connected to the shore by an easily defended causeway. Attended by a Bengalese valet and an American clerk with the homely name of Abraham Jones, Baranov welcomed John's longboat at the wharfhouse below his fort.

Baranov still mistrusted the Kolosh. For his shipments to Russia, he bought pelts not from them but from slaves whom he had imported from the Aleutian archipelago far to the west. The hostile Kolosh, the submissive Aleuts, and some friendly Kodiaks made up the native Eskimo population of Baranov Island. The governor made them all live outside of his fort, at the far end of the causeway. Their sod huts were no better than the wigwams of King Philip at Mount

Hope. Each had a smokehole in the roof, and they stank of fish and train-oil. The men daubed their faces with colored earth. John describes the women thus:

> At the age of 14 or 15 they make a hole in their underlip and insert a small piece of wood like a button. This is increased in size as they advance in age, until it is three or four inches long and one or two wide. I saw an old woman, the wife of a chief, whose ornament was so large that by a peculiar motion of her lower lip she could almost conceal her whole face inside it. You will naturally inquire the reason for this barbarous mode of adornment. I might reply by asking the reason for topknots and stays among civilized women. But I may be allowed to make one observation which has probably occurred to my readers; and that is, that the fair sex of the northwest coast are utterly unable to enjoy the luxury of a kiss.

Inside the fort lived two hundred Russians, exiled to Alaska as punishment for crimes, and bound to service till their terms were up. These miserable men were called Promuschleniks. They hated the Eskimos and one another. They were allotted two dried fish a day for subsistence, but had to buy everything else at the Company store. They made a living by shipping pelts, once every year or two, to St. Petersburg, where they were credited with half the proceeds. Since the accounts were made up long after the furs had been shipped, the Promuschleniks were always in debt to the company.

When John arrived at New Archangel, Baranov was sixty-five. His flaxen beard was turning white. His frail body was racked by arthritis. He eased his miseries by ladling vodka from a bucket which he kept always at his side. His gnarled hands could hardly lift the dipper. One of his rare visitors wrote of him:

> His long abode among so uncivilized a race [the Eskimos], his daily intercourse with a dissolute and licentious rabble, with rogues and cheats [the Russians] and the necessity he has been under of having recourse to severity and harshness in order to ensure his own safety and that of the Company, have indeed somewhat blunted his finer feelings, and rendered him less alive than he probably once was to the voice of compassion and philanthropy.

It would not have been unnatural for him to open fire on the *Juno*, for Alaska was as remote from the events of the Atlantic as Chile or California, and Russia might have been at war with America for a year before the news could reach New Archangel. The few Yankee traders who had visited the country had not left a good reputation. At the massacre three years before, deserters from a Salem trader had helped the Kolosh torture the Russian garrison. Tusks of the sea walrus, known to the trade as "sea-tooth," were accepted by the Eskimos as payment for peltry, just as wampum had passed for money in New England hardly more than a century before. One Yankee shipmaster had palmed off imitation tusks, made of porcelain in England, for a valuable cargo of sea otter, and thus debased the currency. Yankees and Russians both knew that a Kolosh, once he possessed a musket, would almost certainly break it or let it rust after a few firings, and would then be unable to repair it. The Russians feared to let firearms get into native hands, but the Yankee captains made a practice of buying up their unusable muskets for a trifle, having the ship's blacksmith repair them at his forge, and then reselling them at the price of new. Baranov had good reason to mistrust his American visitor.

But he was a lonely man and welcomed John to the fort. He asked only that he trade no guns to the Eskimos, and even offered to lease him some of his Aleutian hunter-slaves. They knew, better than any white man, how to spot the telltale bubbles when the little owl-faced otter rolled off their backs to dive, and how to plant the javelin when they came up for air. Firearms were no good for sea otter anyway, for their noise frightened the herds away from the shallow hunting-grounds into the deep water where they were safe from pursuit.

Baranov knew the value of the *Juno*'s goods if the Eskimos at Newettee did not. He bought up a third of her cargo—the bulky third —over a week of bargaining and dinners in the blockhouse. To get rid of the rest—or perhaps to show Baranov that he was not too eager to get rid of it—John sailed north another hundred miles to Lynn Channel, making a brisk trade with the Eskimos as he went. On one of his trading stops he spoke the Boston ship *Athawhalpa* in distress, and towed her to deep water. The Kolosh had murdered her captain. They might have murdered John too, another day when the *Juno* grounded on a sunken rock, had he not held one of their chiefs aboard as hostage until the tide floated her off, and kept a six-pounder trained on the bidarka which rowed the chief ashore, as long as the *Juno* was within gunshot of the land. (The bidarka is a canoe of sealskin stretched over a wood frame, with waisthole flaps of walrus-skin in the top.) When he got back to New Archangel he had collected a thousand pelts, worth $25,000 or more in any market, and he still had a third of his Bristol cargo in the hold. He confesses he was glad to see the gruff hospitable Baranov and the homelike Jones again.

One day while he was still careened, making repairs from the grounding, the weatherbeaten Russian brig *Maria*, Captain Maschin, with the blue Greek-cross imperial ensign at her masthead, limped into the harbor of New Archangel. Keeping her company was the ship-of-war *Nadejda* (the name means Hope), Captain Urey Lisiansky. On board the *Maria*, with a crew of galley-slaves as wretched as Baranov's own garrison, was the exalted Baron Rezanov, on his way home to Russia from a voyage round the world. He had left Cronstadt in the fall of 1803, a year before John had left Bristol. Of the two, he must have been the more homesick. His was the first Russian expedition to circle the globe, and so far it had been a failure.

Nikolai Petrovich Rezanov, chamberlain and plenipotentiary of Alexander I, the Czar of All the Russias, was a young widower, tall, glacial, cruel, handsome, and thwarted. He had hoped to become the Columbus of Russian trade and make alliances for his imperial master. He had reached Alaska by way of England, Brazil, the Marquesas, Hawaii, Canton, Nagasaki, and Kamchatka. The Spaniards had not let him into Manila. The Chinese had denied him the privilege of sending Russian ships into their ports, though they traded with all other nations. Russia could still barter furs for Chinese teas only at trading posts on the remote southern frontiers of Siberia.

The Japanese had treated him even worse. They would trade with no foreigners at all except the Dutch. At Nagasaki the Japanese governor ordered him to kneel in his presence and to give up his sword. Rezanov properly refused. He offered to unload from the *Maria*, as a present to the Mikado, goods worth 300,000 rubles: a clock in the form of an elephant, an electrical machine, a fifteen-foot mirror, a black fox coat, an ermine cloak, a microscope, and a portrait of the Czar by Madame Vigée-Lebrun. It had taken the Mikado six months to decide whether he would accept them. Meanwhile, when the Baron was allowed ashore for exercise, he was imprisoned behind a bamboo wall no more than fifty feet around, under the hostile and unwinking eyes of the Japanese police. In the end, the Mikado rejected his gifts and ordered him out of the country, forcing him, as a parting insult, to accept two thousand yards of silk as *his* present to the Czar.

New Archangel was a miserable place, but at least it welcomed Baron Rezanov. In Russian America he became important again. His father-in-law had founded the Company; he was a heavy stockholder in it himself. His staff comprised two naval officers, Lieutenant Nikolai Alexandrovich Khvostov and Midshipman Gavril Ivanovich Davidov, together with two shipwrights named Koryukin and Popov. He was attended by Dr. George Langsdorff, a thirty-year-old German naturalist who doubled as his physician. The week following the *Maria's* arrival was spent in festivity and mirth, and business was entirely suspended.

Rezanov had come to inspect his property. His ignorance of Alaska was as profound as the Czar's own. He invited himself to stay with Baranov until his two carpenters had built him a new brig to replace the unseaworthy *Maria*. He planned, when the new vessel was finished, to load her with pelts, live animals, and precious ores, and carry them back to Siberia and thence overland to St. Petersburg, as a tribute from Alaska to the Czar. Captain Lisiansky, meanwhile, would return the *Nadejda* by way of the Cape of Good Hope.

With the improvidence of the exalted, Baron Rezanov had brought too little food. One might not guess, from the banquets in Baranov's castle, that the Russian colonists faced starvation. But Rezanov knew, and so did John, that their blue skins and falling teeth were the signs of scurvy. Their only remedy was wild garlic, for they were too lazy to grow vegetables or milk cattle, even though the climate was favorable: in fact, John was surprised to find Alaska as warm as Bristol. The sixty drunkards aboard the *Maria* ate up the station's meager food supply without producing any in return. Rezanov needed the *Juno*'s provisions to save their lives. He needed the *Juno* herself, for the *Maria* could never sail again, and it became daily more doubtful that Koryukin and Popov could build him another ship before winter. The *Juno* was a ship that suited his rank. She was twice the burthen of the *Maria,* and half again that of the *Nadejda.*

John was as sharp a trader as his uncle James or his great-uncle Simeon Potter. He sold Rezanov the *Juno,* together with the last third of her outward cargo, which was enough to feed the whole company at New Archangel for two more months. It consisted of:

19	casks salt pork @ 200 lbs.	315 lbs.	loaf sugar
42	casks salt beef @ 200 lbs.	2983 lbs.	powdered sugar
31	casks wheat flour @ 178 lbs.	7392 lbs.	biscuit
8	casks rice @ 600 lbs.	660	gallons rum
1955	gallons molasses	10,000 lbs.	tobacco

besides miscellaneous hardware and cloth.

In return Rezanov paid him:

$54,638 by draft on the Russian-American Company in St. Petersburg, payable in Spanish milled dollars

$300 in specie

572 sea-otter pelts worth $13,062

The *Yermak,* a 40-ton sloop of Baranov's, completely rigged, with two suits of sail, 4 carriage guns, 30 muskets, and provisions for thirty days

Promise of safe-conduct across Russia to St. Petersburg

This consideration was worth about $68,000, almost twice what the *Juno* and her whole cargo had cost. In addition, he had the thousand pelts he had bought from the Eskimos, and an undisclosed amount from Baranov for the first third of his cargo. He felt that he had struck a bargain; but Rezanov wrote his directors, along with a record copy of the draft, that he would have bought the *Juno* at any price, to save the colony from famine.

On October 5, 1805, the guns of the fort fired a salute as the *Juno* and *Yermak* changed hands. John hoisted the stars and stripes to the masthead of the *Yermak*. He stowed the peltry in her hold and crowded his Bristol crew aboard, except for five seamen who preferred to earn ten rubles a month by staying with the Russians, and one other:

> As my valet for the voyage to Russia [he writes] I retained in my service Edward D. Parker of Bristol. He was one of my ordinary sailors, but a very useful man of all work. A barber by trade, he was also a tolerably good tailor and performer on the violin and clarinet. This latter accomplishment I thought might be useful in dispelling the blues, if we should at any time be troubled by that complaint.

He gave command of the *Yermak* to George Stetson, the *Juno*'s former mate, and made James Moorfield, her clerk, his attorney for the sale of the pelts in China. He directed Moorfield, when he reached Canton, to sell them, along with the sloop herself, for what they would bring, deposit the proceeds with the Cantonese merchant Hu Qua, lay in the ventures ordered by his relatives, and find passage home to Bristol, with the crew, as best he could. He endorsed the *Juno*'s papers with the words "Sold to a Foreigner" and the date. Stetson, on reaching Bristol, would surrender them to Collins for voiding of registry and cancellation of bond. On October 27, 1805, the nineteen men set sail in the forty-ton sloop for Hawaii and thence for Canton, six thousand miles southwest. She could make only five knots, even before the wind.

There was no reason John should not have gone with them, for the draft in his pocket could have been cashed in Canton as readily as in Saint Petersburg. But though many Americans had seen Canton, none had crossed Siberia. He settled down, until Rezanov should be ready to cast off for Russia, to pass the winter among the strangest company and under the most discouraging surroundings, perhaps, that ever handicapped a bachelor party.

John disliked Rezanov for his gullibility as well as his arrogance. Both are traits which New Englanders despise. He insisted on calling the Eskimos Americans, and the Americans Bostonians, and John himself Wolf instead of deWolf. But John admired the bear-like Baranov, and feared him a little. No one could help liking the hard-working, considerate Lieutenant Khvostov, who never stopped talking, nor the handsome fun-loving young Midshipman Davidov, who never stopped laughing. Khvostov was four years older than John, and Davidov four years younger.

Dr. Langsdorff, the German naturalist, became the best friend of his life. The two merry men were made for each other. Like Khvostov, Langsdorff was twenty-nine years old. Besides his native German, he spoke English fluently, as well as a little Russian, French, Portuguese, and Latin. He was a short fellow with a bulbous lower lip, a pointed nose, says John, "turned up at the end like a slipper," and a triangle of perpetual wonderment between it and the tips of his eyebrows. He loved nothing better than to hunt for the Alpine flowers and volcanic minerals of the unfamiliar island. It was a debt, he said, which he owed to Science. He explored the slopes of eight-thousand-foot Mount Edgecumbe across the bay, and ranged the spruce forests with his fowling piece in quest of wild game. After his specimens had been skinned for his collection, Parker made stew of the remains.

After the *Nadejda* had cast off for Russia and the *Yermak* for China, the settlement made ready for winter by chinking the joints of the loghouses with moss and bark. Baranov kept a guard night and day at the fort in case of attack by the Kolosh. The air was too damp for wood fires, so the colony kept warm by burning the oil of the whale and sea-dog in braziers. There was little snow, but at night the Saint Elmo's Fire danced blue on the sentry's bayonet, the flagstaff of the fort, and the barrel of the single cannon beside it, trained shoreward upon the Eskimos. The colony included a workshop, a forge, an empty cattle-barn, three bathhouses, the tents and bunkhouses of the garrison, and the huts of the officers.

Everyone dressed in a hooded *kamleika*, a sort of raincoat sewn of the entrails of the sea dog, and in the coldest weather added a reversible parka made of the skin of the same amphibian, and a wooden hat strapped under the chin. The sea dog, *phoca vitulina* in Langsdorff's vocabulary, provided food, heat, light, and clothing. Aside from its unpalatable but never-failing flesh, and from the *Juno's* own provisions, the colony's main diet was *ukler*, or dried fish—salmon, halibut, or herring. It took the place of bread. Occasionally someone shot caribou or deer. John's ewe dropped twin lambs, one of which was slaughtered and served up at the Baron's table. The largest of the log houses was converted into a messhall and ballroom. In lieu of glass, its windows were sealed with fish skin. Ten officers dined regularly with the Baron. Dessert was invariably cranberries preserved in candlefish oil.

For the amusements, the friendly Kodiak women, who were always hungry, were allowed into the messhall to flatter the Baron with long speeches of loyalty and amuse him with dances. Their straight black hair hung loose, hiding the earrings in their ears. They may not have worn lip-plates like the Kolosh, but their dancing was primitive. It consisted in hopping up and down and imitating the cries of birds and beasts, while the watchers clapped hands in time. More Kodiak women waited out of sight in the bunkhouses. Baranov, though he still had a wife and two children in Russia, had "married" a Kodiak girl himself. He renamed her Anna Grigoryevna in honor of Rezanov's dead wife; Rezanov, far from being insulted, was flattered by the tribute.

At these *prazniks*, Langsdorff earned Baranov's gratitude by dosing his vodka with vitriolic acid and sugar syrup, to make it more potent; and the blazing candlefish guttered to the thumping of the dancers' feet, shod with the soft sea mukluk, on the earthen floor.

His Excellency Baron Rezanov [writes John] was always with us on these occasions, and would in an emergency take the fiddle, on which he was quite a good performer. Mostly, Dr. Langsdorff and my man Parker took turns at the bow. With plenty of good resin for it, as well as for our stomachs, we made a gay season of it. Our daily ration was a bottle of the Russian brandy called vodka, which contrasted happily with the half-gill of rum issued aboard our Yankee vessels.

Aside from the dances, the chief amusement of the Russians was in watching Billy the ram trying to butt John in the rear. He suspected they had trained Billy to attack him unawares, but he did not much mind amusing them at his own expense until Billy hit him so hard, one day, that he rolled head over heels down the hillock and into the cold water. After that he learned how to sidestep and grasp Billy by the horns as the ram lunged by. It was a battle, he says gravely, between sheep and Wolf.

By spring the generous provisions in the *Juno's* hold were almost gone. Rezanov stubbornly refused to sail home without the sloop which Koryukin and Popov were building. After a year on the stocks, she had got no farther than the keel. She was to be named the *Avoss*, which is the Russian word for "perhaps." Meanwhile the colony would face starvation again unless more food could be found.

Rezanov decided he could get it from the Spaniards at San Francisco, a thousand miles south. It was well known that the mission was rich in cattle and wheat, which he believed the monks would trade for the hardware and cloth still left from John's outward cargo. He sailed aboard the *Juno* on March 1, 1806, taking with him Langsdorff, the two naval officers, the five American deserters, and enough Russians from the *Maria* to make up the ship's complement. John was left alone with Baranov. If only as a means of getting home, he spent his days working on the *Avoss* with Koryukin and Popov.

Rezanov returned to New Archangel on June 21 in triumph. Ten of the garrison had died of scurvy in his absence. Not only had he filled the *Juno's* hold with Spanish beef and grain, but he was engaged to be married. He had won the heart of Concepción Argüello, the youngest daughter of Don José "El Santo" Argüello, the Commandante of San Francisco. She was fifteen, and Rezanov was forty. Langsdorff reported to John that her eyelashes were dark and long, the whites of her eyes were bluish, and she had the prettiest instep and the merriest laugh in both the Californias. Since Baron Rezanov could not marry without the Czar's permission, nor she without the Pope's, the wedding date had been set for May 20, 1808, two years after the formal betrothal. It might well take that long for the Pope's blessing, through the cumbersome protocol of the Spanish court, to reach San Francisco, and for Rezanov to travel to St. Petersburg and return with the Czar's.

Rezanov could flatter himself that at one coup he had justified his whole embassy. He had saved Alaska from starvation, he had won a bride, and he had made an alliance between Spain and Russia. That alliance might have a profound effect on the world's future. The dismemberment of the Spanish Empire had begun, and no one could foresee how far it would go. At sea, the British had seized a Spanish treasure-fleet carrying $3,000,000. Napoleon had practically stolen the Louisiana Territory from Spain in order to sell it to the United States. He had sacrificed the Spanish Navy to Nelson at Trafalgar. He had crushed the Russian Army at Austerlitz, and Russia lay open to his invasion. It was not too wild a dream that the Spanish and Russian Empires, at opposite corners of Europe, might found a third, through the marriage of Rezanov and Concepción, which would stretch from the Arctic circle to Cape Horn, and forever bar America from the Pacific.

According to Langsdorff, the strain of courtship had told on Rezanov, who was moody at best. Angry that Langsdorff had hunted seabirds at San Francisco, instead of chatting Latin with the brown-habited Franciscans as a diplomat should, he had cut off the heads of the doctor's precious specimens and thrown the carcasses overboard. When his crew sneaked ashore to wash their clothes in fresh water, he had them flogged astraddle of the *Juno's* guns. He dared not flog John's five Yankees, but he did confine them to the treeless

island of Alcatraz until he was ready to set sail. Back in New Archangel, he was no more tractable. The four bachelors—John,
Langsdorff, Khvostov, and Davidov—gave him a dinner-party
for which the second lamb was killed. They urged an early start to
Russia, before another winter should make it impossible to cross the
Bering Sea and the vast reaches of Siberia. But Rezanov insisted on
waiting for the *Avoss*. Even with John to help them, and forty
promuschleniks at the command of their knouts, Koryukin and
Popov had got no farther than her ribs. He invented still other
reasons for delay. Perhaps he dared not face the Czar; perhaps he
did not want to marry Concha after all. John simply says, "His
Excellency failed to make any arrangements for the future."

There is nothing like a friend's approaching marriage to make a
bachelor homesick. John looked at the degradation around him—
the Russians and the Aleutians held in slavery by the drunken
Baranov and the arrogant Rezanov for the sake of a few otter skins
—and decided he must get home. As Langsdorff says,

> Captain deWolf, one of the most compassionate and benevolent of
> men, who often made me the sharer of his joys and sorrows, was dis-
> gusted with the lot of the serfs.

John was angry with Rezanov for punishing his sailors, and
Langsdorff was angry with him for throwing his taxidermy overboard. Rather than wait for the *Juno* to refit, and the *Avoss* to be
built, and the Baron to make up his mind, the two friends asked
permission to start without him. Rezanov seemed glad to get rid
of them. He commandeered Baranov's one remaining vessel, the
little twenty-five-ton brig *Russisloff,* and ordered them on their
way.

To the amazement of the slow-moving Russians, John fitted her
out in three days. He presented Billy and his ewe to Baranov. He
said good-by to the five Bristol boys, who, in spite of Rezanov's ill-
usage, still preferred Alaska. On June 30, 1806, with Dr. Langsdorff,
Parker and his fiddle, five Russians, and two Aleuts, he put out on
the 2500-mile voyage to the eastern tip of Asia.

His first stop was Kodiak, two weeks across the gulf. Bander, the company's local agent, showed him over the station. It was more civilized than New Archangel, with forty houses, a barracks, a church, and a school. The priest doubled as schoolmaster—just, John notes, as the Reverend John Usher, Junior, did at Bristol. Everyone called him the Pope. He and his wife were farmers as well, with several milk cows and a fair tract of potatoes, cabbage, turnips, and cucumbers. The Pope cultivated them in his black cassock. In New Archangel, vegetables and milk had not existed. Before the *Russisloff* cast off from Kodiak, Bander stowed aboard a cask of vodka for his colleague Prikaschik at Unalaska, her next port of call. Prikaschik was "drunk as David's sow," says John, when he staggered down to greet her. His predecessor, Larionov, had died a few months before, leaving his widow and daughter at Prikaschik's mercy. A ship might not arrive from Russia for another two years to take them home. When the widow Larionova heard that John was bound for the mainland, she begged him on her knees to take her along, so that she could see her native town of Irkutsk before she died. He promised to make room for her, but Prikaschik objected, for he dreaded what report she might make of him to the company: he was, John says, "a great lover of the ardent." In the end John made Prikaschik release her by threatening to hold up his cask of vodka. The old lady, with her daughter, her barrel of guillemot eggs preserved in oil, plenty of smoked goose and pickled fish, was hoisted aboard. The ladies bedded down on one side of a screen in John's cabin. To make room for them, he and Parker had to take turns in John's own bunk on the other side.

They sailed from the treeless black cliffs of Unalaska on August 16 and hit foul weather at once. Langsdorff was eager to inspect a new volcano called Castle Rock, which was reported to have risen in 1796 from the sea northwest of the station, but a thick fog hid it from sight. By the twenty-eighth, sailing north of the Aleutian chain, they had hardly passed Attu, at its tip. Through the mists, as they crawled along, they heard, but never saw, the seal herds, like thunder, roaring from their invisible islands. When they entered the open waters of the Bering Sea, they were in the haunts of the bow-head right whale, who roamed unmolested in the perpetual fog.

> We were frequently surrounded by whale [John writes]; sometimes they would take a position to windward and bear down as if they meant to sink us. But when they approached within 8 or 10 rods, they would dip and go under, or make a circuit around us. Most of them were much longer than our vessel, and it would have taken but a slight blow from one of them to have smashed her into a thousand pieces.

The brig seldom made more than 2 knots. Once she was actually forced backward. John kept the seas from breaking over her by trailing blubber from the crew's mess over the quarter-rail. It made a slick for nearly a mile to windward, and saved the *Russisloff* from foundering.

Dr. Langsdorff was not frightened. He studied the sea birds that perched on the spars and sails. Once he killed a flock of four wild geese at a single shot, and, still better, put out the brig's bidarka and brought them aboard.

John planned to pass through the Kurile Islands below Kamchatka, and reach Siberia at Okhotsk, a thousand miles across the gulf of the same name. But an early blizzard hit him when he was in the very teeth of the Kuriles. He dared not go forward. He turned his course northwestward to the almost uninhabited peninsula of Kamchatka. On September 22 he brought the *Russisloff* into Petropavlovsk, resigned to another winter half the world away from home. It was a miserable place to hibernate. A rickety wharf led past the fish-drying racks to a collection of thirty weatherbeaten huts, a bunkhouse, a small unfinished church, and a shed which served as office for the Company. The buildings, framed of heavy logs, were anchored against the wind with stones. The Company's agent, Major Ivanah, lived in the only decent house on the station— or, for that matter, in the whole province. It was painted white and had a red tin roof.

John, who had long since learned to make the best of adversity, stowed the ladies with the major's wife, and took lodging in the three-room shanty of an old man named Andra. He shared a curtained bunk in the largest room with Langsdorff; Parker had a cot at their feet. Andra and his wife slept on the stove in a second room; his cow and her fodder occupied the third.

Through the winter Langsdorff combed the high Kamchatka capes for plants, rocks, birds, and insects. John explored the southern half of the peninsula on his dogsled. Together they soaked for hours in the hot-spring baths behind the station. John learned a little Russian. Everyone liked him, for he could laugh at himself, even when he splintered his dog-sled against a tree trunk. The major asked him to stand godfather for his baby, which was a great compliment to a man who, as far as the major comprehended, might have come from another planet.

Back at New Archangel, the departure of John and Langsdorff stung Baron Rezanov into action. A feverish haste to reach St. Petersburg replaced his lethargy. Perhaps he determined to get there before them so that the Czar would learn of his engagement to Concha Argüello from his own lips. Somehow he got the *Avoss* into the water. With Khvostov at her helm, and Davidov in command of the *Juno*, he hurried across the Pacific, leaving Baranov in solitude once more.

He must have passed John deWolf somewhere in the Aleutian fogs. He plunged through the Kuriles and across the gulf to Okhotsk, straining to reach port before the ice closed in. From Okhotsk he headed west, on horseback and by coach. Traveling night and day, outwearing relays of the imperial post-horses, he broke into a fever. Still he kept on, more dead than alive. He never reached the capital. At Krasnoyarsk, just over the Urals, his horse, as tired as he, stumbled. Over its head fell the Baron Rezanov to his death, much as Benjamin Church, a century before, had fallen to his at Fall River.

John awoke one morning in his miserable billet at Petropavlovsk to see the *Juno* at anchor off the fish-wharf. The two Russians, the

German, and the Yankee had a praznik of their own aboard her that night. They had not heard of the Baron's death, and if they had would not have mourned him for long.

In May the Kamchatka ice began to melt. John good-naturedly crowded three more homesick ladies and two men aboard the tiny *Russisloff*. The *Juno* bored a lead for him through the decaying cake-ice of the harbor, and kept company, with her sails reefed to hold her speed down to his own, for the thirty-three days it took him to cross the Gulf of Okhotsk. He was glad she was standing by, for once the *Russisloff* almost capsized when she ran up the back of a sleeping whale and down the other side. He reached Okhotsk on June 27, 1807, and not too soon, for the ice had cleared the harbor only the week before.

He returned the borrowed brig to the governor of Okhotsk. The two Eskimos in the crew begged him to take them with him to America as slaves, rather than send them back to Baranov; but that he could not do. There were too many slaves in America already, he writes. He said farewell to Langsdorff, who decided to linger for more specimens, and to Khvostov and Davidov, who had to stand by the *Juno*. They agreed to meet for another party—a civilized one this time—if ever they all reached St. Petersburg. He sewed his draft, and the safe-conduct which Rezanov had given him, into his coat. He dared not trust his pockets, for after three years, and in spite of Parker's repairs, his clothes were falling apart. With Parker, three guides, and eleven white horses, he started out to cross the Russian Empire.

When they could, they stopped at the imperial post-stations. When they could not, they camped out beside the trail in bearskin sleeping-bags. They made thirty to forty miles a day, which was not much faster than their speed at sea. Sometimes they could ferry the rivers; sometimes they had to swim them. Their horses became streaked with blood from mosquito bites, and the men had to wear gloves, sunbonnets, and gauze veils. John, being skinny, rattled in the saddle between two six-inch pommels till he learned to wedge himself in with pillows. One night four of the horses, including his own mount, broke away from the picket line, not to be seen again; they were probably eaten by bears.

At the end of July his caravan reached Yakutsk, on the Lena. He rested a day before pushing toward Irkutsk, the capital of Siberia. Irkutsk lay twelve hundred miles southwest, counting the bends in the trail and the river. Aching from his saddle, he decided to make it by boat instead of astride. He hired a twenty-foot towboat, with three horses to haul the long stretch upstream. This leg of his trip took him another month, but at least it was a more comfortable one. When the wind held, he sat in the roundhouse watching Parker and his courier Kuznetsov (the name means Smith) working the single square sail. When it fell, he was towed by the horses from the bank. When both sail and horsepower failed, Parker and Kuznetsov had to man the sweeps.

> I had long noticed the great deference shown to the military in these parts [he writes], but I saw it particularly illustrated by Kuznetsov, my cossack. He was scolding the postillions for their laziness in hitching up the horses at one relay, and I could understand he was making a great lion of me. "Start quick, you rascals," said he. "We have a great American captain in the boat, going on government business!" And this seemed to hasten everything, even the horses, for they travelled much better after it.

Irkutsk was a town of thirty thousand. Along the duckboard sidewalks, he saw stone buildings for the first time since he had left his uncle's wharfhouse. He met people who understood a little English. It was a mystery to them how he could have reached Siberia from the east, instead of from Moscow or St. Petersburg. They had curiosity enough to ask him where America was, and what was the name of its Czar. Langsdorff, in his fitful way caught up with him, and they spent a day of sightseeing together. But the flora and fauna of the Siberian capital deserved a week of the scientist's attention, so John went on without him.

He bought a carriage called a *pervoshka*, which proved to be no more than a box rounded at the bottom and fitted to the axletree without springs. He had either to lie down in it or sit bolt upright.

Even stuffed with a featherbed, it was as uncomfortable as his saddle. With Parker and Kuznetsov, he left Irkutsk on August 21 in two pervoshkas. To cover the thirty-five hundred miles to St. Petersburg before still another winter set in, they would have to travel fast. Aside from replenishing his provisions and changing his horses, he stopped only once in the next week. That was in a village struck by a plague of smallpox, where he urged the local Pope to feed his parishioners bread and milk, of which there was plenty, and showed him a kind of primitive vaccination by inoculating the healthy with thread smeared in the sores of the sick.

After eight days in the springless pervoshka, he reached Tomsk with his whole body trembling. There Kuznetsov sold one of the pervoshkas and brought him a new *troika*—a three-horse carriage equipped with springs. Parker and Kuznetsov followed uncomfortably behind in the remaining pervoshka. The $300 in silver which he had got in part payment for the *Juno* was almost gone.

Even with the comfort of springs beneath his swaying troika, he had to rest up for a week when he reached Tobolsk. The night before he left that town, the mayor gave him a farewell which he describes as follows:

> The custom of the gentlemen was for each to lay his right hand on the other's back, and then to kiss each other on both cheeks. Not infrequently their noses came into rude collision. A lady, however, presents you the back of her hand to kiss, and at the same time she kisses you on the cheek. Being all ready for action, the ladies and gentlemen placed themselves in a row around the room, and then the performance was begun. By this time the sweat had begun to start from my forehead; but I saw no use to be lagging, and so, summoning up my courage, I turned to and went through the ceremony like a veteran courtier. The last of the ladies was the mayor's daughter, a great beauty; and I was strongly tempted, in violation of Russian etiquette, to kiss her cheek. But I managed to restrain myself.

At Ekaterinburg, since renamed Sverdlovsk, he passed the Urals. At Kazan he ferried across the Volga. On October 8, 1807, he reached Moscow, which up till a century before had been the capital of all Russia, and was to become the capital again a little more than a century later. John heard the first reliable news in three years. Aaron Burr had been convicted; the British frigate *Leopard* had fired into the American *Chesapeake;* Napoleon had entered Spain and, after his victories at Austerlitz, Jena, and Eylau, had forced on the Czar, on the island of Tilsit in the Niemen, an alliance with France. (On the very day John entered Moscow, the Charleston *Courier* reports that Christian & deWolf offered 120 "prime Angola negroes" for sale at Gadsden's wharf.)

In Moscow, with the rest of his travel money, John had some of his pelts made into a fur coat, for the trip north to St. Petersburg would be cold. He was delighted to meet an educated lady who had heard of George Washington and Benjamin Franklin. He spent a week exploring the ancient city, which looked, he says, like a turtle two-thirds submerged in water. He saw the Kremlin, on the crown of the hill, and the three concentric walled circles outside it: Chinese Town, White Town, and Land Town. He saw the famous two-hundred-ton bell, which was cracked even then. He marveled at the hundreds of gold and silver spires, little guessing that within five years the Russians themselves were to burn the city to save it from Napoleon's hands.

At last he reached the end of the vast country. On October 21, sixteen months after leaving Alaska, he drove into St. Petersburg. He found, as he knew all along, that he need not have made the overland trip at all. The duplicate of Rezanov's draft for the *Juno* had been cashed long before. Moorfield, from Canton, had sent it around the world in the opposite direction from his. Through the American Consul, the Russian-American Company had paid it to Cramer & Smith, the deWolf agents in Russia. Since John had made it payable in Spanish dollars, and Russian and American paper had dropped 15 per cent in the meantime, they had made an unexpected premium. While he was needlessly struggling across Asia and half of Europe, they had already reinvested in Russian hemp and iron, and that cargo had preceded him to Bristol. He had nothing left to worry about except getting there himself.

He went out to Cronstadt, the port of the capital, and engaged passage in a British ship for London. But the day before she was to sail, Napoleon had forced the Czar to declare war on England. Without notice, every British ship had fled from the Baltic. The only foreign-bound vessel left in port was a seventy-ton Dutch galiot, laden with tallow. Her skipper was a little old Dutchman, less than five feet tall. A mate and a cook comprised her crew. John asked if he would take him and Parker aboard.

"Yaw," said the Dutchman.

"Where are you bound?"

"Copenhagen."

"Will you let my man work his passage?"

"Yaw, goot."

The cabin was a doghouse containing two box-bunks with sliding doors. John turned in with the Dutchman; Parker and the mate took turns in the other bunk. After a breakfast of beans and buckwheat, which John had not tasted since he left Bristol, they stood down the Baltic. Parker broke out his fiddle for the sheer joy of being homeward bound, but the Dutchman did not even smile.

On the second day, John was standing on the pier at Elsinore, under the battlements of Hamlet's castle, looking up the sound to Copenhagen, when he saw a ship bearing down with a large American ensign at her masthead.

> At the sight of her [he says] my heart leaped up into my throat. I waited until she came to anchor, and then called a shore-boat and went off to her. She proved to be the *Mary* of Portland, Capt. David Gray, and was homeward bound. This was joyful news, and affected me so deeply that I could hardly tell the Captain my story. At last, after making known who I was, and from whence I came, I asked if he would take me as passenger, and he readily consented. I went immediately to the galiot to settle with the little Dutch skipper. To the question how much I was to pay him, he answered that he only wanted "Was billig ist; das ist mir recht." (Whatever is reasonable; that will be all right with me.) Not knowing exactly what that was, I tendered him 20 Spanish dollars, with which he was well satisfied, and made him a bonus of a pair of my breeches, which he had already been wearing since we left Cronstadt.

John and Parker shipped aboard the *Mary* with Captain Gray. She was bound for Portland in ballast. Except for putting in at Liverpool for repairs, they had a clear passage.

> You may suppose [writes John] that I started from Portland with as little delay as possible for Bristol. I arrived there, by Mr. Chadwick's stage from Providence, on the first of April, 1808. Thus ended an absence of three years and eight months. The owners were already in receipt of the proceeds of the voyage, which resulted in a clear profit of ONE HUNDRED THOUSAND DOLLARS.

This included the profit from the sale of the *Yermak* and her pelts in Canton. After selling her, Moorfield and Stetson had taken passage home in a Boston ship. Oddly enough, she was the original *Mary* which had kept the *Juno* company on her outward passage round Cape Horn. On this return journey from Canton, seven of her crew, including two of John's, had jumped ship in Hawaii, and the *Mary* herself had foundered off Cape Hatteras. Though all hands were saved, the *Juno's* registry and bill of sale were lost, along with the ventures of Farmer John and his family.

Under the law, a ship's bondsmen forfeited their collateral unless they could prove, within two years after she cleared from her home port, that she had been sold abroad. For over a year, Collector Collins, hoping that John might return, had managed to delay the forfeiture of the *Juno's* bond. Stetson's story of the sale might be true, wrote Secretary Gallatin from Washington, but there was no proof of it. When John arrived with Rezanov's duplicate receipt in his coat-lining, Gallatin was satisfied. The *Juno's* registry was honorably canceled without penalty—more honorably than when deWolf slavers were sold abroad to evade the law—and Major William's insurance company paid Farmer John for the loss of his china, and of his tea, his shawls, and his handkerchiefs and trouserings.

The town had pretty well given up John, like his father, for lost by the time he and Parker returned; but it was not greatly surprised that they did return. Disappearances at sea were common, and so were miraculous escapes from it. The village had not changed much

in his absence, except for the completion of Captain Jim's mansion
at the Mount. The sou'wester still threaded up the bay each afternoon, the Congregational church still stood in the middle of Bradford Street, the boys still labbed 'lasses on the wharf, and the gos-
sips still gathered in Pardon Handy's chandlery. They did not care
to hear about his travels much more than if he had made an ordinary
voyage to the Caribbean or the Slave Coast; they had rather discuss
Jefferson's embargo. He met the common neglect of travelers, but
he immediately earned, from the boys on the wharf, the nickname
of Norwest John, which thereafter distinguished him from any other
John deWolfs.

He got none of the hundred thousand for himself, but Russia
was now in his blood. The year after his return, Captain Jim sent
him back to St. Petersburg. As he had hoped, he found Langsdorff
there, and by luck the two of them ran into Khvostov and Davidov
too, who were still officers in the Imperial Navy. The scheduled
praznik took place in Norwest John's boarding house. It turned into
a four-way night of reminiscence. John says dryly that "libations to
the gods of friendship were not omitted." The two Russians had
fought in a war with Sweden since John had seen them, and had
much to tell. Their ship was anchored on the other side of the Neva,
which runs through St. Petersburg. At two in the morning they
started for her, and had crossed the drawbridge before remembering
a last story that must be told. By that time the drawbridge had been
opened for river traffic. They tried to jump across the opening,
which was more than even sober men could have done. They fell
into the swift waters of the icy Neva and were drowned. Norwest
John ends his memoirs, written in his old age:

> Though more than 50 years have passed since the death of these
> young men, I cannot forbear to recall their many virtues and to lament
> their untimely end.

The *Juno* herself, still under Russian colors, was the next victim
of the years. In 1816 she foundered off Petropavlovsk with the loss
of twenty-three men and all her cargo.

Baranov stayed on at his post after the others had left him, growing drunker and gloomier each year. The more he drank, the less he ate. He lived on one meal a day, eaten whenever hunger forced him. He took to wearing a black wig to keep his head warm. He tied it round his neck with a colored scarf. Each year he tried to resign as Governor of Russian America. The Czar would ignore his resignation, award him a new medal, and simply refuse to send out a ship to take him home. When he got too old for anything else, he was suddenly dismissed. By that time he did not want to leave Alaska. But the Czar sent out a successor anyway, with orders to check all the account books of his long service. Not a kopeck was missing, but there was a sad shortage in the Company's supply of vodka. At once bitter and happy at leaving his life's work, Baranov determined to spend the rest of his days in the warm Pacific, where he was well known. He paid a call on King Kamehameha at Hawaii, visited the Marquesas Islands, and then, one day at the Grand Hotel in Batavia, he died. His work for the Czar was undone in 1867, when the United States bought all Alaska for $7,200,000. He would have thought it a high price, for the sea otter had been hunted nearly to extinction.

Langsdorff, after returning to his native Germany, formed a company to promote emigration to Brazil. When it failed, he retired to his home in Freiburg, at the foot of the Black Forest. There he wrote an account of his trip round the world, the first half with Rezanov and the second, more or less, with Norwest John. He described Rezanov's tomb at Krasnoyarsk:

> It is a large stone, in the fashion of an altar, but without any inscription.

He did not forget to mention the golden woodpecker (*picus auratus*) which he had seen on Baranov Island, nor the skunk (*viverra putorius*) at San Francisco. He strayed from the stern objectivity of science only to describe the impact which Concha Argüello had made on the Baron and—who can doubt it?—on himself.

She was distinguished for her vivacity and cheerfulness, her love-inspiring and brilliant eyes, which pierced his inmost soul, and her exceedingly beautiful teeth; for her pleasing and expressive features, and for a thousand other charms. Yet her manners were perfectly simple and artless. Beauties of her kind one may find, though seldom, only in Italy, Portugal and Spain.

He sent a copy of his book to Norwest John in Bristol, underlining his mischievous account of Hawaii—and John, thinking of the seven deserters from the *Mary*, had to admit that it was true:

> The seamen of the United States like so well to revel in a superfluity of the productions of nature without much labor, and to have handsome young girls at their disposal, that a ship scarcely ever touches here without leaving one or more of its sailors behind.*

Doña Concepción Argüello never married. She waited the agreed two years for her fiancé, not knowing that he had been killed. She waited longer, till California became first Mexican and then American. In 1851, when she was sixty, she entered the Sisterhood of Saint Dominic at Monterey, taking the name of Sister María Dominga. By this time Bristol ships were reduced to ferrying gold-seekers around the Horn to the harbor below her father's presidio. In 1854 the Sisters moved to Benicia, across the bay from San Francisco. They opened Saint Catherine's Academy for Young Ladies. By paying fifteen dollars extra a quarter, the pupils could take Spanish lessons. It can be imagined that the Spanish teacher was Sister María Dominga. She died two days before Christmas of 1857 at Benicia, in the white habit of the Sisterhood.

Norwest John outlived the others. Like many of the deWolfs, he seems to have preferred working for his relations to working for himself. His uncle Captain Jim was one who appreciated the achievement of his voyage. In 1812 he sent him aboard a sloop to Hartford, to fetch Minister Griswold to Bristol. In 1815 he made him

---

* A Bristol mariner who had touched at Oahu before the missionaries arrived was asked to describe the scenery. His answer: "Prettiest girls you ever see, all settin' around nekkid." Sam Patterson, one of John's original Bristol crew, later wrote a lurid confession of his two years on the island.

master of his brig *Shannon,* captured from the British in the war, and in 1816 of his ship *Ann,* named for a slaver which the British had seized in 1806.

In 1817 Norwest John bought the brigantine *If,* 160 tons, but sold her the next year to his cousin George deWolf. In 1818 he bought Captain Jim's finest ship, the *General Jackson,* but in two years he sold her too. With the proceeds, he bought the farm behind the Mount where, in the gale of 1815, a fishhawk had miraculously dropped a tautog to the starving Baylies sisters. At thirty-five he was regarded as an incurable bachelor, but no sooner had he bought the farm than he married an out-of-town girl named Mary Melville. She let him name their only son for Dr. Langsdorff. As clippers began to replace the old bluff-bows of his youth, and as steamers began to replace sail, he grew disgusted with the sea. It was no place, he told his cousin 'Fessor, for a married man. He quit it for good in 1829 and settled down, like many Bristol sea-captains, to farming onions. When he grew too old for that, in 1850, he and Mary moved in with their married daughter Nancy Downer in Dorchester, overlooking Boston harbor.

Mary had a nephew named Herman Melville who was writing what became the classic story of whaling, *Moby Dick.* Norwest John did not claim to be a specialist on whales, but he had met some. *Moby Dick* describes the whale the *Russisloff* encountered in the Gulf of Okhotsk:

> A whale bigger than the ship set up his back and lifted the ship three feet out of the water. The masts reeled and the sails fell all together, while we who were below sprang instantly upon the deck, concluding we had struck upon some rock; instead of which we saw the monster sailing off with the utmost gravity and solemnity, leaving the ship uninjured.

To silence doubters, Herman Melville added:

> Now the Captain deWolf here alluded to as commanding the ship in question is a New Englander who, after a long life of unusual adventures as a sea-captain, this day resides in the village of Dorchester,

near Boston. I have the honor of being his nephew. The ship was by
no means a large one, being a Russian craft built on the Siberian coast
and purchased by my uncle after bartering away the vessel in which
he had sailed from home.

Like Benjamin Church so long before, Norwest John wrote his
reminiscences when he was nearing eighty. His grandchildren called
him "White Grandpa." They could always count on finding candy
in his sunny room, but he would make them hunt for it. He would
lean with his elbows on the lambrekin of his arched mantelpiece
as if he still leaned against a quarter-rail. His face had been tanned
to leather. His square hands grasped the lapels of his broadcloth
coat, and his merry eyes twinkled as he watched them search what
he called his cabin. When they saw him gazing out to sea, with his
old spyglass stretched to arm's length, they would ask him, "What
do you see, White Grandpa?"

Norwest John always growled back, "I'm looking at those damned
three-masted schooners."

He died at Dorchester in 1872, aged ninety-three. The Boston
Transcript wrote of him:

> This venerable shipmaster was respected for his courteous man-
> ners, genial disposition, kindly affections, wonderfully retentive mem-
> ory and large intelligence. He continually made friends of new
> generations, and among the sincere mourners of his decease will be
> young kindred and others, whose esteem and love he succeeded in
> arousing by the hearty and tender sympathies which neither time nor
> infirmity could check.

6.

The War of 1812

THE deadly chess game between France and England lasted almost continuously from the execution of Louis XVI in 1793 to
the defeat of Napoleon at Waterloo in 1815. America was the pawn
of both. The French seized American vessels which traded with the
British, and vice versa. Captain Samuel Wardwell of Bristol lost
the sloop *Sally* to the French in 1795. In 1804 James deWolf lost
one of his slavers to the British—oddly enough, her name was *Sally*
too; she was the brig from which Richard Waldron wrote his letter home. In 1806 his brig *Stork,* carrying jerked beef from Bristol
to Havana, was seized by HMS *Cleopatra,* ordered into Barbados,
and condemned as lawful prize by the British court of admiralty. In
the same year Captain Jim's fine two-hundred-ton ship *Ann,* loaded
with slaves for the market at Montevideo, was captured by HMS
Leda. Her cargo was so valuable that Captain Jim sent his brother
John to London to protest the confiscation. The *Ann* was condemned
for running the British blockade of Spanish America, not for carrying slaves. Lovering, the American Consul in London, who pressed
the appeal, probably did not like to let a countryman down, but
he was forced to tell John that the Board of Admiralty rejected
his claim for restitution because it "considered the Trade as of a

[165]

nature entitled to no countenance, and certainly to no extraordinary protection."

The *Ann* was sold, along with her cargo, "to the sole use of His Majesty, his heirs and successors."

After the victory at Trafalgar in October of 1805, the British controlled the seas. Two British frigates, the *Cambrian* and the *Leander,* lay just outside the three-mile limit off New York to search American vessels for contraband and for British deserters. The impressment of American sailors by British men-of-war was a running grievance, and it must have galled an American captain to muster his crew before a British boarding-officer and lose one or two of them for want of proper papers. But there was some justice on the the other side. Many British seamen deserted the ill-paid service of the Navy for the higher pay aboard American merchantmen, and the Americans did nothing to discourage them. In 1803, for instance, British commanders seized forty-three seamen from American ships, but only twelve of them were American citizens. In 1805 Oliver Child of Warren and Ellery King of Bristol, having lost their "protections"—as passports were then called—were taken from Captain Jim's favorite slaver *Andromache,* and drafted into the Royal Navy. It took Captain Jim, Collector Collins, and the State Department two years to get them back. The eccentric 'Fessor John deWolf * wrote an indignant poem about an American seaman

---

* This John deWolf, Junior, son of Farmer John and cousin of Norwest John, was the first of Mark Antony's descendants to receive a real education. He was himself captured during the War of 1812, and thrown into Dartmoor prison. When the warden offered him a cup of grog with the insulting toast, "To Madison, dead or alive," he drank it down with the countertoast, "To the Prince Regent, drunk or sober." He read the Bible in Hebrew and Greek, disdaining the King James translation. He was so absent-minded that once, when a new clerk in the post office asked him his name, he told him, "Why, bless you, *I* don't know it, but perhaps the gentleman behind me can help you out." In later years he taught chemistry at Brown University, where he tried to dissolve his wife's diamonds in acid, to prove they were carbon. He wore dark glasses and a black wig. To hint that he was ready for his tea, he pretended—and perhaps believed—that he was a teapot. Crooking one arm and goosenecking the other, he sidled through the door to avoid nicking his spout, and settled with a hiss of steam on the piazza bench. When his wife

seized by the press-gang and allowed to perish, from an undefined malady, aboard his captors' deck. It ended with these stanzas:

> The sailor's woes drew forth no sigh;
> No hand would close the sailor's eye;
> Remorseless, his pale corpse they gave
> Unshrouded to the friendly wave.
>
> And as he sank beneath the tide
> The hellish ruffians' shout arose;
> Exultingly the demons cried,
> "So fare all Albion's rebel foes!"

Although Captain Jim had little use for poetry, he loved to repeat his nephew's verse in full to any of his family who would listen, clutching his satin lapel and glaring at them from under his bushy eyebrows. The seizures enraged him out of all proportion to his losses. He waited restlessly to avenge himself on England, and to make money as fast as he had made it in the four years of Charleston's open port. He preferred risking his fleet in battle to seeing it rot at the wharves from fear of seizure. But Willian Gray and the Crowninshields of Salem were almost the only New England shipmasters who agreed with him. The rest, Federalists to a man, were opposed to risking war with England.

The War of 1812—"Madison's War," as they called it—might have been waged against the French with as good reason as against the British. In 1810 Napoleon seized between two hundred and three hundred American ships, worth ten millions, which happened to be lying in Continental ports. Or it might not have been waged at all. It was declared by Congress on June 18; only the day before, in London, the British cabinet had rescinded the Orders in Council which authorized the seizure of American ships trading with France.

---

finally brought the tea, he quaffed the bowl down and poured the dregs over the piazza rail, exclaiming, "The whole world is my slopbowl!" His foible so enraged Farmer John, his father, that he once brought his cudgel down on 'Fessor's head, shouting, "Teapot, eh? Then *break!*" Only the wig saved him from a fractured skull.

The news reached America too late. The whole course of the war seems to reflect the indecisive character of President Madison. Most New Englanders felt that Napoleon had duped him into war with England to tie up British forces on the Atlantic and in Canada, and they may have been right, for within a week of the declaration Napoleon opened his fatal invasion of Russia. Not only had the causes of hostilities been removed before the war began, but they were not even mentioned in the treaty when it ended; and its most important battle was fought at New Orleans with the combatants in ignorance that they were already at peace.

The Rhode Island militia were enlisted for terms of six months. They could not be sent out of the state without the Governor's consent. Even if they had wished to join the ten thousand troops of the regular Army on the Great Lakes and in New York state, Governor Jones, being a Federalist, would probably have refused to commit them. As far as Rhode Island was concerned, the war was to be fought at sea, and by private warships, not by the Navy.

President Adams, threatened by war with France, had bought a few frigates (James deWolf's *General Greene* was one of them), but Jefferson, who opposed a Federal navy on principle, had decommissioned them as soon as he took office in 1801, and Madison, in his first term, had done little to rebuild the establishment. By 1812 the British Navy counted 1060 sail, while the American consisted of only 16 seagoing vessels, ranging from 12-gun brigs to seven 44-gun frigates. The deWolfs owned 23 ships, 17 sloops, 20 schooners, 29 brigs, 3 snows, 1 bark, and 1 packet. Though none measured more than 250 tons, their private fleet exceeded the tonnage of the United States Navy.

Privateering had always been illegal in peacetime, and was to be abolished as an instrument of war by the civilized nations of the world (the United States excepted) by the Declaration of Paris in 1856. In 1812 it was technically legal and officially encouraged, but only a little less shady, in the eyes of Federalist New England, than piracy or the slave trade. J. Fenimore Cooper writes in his *History of the Navy*:

Privateering in the abstract is a profession which reason and good morals can scarcely approve; for whatever may be its legality, its aim is to turn the waste and destruction of war to the benefit of avarice.

Such scruples were lost on the Bristol shipowners. Many of the country's greatest naval heroes—Barry, Cassin, Decatur, John Paul Jones, Rodgers, and the senior David Porter—served aboard privateers during the Revolution and the War of 1812. Collector Ellery at Newport, being a Federalist, opposed the war, but he could not interfere with the Bristol privateers, for their commissions were filled out by his colleague Collins at Bristol and signed by President Madison himself. Collins kept blanks in the customhouse on Bradford Street, and forwarded them as applied for to Washington for signature. One of his letters to Monroe, then Secretary of State, ends with these words:

P. S. I have not one commission now in the office. I therefore request that a few may be transmitted.

These documents licensed the holder to

subdue, seize and take any armed or unarmed British vessel, public or private, which shall be found within the jurisdictional waters of the United States, or elsewhere on the high seas and within the waters of the British dominions, and such captured vessel, with her apparel, guns and appurtenances, and the goods or effects which shall be found on board the same, together with all British persons and others who shall be found acting on board, to bring within some port of the United States; and also to retake any vessels, goods and effects of the people of the United States which may have been captured by any British armed vessel.

During the two and a half years of war, President Madison signed 515 such commissions. One hundred and fifty of the privateers hailed from Massachusetts, 112 from Maryland, 102 from New York, 18 from Rhode Island, and the rest from other seaboard states. Salem, which had sent out 158 in the Revolution, sent only 40 in the War of 1812, partly because her merchants opposed the war, and partly because most of her ships, being built for the China

trade, were too sluggish for combat. Of the Rhode Islanders, four
hailed from Newport, five from Providence, and nine from Bristol.
James deWolf owned six of the nine, in whole or in part, and shared
with William Gray of Salem in another ship commissioned from
that port.

One of the Bristol privateers, the *Hiram,* blew up at sea,
sabotaged, it was said, by four Englishmen who joined her crew for
the purpose. She was the only one of the nine in which no member
of the deWolf family had an interest. The *Curlew,* the *Rambler,*
and the *Yankee Lass* were captured by the Royal Navy. The
Blockade and *Fourth of July* made no prizes. The tiny twenty-ton
Water-Witch captured seven hundred barrels of flour being trai-
torously smuggled to the British garrison at Halifax. The *Macdonough,* commissioned toward the end of the war, took two ships,
five brigs, and two sloops after the peace treaty was signed at Ghent,
but had to give them up. Privateering was like horse-racing: one
lucky ship made up for many failures. Captain Jim's *Yankee,* one-
quarter of which was owned by his partner John Smith, proved to
be the most successful privateer of the war. She was even luckier
than the famous *Rossie* of Baltimore or the *America* of Salem. Before
studying her record, let us glance at the nature of a privateer.

The privateer was a civilian warship, authorized by the government to capture and destroy enemy shipping for her own profit.
She carried no cargo, in distinction to the armed merchantman,
which was authorized by letters of marque to do the same thing.
The letter-of-marque was "registered to voyage." The privateer
was "commissioned to cruise."

The privateer's owner had to find two sureties (in the case of
vessels under twenty tons, only one) to post bond that she would
not evade the revenue laws, just as he did for a slaver or other
commercial carrier. The bond was $5000 for ships with crews up
to one hundred men, and $10,000 beyond. Provided her prize was
legally condemned by an American court or consul, and provided
the customs duty was paid on it (the tariff averaged 13 per cent

ad valorem) and 2 per cent was deposited into the Hospital Fund for Seamen, she was subject to no more restrictions than a merchantman. Napoleon himself was always ready to lend the machinery of his courts to the condemnation of British shipping captured by an American privateer.

Among the trained seamen left idle by the embargo and the end of the slave-trade, it was not hard to make up the complement of a Bristol privateer. Scores of them, idling in the taverns and boarding houses along the Thames Street waterfront, or working for a quarter a day in the onion fields, waited for a chance to ship. The 413 privateersmen who manned the nine Bristol vessels were almost one-seventh of the population. There were not enough men-of-war in the Navy to absorb them, and the Thames Street boys were too adventurous anyway for the long enlistment, low pay, and slow promotion of government service. A single British prize, they hoped, would make them rich forever. In Simeon Potter's day, half of a privateer's prize money had gone to the Crown, and during the Revolution half went to the Continental treasury; but now, to encourage the profession, President Madison let the owners and crew keep all they captured.

By the usual ship's articles, half the prize money went to the owners. The other half was divided among the company in shares ranging from sixteen for the captain down to one apiece for the Negro messboys. The chance of sudden riches gave rise to a class of adventurers called variously Marines, Gentlemen Sailors, or Landsmen, some of whom had never gone to sea before. (Personnel of the regular Navy were called Statesmen.) They were the combat force taken aboard to supplement the sailing crew. Bristol was thronged with these tars of long lineage and short experience.

The sailing crew were paid the old wages of $10 to $15 a month. The Marines got no pay at all, but had a larger share in the prize money. Being trained to arms from service in the militia, they were welcome aboard the privateer. They were not assigned to ordinary details, but formed a *corps d'élite*, standing between the ship's officers and the working crew, and commanded by their own officers.

They wore red shirts; the crew wore blue. While the crew slept in the forecastle, as they always had, the Marines swung in hammocks tween-decks, in the space once taken up by the slave cargoes. Government orders required that at least one-third of the privateer's complement must be Marines. Since the same number of men was needed to work the ship as in peacetime, the privateer was always overcrowded.

The sailing crew and Marines on a well-found privateer practiced gunnery daily, and scoured the deck with two-hundred-pound holystones, two to a team, hauling the heavy stones across the sun-bleached decking by the iron ring in each end, and sanding the corners with a smaller stone called the Prayer Book. At mess they ate cold beef, crusted with salt, from wooden kids laid out on the hatchway by the messboys. The beef was affectionately called "Old Horse." At each meal there were biscuits and dried peas, washed down with tea served in horn tumblers. The only tableware was iron spoons. One jug held vinegar, to cut the salt on the beef; another held molasses for sweetening. Dessert was duff, made by mixing flour with dried apples or plums and drippings from the slush-barrel. When the duff was served up, each man squeezed his portion into a ball the size of his fist, coated it with molasses, and ate it with the iron spoon. At dinner half a gill of rum was served aft, but in heavy weather, or after a fight, the captain would usually issue an extra round.

Discipline was severe. Ratings were not allowed to set foot on the quarterdeck or talk with each other on watch. Cowards and drunkards were spread-eagled on the shrouds and flogged with the cat-o'-nine-tails by the mate, or confined on bread and water amidships in a grilled hole called the lazaret, no bigger than a sunken barrel.

When the captain felt obliged to knock a man down, he used a walrus-tusk "persuader." The sailing crew handled the ship barefoot and stripped to the waist, except in cold weather. One detail hauled on the inch-thick lines which lifted the sodden sails to the yardarm or squared them to their course, while another, bent over the timber, clewed them up to their grommets with no more purchase than their toes on the footrope, at the imminent risk of a fall to the deck below. If the sails were frozen, they could tear out a man's finger nails. The foretopman, far aloft, swayed in his crow's-nest, scouring the sea by sunlight and moon for glimpse of a sail. On Sundays the off-watch dressed up in blue roundabout jacket, white duck trousers, patent-leather pumps, check shirt, and black silk neckerchief, tied with the same knot the Navy uses today. The captain read morning prayers from his service-book, beseeching the Almighty, on their behalf, that "the coral pillow and the seaweed winding-sheet might have no terrors for them." In the afternoon they washed and mended clothes, trimmed beards, embroidered scrimshaw on their pants, watched the Negro boys dance on deck, or simply slept. The ship's log of the *Yankee* for one Sabbath records that the sailing crew sang hymns while the Marines joined in secular ditties like "Yankee Doodle" and "Old Tom Tough." Allowing for the changes of fashion, the contents of a privateersman's sea chest were not much different from what goes in a duffel bag today. Benjamin Barker, killed in action aboard the *Yankee,* left the following effects:

1 bed tick	2 pr. drawers	2 pr. shoes
2 quilts	1 thick shirt	1 shaving box
1 knitted nightshirt	2 light shirts	1 pr. earrings
1 pillow	4 handkerchiefs	1 Testament
7 pr. stockings	2 blankets	1 segar box
5 " pantaloons	4 towels	1 thick jacket
4 vests with trimmings	1 cap	2 pr. gloves
2 red shirts	1 covered hat	

The sailing crew were jealous of the Marines, and the Statesmen were jealous of both. At the time of the Battle of Lake Erie, Commodore Oliver Hazard Perry's annual pay was $720, which was less than the lay of Jack Jibsheet, the Negro messboy, on a single cruise of the *Yankee.* Ashore there was jealousy too. The Bristol farmers and clerks envied the prize money which the swashbuckling privateersmen, in white ducks, blue jackets, and jaunty varnished hats with a foot of ribbon over the eye, squandered in the taverns of the waterfront. Privateers, being semi-official, paid no tonnage fee for entering the harbor, and thus cut down on the perquisites of the customs officers. Collins probably did not mind, for he was on the deWolf payroll as well as the government's. But there is a pathetic entry in the journal of honest Samuel Bosworth, who had toiled on as surveyor at the same salary of $250 ever since the affair of the *Lucy* in 1799. Rich as the privateersmen were after a successful cruise, they were stingy tippers. He writes on the margin of his diary for 1814:

> Such scanty fees
> My spirits freeze;
> They're scarce enough
> To buy my snuff.

Next year, when the war ended, he hoped for better usage, and wrote:

> Now may the Peace
> My fees increase,
> For God knows How I need them.
> I children have
> Who soon must starve
> If I have naught to feed them.

All of the privateers were small—few were even as large as the Pilgrims' *Mayflower*, which had measured 180 tons. The deepest draft possible in Bristol harbor was twenty feet. To overtake the enemy, as well as to escape him, they had to be fast, and to be fast they had to be "tender-sided." They were overcrowded and over-armed, but they were famous for their speed, especially into the wind. Their favorite tactic was to overhaul a prize, lie to windward just beyond her range, and lob shot at her every quarter-hour until she struck her colors. Their muzzle-loading iron guns, cast at John Brown's foundry in Scituate or at the Taunton Iron Works, weighed up to six tons; they threw balls of twelve pounds at an effective range of half a mile on a light sea. For reloading, they were run inboard by tackle. Some, on fixed trunnions, were emplaced in the tween-deck ports; some were above on carriages or swivels; and Long Tom, the brass chaser, was securely lashed amidships on a broadside carriage, ready to be wheeled into position fore or aft according to need in combat. The blunt carronades, for close in-fighting, were always in the gunports; the light swivels were sometimes posited in notches of the rail, or even in the crosstrees. American guns were painted blue; British guns, purportedly to hide blood-stains, were red. So ponderous was the privateer's load of metal that in a heavy sea, or when she was closely pursued, some of the guns had to be jettisoned. On her third cruise the *Yankee* carried the incredible number of nineteen guns and a complement of two hundred men. She sailed with the *Blockade* in company; privateers often hunted in pairs, so that while one engaged, or at least drew off, a hostile man-of-war, the other could cut out a single ship from the convoy at her leisure.

The privateersman's object was not to destroy his prize—it was the last thing he wanted to do—but to terrify her into surrender, or at worst disable her slightly. Once she had struck, a prizemaster, with a guard from the surplus Marines, would be thrown aboard her. After disarming her crew and taking their surrender, he would order them to sail her to the nearest American or consular port, where they would be released for exchange, and the vessel put up for condemnation and sale. One letter home from the *Yankee* records that "our instructions require that we shall treat our prisoners with kindness and humanity."

II

The brigantine *Yankee* was 120 feet long, with a good deal of dead rise to her sides, but fine sections fore and aft above the water-line. She was square-rigged at the foremast and schooner-rigged at the mainmast: what mariners called a "morphydite" brig. Her cruising speed averaged 7 knots, but under a heavy press of canvas she could make 12. "What we can't lick we can run away from,"

Captain Wilson boasted. There was no cowardice to that; it was plain good business. He had no scruples against flying false colors, and once escaped from a British cruiser by running up the Union Jack.

The *Yankee,* built at Haddam, Connecticut, was not a new ship; there is reason to believe she had been in the slave trade before 1808. She was completely refitted within a month after the declaration of war. Her commission was issued July 13, 1812, and she sailed from Bristol a few days later.

James deWolf owned three-quarters of her and John Smith one-quarter. Her sureties were John deWolf, Captain Jim's brother, and Hersey Bradford, his son-in-law. Her commander was Joseph Oliver Wilson, twenty-four years old and English-born. Her armor was twelve guns, divided between six- and nine-pounders and reinforced by a long brass nine amidships, pivoted on a metal track countersunk in the decking. Although credited with a complement of 120 in her application, and 110 on Collector Collins' rolls, she carried only ninety-four men, perhaps to avoid the heavier bond. They still overcrowded her. They were divided as follows:

Captain	Cook's mate
1st, 2nd and 3rd Lieutenants	Gunner
Clerk	Gunner's mate
Surgeon	Armorer
Lieutenant of Marines	Cabin steward
Master's Mate	36 Seamen, able-bodied and ordinary
6 Prizemasters	Captain of forecastle
Boatswain	" " foretop
3 Boatswain's mates	Sailmaker
Carpenter	Drummer
Carpenter's mate	5 Boys
Cook	22 Marines

The Marines were divided into two companies, one for each watch. Each of the guns had a four-man crew: captain, boarder, shotman, and sponger. One mess was billed for the cabin, one for the wardroom, and seven for the crew. The company's half of the prize money was, by the articles, divided into 145 shares, with an additional bonus of $50 for the first man to sight an enemy sail and the first to board the deck of a chase.

During the war the *Yankee* made six cruises under four different commanders. On the first, which lasted three months, Captain Wilson made for the coast of Nova Scotia, and returned after taking ten prizes. One was the full-rigged ship *Royal Bounty*, four times her burthen, but manned by only twenty-five men. Three of her crew were killed in the running fight. Another was the ship *Francis*, which carried a cargo worth $200,000. A third was the *Henry*, taken the day the ill-fated *Hiram* blew up.

Shares on this cruise amounted to $700 each. From his own profits, Captain Jim ordered a warship from Caleb Carr's yard in Warren. He presented her, fully rigged and armed, to the Navy, only fifty-seven days after her keel was laid. She was the 400-ton *Chippewa*, a full-rigged brig 112 feet long by 30 feet beam, mounting eighteen 32-pound carronades. But she saw less action than the *Yankee* herself, and broke up on an uncharted reef in the Caicos Islands in 1816. She had cost him $52,000.

Bristol sailors fought in the streets for places on the *Yankee*'s second cruise. It took her to the familiar coast of Africa, and home on the track of merchantmen returning to England from Brazil and the West Indies. In those days the favorite sport of boys too young for sea, next to labbing 'lasses, was swarming up the shrouds of vessels tied up at the wharves, and, after reaching the crosstree, shinning up the smooth topgallant mast and setting their caps atop the truck. One March day in 1813, a boy named Benny Waldron had just capped his mast when he saw something that made him slide all the way down, burning his hands and tearing his breeches. The *Yankee*, five months out, was coming up with a prize each side of her. Beyond Prudence Island, still out of sight from the ground, she gave the town a salute from each of her guns. She cleared the pole-and-keg beacon of Castle Rock with the Blue Peter of the privateer at her foremast, the homeward-bound pennant at her mainmast, and the Stars and Stripes at her gaff halyard. On one side of her was the British letter-of-marque *Thames*, and on the other the fine two-hundred-ton brig *Shannon*. She had taken or destroyed eight prizes worth $300,000, not counting 52 cannon, 401 stand of small-arms, and 196 prisoners, for each of whom a bounty of $20 would come from Washington. She tied up at the Pump Lane wharf with $45,000 worth of gold dust, 6 tons of ivory tusks and 32 bales of dry goods, all taken from her victims. Manning her prizes had reduced her complement of Marines by half, and each share was worth $338.40. That night rum was served free at the Old Bay State, and champagne at the Mount. Captain Wilson made enough from his lay to buy a plantation on the island of Cuba, where he lived after he had retired from the sea.

Her third cruise, under Elisha Snow, starting May 20, 1813, carried her into the British Channel and the Irish Sea. She took seven prizes, but two were retaken by the British. She ordered the five others to France for sale. Each share proved worth $173.84. Her fourth, under Thomas Jones, covered the Grand Banks, but was almost a failure, with only two prizes and dividends of $17.29. There was no competition for places on her fifth; in fact, some of the crew swam ashore before she could cast off. Snow was commander again. After several months without sight of a sail, he mistakenly captured the neutral Swedish brig *Maria,* and had to restore her at his owners' expense. In disgust, the crew of the *Yankee* deserted to a man when she put in at New Bedford with her indigestible prize. If Captain Snow had not rounded them up from the boarding houses with his persuader, he would not, a few days later, have taken the heavily laden British ship *San José Indiano*. She was the richest prize made by any privateer during the war. He sent her into Portland, where ship and cargo sold for $379,024.62. The shares of the messboys, Cuffee Cockroach and Jack Jibsheet, were $738.19 and $1121.88 respectively, though history does not explain why one got more than the other. James deWolf bought her in for his own account.

Captain William C. Jenckes commanded her sixth cruise, which lasted 105 days and ended at Beaufort, South Carolina on January 21, 1815, after the signing of peace. None of her six prizes was valuable except the ship *General Wellesley*, a six-hundred-ton teak-built Indiaman. Unhappily she grounded on Charleston bar as she was entering the port for sale, with the loss of her cargo, all her lascar crew, and two of the *Yankee's* prize-crew. She might have brought more than the *San José*; even so, Ben Churchill, her mate, made enough from the sale of her hull to buy a house on Hope Street from Captain Jim's nephew John Howe. He had lost a leg in action; to console him, the *Yankee's* carpenter carved him the four spread eagles which still adorn the balustrade.

On her six cruises the *Yankee* made forty-one prizes: twenty-five brigs, nine ships, five schooners, and one sloop. A privateer was accounted lucky if she made one prize per gun; she had made four. Half the lay went to her owners, and of that, Captain Jim received three-quarters. She had captured British shipping worth three million, and poured better than a million, aside from the owners' shares, into the village of less than twenty-seven hundred souls. And a dollar bought many times what it does today.

It was such privateers as the *Yankee* which forced Lord Liverpool's ministry to open negotiations for peace. On every other front Britain was winning the war. The American campaign on the Canadian border was a failure. The Royal Navy blockaded all ports south of Cape Cod, burned Washington, and forced President Madison to fly to the woods of Virginia. The frigates with which the American Navy began the war were sunk or bottled up by the fall of 1814. In September the Treasury defaulted the interest on the public debt, and New England threatened to secede from the Union. But because of the privateers, British merchantmen had to be convoyed by warships, just as American shipping was convoyed in World War II for fear of submarines. Insurance for crossing the Irish Sea rose to 13 per cent at Lloyds—in 1814 the *Lutine* bell tolled as often as thrice a day—and in Halifax British owners could not buy it at any price. On November 7, although the Admiralty claimed the capture or destruction of 228 American ships, Lloyds admitted that 800 British ones had been taken by American privateers since the start of the war. "If they fight," complained the

London *Times*, "they are sure to conquer; if they fly, they are sure to escape." After the war, Niles' *Register* published a list of 1551 prizes sent in or sunk; though it included those taken by the regular Navy, it is safe to assume that the privateers accounted for more than a thousand.

On June 18, 1815, the British crushed Napoleon at Waterloo; but it was lucky for the United States that our own treaty had been signed at Ghent six months before, for the Royal Navy was intact, and could soon, when released from European duty, have driven our privateers from the sea.

In after years, Dr. S. Compton Smith, a Bristol-born physician, was privileged to hear the reminiscences of Captain Wilson of the *Yankee* as they both sat drinking rum on the veranda of the Captain's plantation at San Juan de Camarioca, a little east of Matanzas, in Cuba. The doctor, himself too young to have seen action in the war, recorded one adventure which cannot be confirmed from history, but which, even discounting the exaggerations of retired skippers, is worth repeating here, slightly shortened and occasionally paraphrased, from the story he published in the *Phoenix* on May 8 of 1875.

THE *YANKEE* AND THE *TIGRESS*

We sailed from Bristol [Captain Wilson told him] on the first day of October, 1812, and stood away for southard and eastward in a fresh westerly wind. Our intention was to cruise in the southern Atlantic on the track of the homeward-bound British Indiamen. We were in quest of noble game. It is true we were very liable to fall in with the convoying English men-of-war in those latitudes, but we had all confidence in the sailing qualities of the *Yankee*. Running in the eye of the wind, the little craft could outsail anything she had yet met on the high seas. In this respect we had a great advantage over the enemy, whose merchantmen and warships were famous as dull sailers, especially on the wind.

The *Yankee* was as good as new. We had returned from our first long cruise, and had put her up in Caleb Carr's drydock in Warren. She had been newly coppered, and new spars put aboard. A brand new suit of canvas had been set, and all the standing and running rigging had been overhauled and made taut. She had been painted over. In lieu of the broad white stripe which had ornamented her sides on the first cruise, she was now surrounded by a narrow belt of vermilion which contrasted strongly with their bright black. The inside of her ports was also painted vermilion. When they were thrown open, and the *Yankee* showed her teeth, she looked as proud and saucy as a young vixen with her first litter of cubs.

She had already established her fame on the seas. Every British man-of-war between the two continents had standing orders to keep on the lookout for us, and sink us without quarter. On this voyage, therefore, we changed appearance somewhat. When occasion demanded, too, we could make her appear as harmless as any plodding coaster. Yet all was snug alow and aloft, and the run from stem to stern was in such perfect good taste and proportion, that the grace of the almost imperceptible rise in her quarter-deck and forecastle, which, added to the elegant and symmetrical form of her hull, the delicate and clean taper of her polished spars, her bright and taut rigging, her beautifully fitting canvas, and the neatness of her general trim, that she excited the admiration of every genuine sailor. [Captain Wilson, or possibly Dr. Smith, seemed unable to find a verb for this long sentence.]

Her armament consisted of 12 guns: 8 nine- and 4 six-pounders, beside a long brass swivel nine-pounder amidships. We had an extra quantity of boarding-pikes, muskets, blunderbusses, pistols, sabres and the like, in the use of which the crew was drilled every day.

The crew was made up of the picked young men of Bristol, and a braver or more noble-hearted set of boys never trod the deck of a vessel. If there was ever a commander who had a right to be proud of his ship and crew it was I. I hadn't a man who, in an emergency was not qualified to take command of any vessel, so I was never at a lack in selecting a prize-crew. In any cutting-out, or expedition ashore on English ground, I never had to call for volunteers, as every man and boy aboard would beg to be sent on the service. Mine was indeed a crew to be proud of, and I loved my boys.

By the 20th, we passed through the sailor's purgatory, the doldrums: that region of perpetual calm where the tropical rains

pour a ceaseless torrent from the leaden clouds. The next morning found us running up into the southeast trades. At nightfall
the wind had nearly died away. The monotonous slush-shuck of
the waves upon her cutwater and quarters, and the easy rolling
of the vessel, had a soothing influence on the senses of the watch
on deck, and they had to keep moving to shake off their drowsiness. I happened to come up from my cabin, and had been on
deck only a few minutes when the watch in the fore-top called
out "Sail ho!"

"Where away?" called Mr. Richmond, who was officer of the
watch.

"Right off the lee bow, Sir," replied the sailor.

"What do you make her out?"

"Can't tell yet, Sir. She's hid in the mist partly. Now she clears
a little. It's a ship, Sir."

"What does she look like?"

"Like a Canton trader, Sir. I'm sure she's English-built."

"What's her course?"

"She's heading sou-sou-west, Sir."

By this time all was commotion aboard the *Yankee*. As I
sprang into the main rigging with my night-glass in my hand,
a moonbeam broke through the clouds and fell directly on the
white sails of the stranger, not a mile away. She was an English
Indiaman beyond a doubt.

Our quarterdeck was now swarming with officers, who, some
with glasses and some with the unaided eye, were intently scanning her.

"What the devil is she doing on that tack?" muttered Mr. Richmond. "It strikes me somewhat odd that a homeward-bound tea-
wagon should be running down in that direction."

But while the officer was still speaking, the mystery was explained. The stranger shook out her canvas, ran up her light
sails and dropped two more points off the wind. She had evidently seen us before we saw her, and now evinced a willingness
to give us a wide berth.

"Mr. Richmond," said I, "we must overhaul that fellow and
find out what he's made of."

"Aye, aye, Sir," he replied. Hailing the watch, he gave orders
to crowd all sail.

In a few minutes we were bowling along on the same tack
with the stranger. She sailed well before the wind. For several

hours we did not seem to gain an inch on her. In the meantime the clouds had been lightening up a little, and the moon poured her light more steadily upon the sea, enabling us to keep sight of the chase from the deck without the aid of glasses. When the day began to break, we saw that for some unaccountable reason the stranger changed her tack and lay close under the wind, which now blew a steady ten-knot breeze from the southeast. This was our best tack, and soon it was clear we were gaining on her. She was a small ship and lay deep in the water, as if heavily freighted. Her sides were rusty as if long at sea. In many other ways she had the usual look of homeward-bound vessels from India.

But there was something in the perfection of her rig and the easy manner she was handled that excited my suspicion, besides her conduct in changing her tack to the course on which she was sure of being overhauled by us.

"What do you think of her, Mr. Richmond?" I asked my first officer, who for some minutes had been gazing intently at the stranger.

"She's evidently less anxious to get out of our way than she was last night," he replied. "In my opinion, Captain, she's either a neutral or a rogue."

"I'm beginning to have my own doubts," said I. "At any rate, we'll make her show her colors. Give her a shot from one of the starboard guns and have all hands piped to quarters."

The order was executed promptly. As the crew came pouring up the hatches, in obedience to the shrill whistle of the boatswain, the brazen throat of the nine-pounder disturbed the silence of the sea with its roar. As the breeze lifted, the white smoke, blown into the foretop of the chase, showed that the charge had told. Still the stranger kept on her course in dogged sullenness, condescending neither to show her flag nor to answer our shot.

"Give her another; we'll bring her to reason yet. Clear the decks for action. I perceive, Mr. Richmond, there's fight in that fellow if we can coax it out of him."

In the meantime we continued to gain on the ship, coming up under her windward quarter. When we were within musket-shot I directed the officer to hail her.

"Ship ahoy!"

"Ahoy!" came back in a sullen growl.

"What ship is that?"

No answer was given to this last hail, but an officer was seen to be engaged in sending a flag to the gaff halyards. When the hail was repeated in no very gentle tones, a dark ball of bunting rose slowly aloft, and with a skillful jerk of the halyards fell from its confinement, and the BRITISH JACK floated gracefully out upon the breeze. At the same instant our hail was answered: "His Majesty's ship-of-war *Tigress!*"

Simultaneously with this hail, the stranger opened a long line of ports, and exposed to our astonished gaze twelve guns of heavy calibre bearing directly upon our decks.

"Surrender, you damned Yankees, or I'll blow you to Hell in an instant," yelled the Englishman through his trumpet.

This insulting demand was answered by a shot from our midship gun. It went crashing through his roundhouse and carried away a part of his bulwarks. The next moment the *Tigress'* heavy broadside was poured into us, strewing our decks with ruin and blood, and making sad havoc of our spars and rigging. But the smoke of our enemy had not risen when we returned our entire broadside of six guns and swept her deck almost as effectually as she had ours. We had caught a Tartar, my boy, and our legs were no use to us now. Besides, we were badly crippled. Our foremast was shattered to splinters and would soon go by the board. We were in for a fight. I determined to give John Bull all he wanted or sink in the attempt. He would blow us out of the water with another broadside like that.

"Call away the boarders!" I shouted. "Men, fill your bills from the arms-chest and follow me. Mr. Richmond, send some men into the foretop with muskets, and lay us foul of that fellow without a moment's delay."

"Aye, aye, Sir"; and in less time than it takes to tell it, the jibboom of the *Yankee* fouled through the fore rigging of the *Tigress*, and the two vessels fell side by side in a deadly embrace. In an instant my crew followed me with a yell upon her crowded deck.

Muskets, pistols, sabres and boarding-pikes were the weapons. My boys fought like devils, and although the crew of the man-of-war outnumbered us more than two to one, we knew it was to be victory or death. The enemy, we were aware, would give us no quarter. In the meantime, my men in the rigging of

THE DE WOLF
FAMILY TREE

The deWolf Family Tree

Numbers opposite names on this partial chart are taken from "The deWolfs," by the Reverend Calbraith Perry, #632, published in 1901.

Abigail Potter (1726-1809)

August 25, 1744,

#14 Charles
1745-1790
m. Mary Taylor

#15 Mark Antony, Jr.
1747-1779
d. at sea with #18

#16 Margaret
1748-1810
m. Joseph Diman

#17 Abigail I
1750-1752

#18 Simon
1753-1779
d. at sea with #15
m. Hannah May

#19 Abigail II
1755-1833
m. Perley Howe[2]

#20 Samuel
1750-1778
d. at sea on privateer "Oliver Cromwell"

#21 Nancy[2]
1750?

#22 John, "Farmer John"
m. Edward Kinnicutt

Also 3 sons lost at sea with 2 sons of #23

#36 George, "General George"
1779/1844
m. Charlotte Goodwin

#37 Charles, Jr.
?-1834
m. Mary Goodwin

#39 Martha
m. Thomas Warren, "the blue goggled scientist"

#47 Mark Antony III
1777-1796
d. on Slave Coast

Simon, Jr.[1]
?-1796
suicide on Slave Coast

#55 John II, "Norwest John"
1779-187—
m. Mary Melville

#59 John "Squire" Howe
1783-1864
m. Louisa Smith

#60 George Howe
1791-1837
m. Abby Turner

#137 Buckmaster
1805-1845
m. Mary Smith

#39 Mariana
1811-1859
m. #147

#141 Charlotte
1818-?
m. Edward Good

#142 Theodora, "Madam Colt"
1822-1901
m. Christopher Colt

#147 Charles Henry
1806-1846
m. #39

#185 John Langsdorff
1819-1886

#186 Mark Antony DeWolfe Howe, "the Bishop"[8]
1808-1845
m. Mary Emory
     Elizabeth Marshall
     Eliza Whitney
18 children, 31 grandchildren

#190 Lavinia Howe
1811-1902
m. #234

#405 Francisco "Hungry Frank"
1843-1924
m. #487

#407 Isabella "Belle" Colt
1840-1923
m. #405

#410 Le Baron "Judge" Colt
1846-1924

#411 S. Pomeroy "Unkie" Colt[4]
1852-1923
m. #601

#5 Mark Antony deWolf (1726-1793) married

2 sons lost at sea with 3 sons of #19

1761-1846
m. Samuel Lee

m. #236 ?

#24 William "the Major"
1762-1829
m. Charlotte Finney

  #75 Henry
  1786-1857
  m. Anne Marston

  #78 Maria
  1795-1890
  m. Robert Rogers

    #222 Annie
    1815-1908
    m. Russell Middleton

      #617 Annie Middleton, "Cousin Annie"
      1847-1915

      #618 Alicia Middleton, "Cousin Alicia"
      1849-1938

    #226 Abby
    1822-1901
    m. Charles Dana Gibson

      #621 Charles de Wolf Gibson [5]
      1849-1890
      m. #254

#25 James "Captain Jim"
1764-1837
m. Nancy Bradford

  #80 James, Jr., "Gentleman Jim"
  1790-1845

    #221 James de Wolf Perry
    1815-1846
    m. Julia Jones

      #630 Raymond Perry
      1836-1903
      m. widow of #236

      #631 Rev. James de Wolf Perry [6]
      1838-1927

  #82 Marianne
  1795-1834
  m. Capt. Raymond Perry, U.S.N.

    #234 Alexander Perry
    1822-1888
    m. #190

      #632 Rev. Calbraith Bourn Perry
      1846-1914

      #638 Marianne Perry, "Miss Minnie"
      1850-1932

  #83 Francis Le Baron
  1797-1834
  m. Ellen Post

  #84 Mark Antony IV, "Don Marcos"
  1797-1837
  m. Sophie Chappotin

    #236 James
    ?-1870
    m. Ellen Rodney

  #85 William Henry, "Commodore"
  1802-1853
  m. Sarah Ann Rogers

    #239 Rosalie [3]
    1816-?
    m. John Hopper

      #650 William de Wolf Hopper [7]
      1858-1935
      m. #657

    #241 Sarah Ann [3]
    1833-1889
    m. George Gardner

      #654 Nellie Gardner
      m. #650

    #243 Mary [3]
    1835-?
    m. John Wheeler

    #245 Madeline [3]
    1838-?
    m. Benjamin Smith

  #87 Catherine
  1806-?
  m. Joshua Dodge & A.J. Davis

  #89 William Bradford, "Bradly"
  1810-1862
  m. Mary Soley

    #249 William Bradford, Jr., "Willy B."
    1840-1902
    m. Marian Mora

  #90 Josephine Maria
  1812-1901
  m. Charles Lovett

    #254 Josephine Elizabeth Lovett
    1841-1922
    m. #621

  #91 Lydia
  1794-1825
  m. Luke Drury, the Collector

  #95 Abigail "Miss Abby Levi"
  1804-1888

#26 Levi, "Quaker Levi"
1776-1848
m. Lydia Smith

#27 Mary
1765-1768

#28 Elizabeth
1768-1768

NOTES

1 Simon deWolf, Jr., was unknown to the genealogist and is hence unnumbered.

2 All that is known of Perley Howe is that he wore a large ruffle to conceal a goiter, and that he lost all his savings in Continental paper currency.

3 #239, 241, 243, and 245 all eloped with their respective husbands.

4 #411 was the father-in-law of Ethel Barrymore.

5 #621 was the father of Charles Dana Gibson II, creator of the Gibson Girl.

6 #631 was the father and grandfather of clergymen of the same name.

7 #650 was a much-married actor better known to fame as DeWolf Hopper.

8 Among the grandchildren of #186 is the author of this book.

Abigail Potter deWolf

Mark Antony deWolf

Charles deWolf

John deWolf ("Farmer John")

General George deWolf

John deWolf, Jr. ("'Fessor John")

Father
of the second an

William deWolf

James deWolf ("Captain Jim")

Henry deWolf

William Henry deWolf

d Sons
rd generations

Theodora Goujaud deWolf Colt

S. Pomeroy Colt ("Unkie")

Russell G. Colt

An orgy at the Casino, September 20, 1914, showing (A) Bell
Senator LeBaron ("Barry") Colt, (D) Colonel S. Pomeroy Co[

Ethel Colt Miglietta
John Drew Miglietta
(inset)

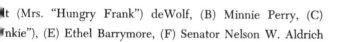

...lt (Mrs. "Hungry Frank") deWolf, (B) Minnie Perry, (C)
...nkie"), (E) Ethel Barrymore, (F) Senator Nelson W. Aldrich

General Ambrose E. Burnside

The Fourth at Bristol, 19
(*opposite*). Bristol Train
Artillery in foregroun
Captain Jim's light coach
rear, with Pomeroy and Bar
Colt insi

Bristol Harbor, looking east from Poppasqua

, Mount Hope in rear center

Old-time Bristol building

JOHN DE WOLF · c 1793

T · 1805
DE WOLF

THE COURT HOUSE · 1817   THE ACADEMY · 1791

HOWE-DIMAN 180?

PLACE   GEN GEORGE DE WOLF   ST. MICHAELS CHURCH
              1840   1793

OLF · 1835   HENRY DE WOLF-MIDDLETON 1811

·SELECTED·ARRANGED·&·DRAWN·BY·WALLIS·E·HOWE·1955·

drawn by Wallis E. Howe, 1955

George deWolf's Mansion

the *Yankee* poured down a hailstorm of shots upon the heads of the English. But I'll give the man-of-war credit for fighting with coolness and courage. She had doubtless at first counted on an easy victory, but had not looked for so desperate an assault.

The *Tigress* had been cruising for us, thus disguised, for some months. After scouring the African coast without finding us, she had finally sought us in the eastern latitudes. She had skillfully covered her true character. Had we guessed who she really was, we would by no means have courted an engagement with her, but would have shown her a fine specimen of superior sailing on the wind. She carried more than double our weight of metal, too, having 24 nine- and four-pounder guns. Now we stood upon her decks struggling breast to breast and knife to knife. Pistol and musket shot hunted through our crowded ranks like hail, and covered the decks of both vessels with blood. Dead and dying lay in heaps about me.

We soon had a footing on the forecastle of the ship, and drove the English toward their quarter-deck. They continued to pour shot into us at a fearful rate, but my boys, maddened by the sight of their fallen comrades, fought blindly. It was blood, all blood; even now I sicken at the recollection of it.

At one time I glanced toward our little vessel. As she continued closely entangled in the rigging of the ship, not a single man or boy of her surviving crew could I see on board of her. They were all struggling with me upon that slippery deck. Then it occurred to me, as I saw the disparity in size between the two, that I had best finish the fight aboard my own. The *Yankee's* guns lay below those of the *Tigress*, bearing upon her sides between wind and water. We could thus soon cripple her, while her broadsides would spend themselves on our sails and rigging, passing harmlessly over our heads.

"Back to your deck, men!" I shouted.

In another minute they had cleared away the wreckage and the wounded from the deck, and were ready to work the guns with renewed energy. As the last surviving man of my crew sprang from the enemy's bulwarks to our own, they poured a broadside into her, which crashing through her timbers, drove a hurricane of shot and splinters across her decks and made her scuppers run afresh with human gore.

"Give it to them again, boys!"; and once more the iron death thinned the ranks of the English.

But all this time the foe was by no means idle. After our second broadside they quickly returned to their guns and rapidly discharged them over our heads. But they were comparatively harmless because of their high range. We continued to fire, for we could see that our shots were telling fearfully upon the ship, and tearing great breaches through her sides.

At length her firing ceased, and there seemed to be a new commotion on board of her.

"They're preparing to board us. Stand to your posts, men!" I called.

But no! She had now another foe than man to contend with. A little cloud of blue smoke was seen to issue from her main hatch. Presently we heard a running to and fro over her lower decks, and then the splash-splash of water dashed violently upon her side. She was afire!

"Cut loose our fore rigging!" I shouted to the men of the forecastle.

Soon axes were lashing among the hamper which held the two vessels together; we broke away from the ship and forged ahead of her, where we obtained a raking position. When I was about to improve it, my attention was called to a dense column of black smoke that poured out of her hatchways and ports. At the next moment a bright scarlet flame shot upward from her hatch. Spreading, it streamed out of the ports and crept up her masts and rigging. The fiery serpents crawled over her decks, upon the bulwarks and over the tarry ropes, devouring the sails—down they came by the run—licking up the splinters and litter which lay confusedly about and scorching the dead and dying. Soon the gallant ship was enveloped in her fiery pall. But still, through all this terrible scene, the proud old British Union waved defiantly upon the breeze, and the guns, as they became heated, continued to give out their sullen notes of battle.

The surviving officers and crew of the *Tigress* gathered upon her quarter-deck, too proud to ask for mercy. They stood together, heroically awaiting their doom. I hailed them with my trumpet, and begged them for God's sake to seek safety aboard the *Yankee*. But they did not or would not hear. Though all my boats had been lowered into the sea, and my brave fellows, forgetful of their recent hot blood, now stood ready for the word to fly to their rescue, our enemy refused all aid.

Our vessel had now drifted some distance to the leeward of the burning ship. While we were still gazing in tears upon the fearful sight of the ship and her noble crew, who preferred certain death to surrender, a black mountain of vapor and smoke rose suddenly from the sea where she lay; a bright blinding flash gleamed over the waves; a dull heavy roar seemed to vibrate to the very floor of the ocean, and we were alone upon the deep. Only a few broken spars and dismembered bodies remained of what had a moment before been His Majesty's ship-of-war *Tigress* and her valiant crew.

❈   ❈   ❈   ❈   ❈   ❈   ❈   ❈

When the Bristol *Phoenix* published this reminiscence of Captain Wilson's, the rival Warren *Gazette* countered by reprinting the *Yankee's* log for the same day, October 21, 1812, written down by Noah Jones, the ship's clerk, and sworn to by Captain Wilson himself. It was less glorious, but the reader can take his choice. It ran:

½ past meridian the island of Goree hove in sight distant about 2 leagues to windward. 1 P.M. saw a schooner under full sail standing out of Goree harbor toward us. Piped all hands to quarters. 2 P.M. the schooner tacked to windward; immediately tacked ship and set all sail in chase. At 3 passed within 5 miles of Goree. Discovered a large English brig and several small craft at anchor under the fort. Finding we came up rapidly with the chase, and believing her to be an armed vessel, again piped all hands to quarters and cleared for action. 9 P.M. hoisted a light on our fore rigging, and discharged several muskets as a signal for the chase to heave to; not obeying these signals fired a shot under her stern; still continuing her course fired one of the bow guns, well loaded, directly into her; upon which she immediately bore away and ran down close under our lee. As she passed us, Capt. Wilson hailed her with the usual questions, and by the answers found her to be His Brittannic Majesty's schooner *Santiago,* from Goree bound to Senegal. After which the British commander was told we were the American armed brigantine *Yankee;* after which he demanded "how we dared to fire into His Majesty's schooner," and ordered us to send our boat on board. Capt. Wilson replied, "I will not; strike your colors or I will sink you." Instantly

His Britannic Majesty's schooner wore upon her keel and luffed up close to the wind, to prepare (as we supposed) for action. Not thinking it advisable to engage a King's vessel without knowing her force, at close quarters during a dark night, we resolved to wait until daylight, and therefore stood after her under easy sail. At 11 A.M. the *Santiago* fired a shot which passed over us; we returned the compliment by giving him Long Tom, doubly charged with round and langrage. We thus returned shot for shot until 1 P.M., when Capt. Wilson, thinking it inadvisable to engage a Government vessel, where we should only get hard blows, and probably lose some spars and men, ordered the sailing-master to make sail and stand to the W.S.W. to deceive the Enemy as to our cruising station. At 2 P.M. lost sight of him astern. The officers and men remained at quarters upwards of 5 hours and displayed great courage and resolution. Lat. obs. 1402.

III

New England commerce at once revived with the return of peace —though in Bristol, thanks to the *Yankee*, it had not declined as it had in Salem and Boston. Customs duties paid to Collector Collins had been $72,000 in 1814; in 1815 they rose to $120,000. The Federalists of New England, who had opposed the war, and even threatened to secede, suddenly became a party without a cause. They took to calling themselves "National Republicans" to distinguish themselves from the "Democratic Republican" coalition of the southern and central states which had elected Jefferson and Madison and was soon, almost without opposition, to elect Monroe. The Era of Good Feeling had begun.

When the war ended, Captain Jim was fifty-one years old. The profits of privateering, piled on those of the round trade and the cotton mills, had made him the richest man in America, except for old Charles Carroll of Carrollton. Ever since his victory over Wardwell in the election of 1802, he had sat continuously as a Republican in the Federalist legislature at Providence and Newport. (Rhode Island, like Connecticut, then had two capitals.)

The gale of September 23, 1815, blew down the fence around his deer park, and the red deer leaped the granite wall, never to be seen alive again. In the same gale, brother Charles's watergate steps washed away, and brother William's urn-shaped elm blew down. Captain Jim never repeated a mistake, and he had reached the age when a man starts to think of the hereafter. Rather than replace the fence and restock the deer, he converted the park into a graveyard for his family. It was as big as the burying ground which served the whole of Bristol, but it is still restricted to his own descendants: Charles's and William's must lie elsewhere. In the center he piled up an earthen tumulus twenty feet high for Nancy and himself, with an iron openwork door.

"In years to come," he told his children, "you can look through the door at us. As long as any of you are around, you'll see my gold teeth, even when the rest of us is dust."

But he had a long time to live. In 1820 the Republicans at last controlled the Rhode Island legislature. He was chosen Speaker of the House, and in 1821 appointed Senator—it was long before the days of direct election. He hurried alone to Washington in the yellow and blue coach, with Ben Mann, his coachman, on the box. When he passed through a city, Polydore, as groom, would mount the jump-step and cling to the straps with white-gloved hands, lurching over the cobblestones to the cheers of the crowds. On the long stretches between towns, when no one was looking, Captain Jim let him sleep on the floor inside. The trip took four days. Nancy and the unmarried girls followed more comfortably by packet. In the capital, the Senator-elect and his family put up at the Franklin Hotel.

From the first, Captain Jim disliked Washington. The Rhode Island legislature had directed him and Burrill, his Federalist colleague, to oppose the admission of Missouri unless slavery were forbidden in her territory. Captain Jim had not even taken his oath before Senator William Smith of South Carolina made an angry speech attacking the Bristol slave trade. He read aloud the Rhode Island statute by which any Negro found outdoors after nine at night got ten lashes from the constable—a law that dated back to 1760, but had never been repealed and certainly not enforced. He held in his hand the records of the Collector for Charleston for the four years of open port. They showed that in the single year of 1807 Christian & deWolf had imported 1164 slaves, and that of the 95 slave ships admitted, 17 belonged to Senator-elect deWolf; that in the whole four years, Rhode Island merchants landed 7958 Negroes, and Charleston merchants themselves only 2006; and that of the Rhode Island imports, 3488 were owned in Newport and 3914 in Bristol, making the village, which was only one-third the size of Newport, the largest shipper of slaves of any port in the country, if not the world.

"We are reproached for our dealings in slaves and human flesh," the Senator said, "whenever gentlemen choose to indulge themselves. But they become very fastidious when we mention facts that apply to their side of the house. The people of Rhode Island have lately shown bitterness against slaveholders, and especially against the admission of Missouri. This, however, cannot, I believe, be the temper or opinion of the majority, from the late election of James deWolf as a member of this House, as he has accumulated an immense fortune in the slave trade."

At this point Senator Burrill raised a point of order: the Senator from South Carolina was impugning the state of Rhode Island and attacking a Senator by name. But Vice-President Tompkins overruled him, on the ground that deWolf had not yet taken his seat. (He was listening uncomfortably in the gallery.)

"Here ends the black catalogue," Senator Smith concluded. "I dare not ask whether citizens of Rhode Island have trafficked in slaves since such traffic became illegal—that were indeed out of order—but would show the Senate that those people who most deprecate the evils of slavery and traffic in human flesh, when a profitable market can be found, can sell human flesh with as easy a conscience as they sell other articles."

This attack did not escape the notice of Captain Jim's enemies at home. He defended himself in a letter to the press, saying that it was "many, many years" since he had trafficked in slaves, and that the greater part of his property had been earned in honorable employment. To which the Providence *Gazette* retorted, "More humane, honorable, successful and constitutional business—privateering!"

But it was true that he had long abandoned the trade. A letter to his brother John, as far back as 1811, reads:

> I learn that Parkman of Boston sends you a schooner to Bristol to be outfitted for an expedition to the eastward, and that you refuse to have anything to do with her, which in my opinion is a very proper determination of yours. I would not touch a finger, nor have the least thing to do with any such business.

Captain Jim made no speeches during his term. The only legislation which bears his name is an amendment to the treaty of 1819 with Great Britain. The treaty provided for a joint patrol of the African coast by the two Navies. His amendment forbade British cruisers to search vessels which flew the American flag. The slave trade was dying hard.

His wife and daughters enjoyed Washington society, but to him it was just more of the frivolity which he disliked at home. Every week he wrote imperious letters in his angular hand to his dependable brother John, giving him orders for the fleet and the counting-house, and urging him to make sure that his sons stuck to their work and kept away from the rum-bottle, and that their slippery nephew George signed no mortgages. He was homesick.

"I'd rather hear the cackle of one Bristol goose than all the bands in New York," he told his wife one night when they stayed at Niblo's on their way down to a session of Congress.

In the fall of 1824 the atmosphere in Washington was electric. In the November election, Senator Andrew Jackson of Tennessee won the highest electoral vote. John Quincy Adams, who was Monroe's Secretary of State, ran second; William H. Crawford, the Secretary of the Treasury, third; and Senator Henry Clay of Kentucky fourth. Jackson still did not have a clear plurality. The choice was thrown into the House, which was empowered by the Constitution to choose from the highest three. A few days before it voted, Adams gave a great ball to celebrate the tenth anniversary of his rival's victory at the Battle of New Orleans. Captain Jim reluctantly let his wife take him to it. He dressed, as he always had, in old-fashioned knee-breeches with ruffled shirt and silver shoe-buckles. He had no fun at all, but he enjoyed the poem which appeared next day in the papers:

Wend you with the world tonight?
Brown and fair, and wise and witty,
Eyes that float in seas of light,
Laughing lips and dimples pretty,
Belles and matrons, maids and madams,
All are gone to Mrs. Adams'.

Websters, Hamiltons are going,
Eastern Lloyd and southern Hayne,
Western Thomas, gaily smiling,
Borland, nature's protégé,
Young deWolf, all hearts beguiling,
Morgan, Benton, Brown and Lee:
Belles and matrons, maids and madams,
All are gone to Mrs. Adams'.

The reference to him was a pretty compliment, but he was sixty years old and knew he was no heartbreaker.

Henry Clay threw his electoral votes to Adams. Jackson was defeated, but there was no doubt he would win in 1828. Captain Jim had grown to mistrust Jackson. Both men professed to be followers of Jefferson, but when Jackson attacked the United States Bank, in which Captain Jim was a stockholder, and opposed a tariff to protect the infant textile industry, he turned against him and deserted the party he had served all his life. Captain Jim resigned his seat on October 31, 1825. He told the legislature which had elected him that all the country's problems were settled for many years to come, and that he had so much to do at home that he could not afford the time to live in Washington. But he confessed to his brother John that the real reason he came home was to keep an eye on his slippery nephew George.

The Mount was crowded, day and night, with his own children and his in-laws, with visiting celebrities, and with a collection of poor relations and miscellaneous friends and beggars, all eager to help him spend his money. He complained to John that their appetites would ruin him. A letter is extant in which, rich as he was, he had to beg his father-in-law for food:

Dear Sir:
   I yesterday invited Severall gentlemen to Dine on Presumption I could find something for them to eat, but not a thing can be found. I have a peace of Mutton to Boil, & if you could oblige me with Something to rost, and come & Dine with us, you will confer a very particular Favor on me, who is,
                         Constantly, Sir,
                         Your friend and obdt. humble Servant
                         Jas. deWolf.

Daniel Webster came; he tried to learn Polydore's recipe for chowder, but Polydore refused to sell it. Margaret Fuller, the famous bluestocking, came, and ran head on into Webster at the door of the six-hole privy as she was coming out and he was going in. Even the emancipated feminist had to blush at the head-on meeting; but Webster, who did not know what embarrassment was, saved the situation by lowering his head as she passed him, and murmuring reverently, with his beaver hat at his breast, "Madam, we are fearfully and wonderfully made."

Nancy Bradford deWolf nagged her husband unmercifully. She rustled around the place in her black silks, with a frilled cap on her bird-head and a bunch of keys at her waist. He told her the dress was too tight across the bosom, and she came back with the pointless remark that *her* family had come over in the *Mayflower*. As they said in town, she took the salt out of him. He would tease her by roaring out a chanty at the crowded dinner-table:

> Oh, I sailed in a brig called the *Nancy;*
> By Jib, how she smacked through the breeze!
> She's a vessel as tight to me fancy
> As ever cut through the salt seas.

Ben Mann the coachman he loved for his impudence. He would call him in from the stable, still manure-stained, hand him a glass of champagne, and ask him, to Nancy's mortification, to repeat his favorite toast:

> Here's to them as sails on the piratical ocean of the Main,
> Not for pleasure, but for gain.

He drove his gig the two miles to the old stone counting-house every day. Once, when he had finished his business, he forgot it was there and drove home with his brother John. So Ben had to walk into town to fetch it. He stopped for a dram at Pardon Handy's. As soon as he climbed into the gig he fell asleep. But the mare knew the way home as well as he, and drove up to the Mount with Ben still unconscious behind her. Captain Jim shook him awake.

"Ben," said he, "you're drunk again."

"Not so drunk, Cap'n, but that I knew Jewel was waiting for me."

Captain Jim could not help laughing, and led Jewel back to her stall himself before Nancy could start her scolding.

He loved his children, but seemed unable not to spoil them. Not one of his five sons went to college. He built a house for each of them. William Henry made a show of managing the family fleet and talked of converting it to the whale fishery; but he was lazy and never completely sober. Young James had set up in New York as the family agent, back in the time of the round trade. He signed himself "James deWolf, jr., Gentleman" and was known as Gentleman Jim. But he seemed to spend most of his time abroad, where, says his obituary, he "graced the court circles of Europe." Mark Antony—he was the fourth to bear the name—dabbled in mysterious "scientific studies" behind the pillars of the Greek temple which Captain Jim built him on Poppasquash. He made frequent trips to the Cuban plantations, where he signed himself "Don Marcos." He was the most arrogant, perhaps, of all the Great Folks. Francis managed the cotton mills, but died too young to prove himself.

Bradford, the youngest, was his father's favorite, with the dark blue eyes and black hair that were the mark of the family.

Two of his daughters married businessmen from out of town but brought them back to the Mount to help him manage his fortune. Kate, his third daughter, married twice and divorced both husbands. One was a foreign consul and one the notorious Andrew Jackson Davis, who made a living—which Captain Jim would far rather have given him out of his own pocket—by lecturing around the country in a hypnotic trance, to prove Mesmer's theory that the mind could control the body. His youngest, Marianne, married a naval officer, a younger brother of the great Commodore Perry. At the wedding, the officers of the *Chippewa*, which Captain Jim had built for the Navy, formed an arch of swords as the couple marched out of Saint Michael's.

He continued to make money up to the year of his death. The Bristol *Gazette* in the spring of 1837 carried advertisements over his name, urging the townsfolk to buy stock in the Rhode Island Cloth Hall, a corporation he had formed for the sale of cotton fabrics on consignment. In the first year of business, it paid a dividend of 7 per cent. There were two hundred cotton mills in the state by now; a steamboat plied each day from Bristol to Providence, and a railroad ran from there to Boston. Martin van Buren was president; for the first and last time in history the government was free of debt. One American in every six was a slave, but the country seemed no worse off for that. Captain Jim could still feel, as he had told his fellow citizens, that its problems were solved for many years to come.

He died at the Mount on Christmas Eve of 1837. At his funeral Bishop Griswold mourned in Saint Michael's: "A rich man who makes good use of his wealth is a blessing to society, and his death is a public loss."

His estate was worth five millions, which was far more then than it would be now. His will still makes the mouth water. He left Nancy $60,000 outright, and an annuity of $3000; but she lived only two weeks before following him to the deer-park graveyard. Her share then went to the public schools. Among his sons and daughters he divided his ships and rigging, his wharfage, his lands in Rhode Island, Kentucky, Maryland, and Ohio, his sugar plantations and *cafétals* in Cuba, his Dighton and Coventry cotton mills, and his banks. To little Jimmy, the son of his dead son Francis, he left his horse Cub, his cow Cleopatra, his bull Sir Robert Peel, his gold watch, and his wines. The share of his daughter Kate, who had married the hypnotist, was left her in trust "free from the control and disposition of past, present or future husbands." To his favorite son Bradford he left the Mount and the residue of his estate. He appointed Gentleman Jim and Don Marcos his trustees, along with his son-in-law Fitz Henry Homer. The will ended by solemnly warning his heirs against gambling with the fortunes it left them.

But man heapeth up riches, and cannot tell who shall gather them. Even before the funeral, Gentleman Jim persuaded Byron Diman, the family cashier, to hand him over, without a receipt, all the negotiable assets in the counting-house. Captain Jim had counted on his gold teeth to survive him forever, but they were the first memorial of him to go. On May 11, 1842, when they had lain only five years behind the grilled door, a certain John Dickinson rowed over from Fall River to loot the tomb. He believed, as all Bristol did for years, and as some still may, that it was filled with gold. He waited for a stormy night, when the thunder would drown out the noise of his gunpowder. He blew open the door without rousing the revellers at the Mount, no more than a hundred yards away. All he found, besides the teeth, were a few gilt buttons and the engraved coffin-plate. He sold the lot for $6.52. It was Captain Jim's nameplate which trapped him. After expiating the theft in the stone jail on Court Street, Dickinson moved west to Cleveland. There, in 1855, he was hanged—not for the grave-robbery, but for a murder he had committed on the way.

Occasionally one of Captain Jim's descendants is buried in the deer park. The only outsiders who lie there are Polydore and Agiway, and they are not really outsiders. The iron gate is sealed up

again, but tramps sometimes camp on the sunny side of the mound
(the whiff of mulligan filters out to Tanyard Lane, and blue jeans
can be seen flapping on the boughs of the jungle between), and
lovers make it their unholy bed. Except for its curved stone wall
and a few foundation stones, nothing is left of Captain Jim's proud
house, nor of the privy where Daniel Webster encountered Margaret Fuller.

For years it was whispered in the cabins of Goree that Captain
Jim had never died at all, but had been carried off by the same
Devil who incited him to drown the slave girl in 1790. Black Violet,
the same old Negress who saw him divide the gold with his brother
Charles, described his departure thus:

"When he was old he shut himself up in his study. Wouldn't see
nobody. One day a fine coach and four stops at the Mount. A
gentleman richly dressed in black, with silver shoe-buckles just like
his own, steps out and asks to see the Captain. 'You can't,' says
Polydore the houseman.

" 'Then I'll call again.'

"So later he calls and is told the same thing, but this time he says,
'That won't do,' and pushes into the hall and climbs upstairs.
Presently he comes down arm in arm with the Captain, him looking
down Fox Hill to the harbor and saying good-by to Polydore, but
no whiter than what he had been. They get into the stranger's coach,
who clucks and drives away, and no one ever saw Captain Jim
deWolf again, never."

7.

Piracy

THE seaborne commerce of America revived with the return of peace. Dutiable imports, which had dropped in value from $27,000,000 in 1807 to $5,000,000 in 1814, rose in 1815 to $39,000,-000. In 1817 there were sixty-nine vessels, totaling seven thousand tons, on Collector Collins' register at Bristol. Receipts for duties were $100,000. Since the tariff averaged one-eighth of the value of a cargo, the town must have imported nearly a million dollars' worth of foreign freight, apart from the tax-free coastwise trade. The exports of Bristol were the standard freight of New England seaports: beef, pork, salt fish, potatoes, hardware, cheese, flour, soap, candles, and rum, with the addition of onions, which were the village staple.

Bristol ships sailed to the Baltic for iron and hemp, to England for cloth, to France for wines, to Spain for fish, olives, and oil. The greatest trade was made to Central America and the West Indies. Ice and hay were even shipped to Havana. Salt was imported from the Turks Islands; sugar, molasses, coffee, cigars, and cocoa from Cuba and Hispaniola; cotton from the Guianas; and mahogany, coconuts, logwood, indigo, cochineal, and sarsaparilla from Honduras. From the Portuguese colony of Brazil came coffee, hides, and sugar; from the Spanish possessions of the Rio de la Plata, beef, horsehair, feathers, and wool; and from both, specie in gold and silver. Some cargoes were sold piecemeal at the Thames Street wharfs, but most found a readier market in the larger ports, where the carriers would be emptied and reloaded without touching the home port. Bristol ships rarely visited Africa now; when they did, they returned not with slaves, but with ivory, beeswax, palm oil, and gold dust. For the hazardous two-year voyage to the Orient they were too small to compete with the great freighters of Salem, Boston, Marblehead, and Providence; between the voyage of Norwest John and the massed whaling cruises of the late 1830s, no Bristol sail entered the Pacific. The village was becoming a freight station, with much of its shipping chartered by out-of-towners and many of its cargoes on consignment.

Meanwhile it could live on the accumulations of privateering and the slave trade. It boasted two distilleries, five banks, two schools, and the three-story building of William deWolf's insurance company, where the ground floor doubled as the Hope Tavern, much frequented by the diehard Federalists. The population was just under twenty-seven hundred. There were four ministers: Bishop Griswold at the Episcopal church, Parsons Wight and Bates at the Congregational and Baptist churches, and Elder Tucker at the Methodist church. There were two doctors, not counting Sweet, the itinerant bone-setter; all three eked out their professional incomes by selling nostrums and cure-alls. Russell Warren the architect, like William deWolf, was a major in the militia. John Howe was entitled to be called Squire, Benjamin Bourn and Farmer John deWolf to be called Judge, and John, Junior, to be called Professor. Captain Jim's fourth son, William Henry, who had been a seaman in the Navy at fourteen, was beginning, at seventeen, to be called Commodore. Almost everyone else was called Deacon or Captain—even though some of the captains had risen no higher than apprentice aboard a privateer.

The appearance of the village reflected the profits of the outlaw professions. Many new houses were built, larger and lighter than the old camelopards. In those of any substance, there would be a back stairway for the carrying of food from the kitchen below and the slops from the bedrooms above. In place of a single keeping room, there would be a supper room, a sink room, a parlor (used for weddings, funerals, and the minister's visits) and a sewing room—which we should call the living room, where the family sat at night around the tallow candles or betty-lamps. Every room had a fireplace. In the back yard were a brick cistern to catch the soft rainwater, a well, a pigsty, a shed for the horse, and usually a pear tree, besides the building known variously as the necessary, the earth closet, the backhouse, the privy, or (by the ladies) the arbor.

In these years just after the War of 1812, Bristol shared, less actively than before, in a complacent general prosperity. But the swashbuckling adventurers of the earlier days when a fortune could be made from a single voyage to Africa or a half-hour's engagement at sea were not so easily satisfied. This is how a later historian, Maclay, describes the lot of the American privateersman at the time:

> The vessels engaged as privateers were laid up, used in commerce or destroyed. Their officers and men were compelled to seek employ-ment in the more peaceful pursuits of life. Years after the war, it was not unusual to observe men who had once commanded the quarterdeck of an armed vessel, whose orders meant instant obedi-ence and whose frown was more dreaded than the heaviest gale or hostile cannon, bending over ledgers in the counting-rooms of shipping ports, or engaged in menial service. Finding their calling as sea-warriors gone, these men entered any trade or business that offered. They soon found out that the qualifications peculiar to and needful for a successful privateersman were not only out of place, but a positive hindrance in their new field of activity. As a rule, these mighty men of the sea reverted in the scale of promotion, and for the rest of their lives ground out a humble existence as drudging clerks, longshoremen or wage-earners. Like the noble ships they once commanded, their occupation was gone, and they were laid up to rust and wear out the balance of their days in an inglorious existence, waiting for Father Time, the conqueror of all, to remove them to their final haven of rest. They have, however, left a record

in the history of their country which is well worthy of preservation, and it will stand as an imperishable monument to the gallant part they played in the defence of their native land.

Captain Joseph Oliver Wilson of the *Yankee* had escaped this fate by moving to Cuba, where he became almost as Spanish as the Cubans themselves, and was known as Don José. His plantation, the San Juan, stood on a hill above the mouth of the Camarioca River, east of Matanzas and due south of the still-Spanish colony of Florida. From a lookout in his garden he could sweep the Florida Straits with his spyglass, and give warning of—or to—the pirates who infested the sea-lanes leading to Havana.

Most of the Gentlemen Sailors of the village were not so lucky. It was humiliating for Marines of spirit to spend the day sitting around Pardon Handy's rum casks, or gazing out to harbor in toggery that grew more threadbare every month. They found merchantmen too slow, and whalers as dirty as slavers. There was no chance for a quick profit in either. Captain Jim deWolf had spoiled them. But his nephew George came to their rescue.

George was the oldest son of Charles, who had been the oldest son of Mark Antony. Even as a boy, they say, he regarded himself as the head of the whole family of the Great Folks. His wife, née Charlotte Goodwin,* was a niece of Mrs. James deWolf and of Mrs. Collector Collins, and since he was a nephew of Captain Jim himself, he was more than kin to the family at the Mount. He was close enough to Captain Jim's age—only fourteen years younger— to treat him as a rival, and it is hard to read his life without feeling that the rivalry was its whole obsession.

Unlike his uncles, George never went to sea. But in 1803, when he was only twenty-four, he bought the slave brig *Minerva* from Collins. In 1804, as we saw, he owned a share in the *Juno*. In the four years of Charleston's open port, he owned the slaver *Charlotte*, named for his wife. On one of her voyages to Africa, her first officer

---

* His brother, Charles, Junior, married her sister. The girls' father, Judge Goodwin of Newport, was subject to fits, and burned to death in a fireplace the year of George's marriage.

went berserk from the heat and threatened to shoot Captain Sabens. When George heard the news, he sent orders to confine the mutineer on bread and water in the lazaret for the whole stretch of the Middle Passage and the return to Bristol.

There was not a more dashing man in the state than George deWolf. He had wide black eyes and long lashes, a romantic flood of dark hair which swept, in the manner of Lord Byron's, over his ears to the edge of his stock, a chiseled nose, a thin-lipped mouth, and a small pointed chin. The pallor of his cheeks was strikingly different from the sea-tanned complexions of Captain Jim and Norwest John, or even from his own father's. His uncle William was fair-skinned too, but where he was chubby, George was gaunt. He was often told that he looked like Napoleon. There is something too flamboyant, even for a deWolf, in his portrait and his handwriting. "A smiling quick-spoken man," his cousin 'Fessor John wrote, "but a cruel one withal." He was known to have read the books of Baron Holbach, the French atheist.

Unlike his relatives, George continued to trade in slaves after 1808. In 1809 he bought the slave ship *Monticello*, the brig *Rambler*, and the schooner *Eliza*, all from Captain Jim. In 1810, from their profit in a single year of the outlaw trade, he had Russell Warren build him a house on Hope Street which outshone his Uncle William's on Poppasquash and his Uncle Jim's at the Mount. It is the only one of the deWolf mansions left, unless you count the thrifty houses of Levi and John, which do not pretend to be mansions at all. It cost him $60,000, which was enormous then and is not contemptible now. It stands impressively far from the street, approached by an iron archway and an aisle of marble. At the time he built it, it was wedged between Chadwick's stable on one side and Benjamin Norris's house on the other, so he wasted no adornment on the flanks, for they could not be seen by the public. The front, which is all they saw, is as flamboyant as George himself: two-story fluted Corinthian columns on top of a reviewing-stand of sandstone, and between them not one Palladian window but two, superposed. Inside—when they could get inside—callers saw a hall ceiling vaulted all four ways, two drawing rooms on the left and a dining room on the right, a spiral stair sweeping up three stories from an ivory-tipped newel to a bullseye skylight, and, through another lacy Palladian doorway at the back, the summerhouse from his father's garden on Constitution Street, with a lead Cupid at its peak, peering through a quadrant. His six Negroes lived in a long leanto at the right, back to back with those of Captain Norris. Parson Wight, in his diary, describes the house as a "splendid mansion," and "the Mansion" it was called for half a century.

Although George was just the right age for service in the national Army, he remained in Bristol with the militia through the War of 1812. No disgrace attached to militiamen who remained in their state regiments, for the purpose of the militia was to protect the state itself. The occupation of Newport by the British, and the bombardment and burning of Bristol, were fresh in many memories. It would have seemed cowardly, rather than courageous, for the local Train of Artillery and the Bristol Grenadiers to desert their native town. Every man from sixteen to sixty was liable to weekly drill on the Common. Annual muster in the fall was the greatest fête-day of the year. During the war, the Bristol militia threw up earthworks along the whole harbor front from Mill Gut to Love Rocks. The federal government presented them with two brass field pieces. The town was ready for the invasion that never came.

Soon after the return of peace, George deWolf acquired the grandest title in town. He was elected, by the troops themselves, Commanding General of the 4th Brigade of the state, made up of the 1st, 4th, and 10th Regiments. It included the levies from Warren and Newport as well as from Bristol itself. He proved to be a stern officer. When a certain Colonel Blodget paraded his men in careless formation at a muster, he ordered him "broke from the service." The sentence was so severe that it was reversed by a board of review. His uniform became him well: blue double-breasted swallowtail with gold-lace epaulets, white satin breeches, a scarlet cloak, and a fore-and-aft chapeau de bras with a white cockade. There was a dwarf in town named Sammy Usher, a grandson of the missionary whom Simeon Potter had assaulted. Sammy described himself as "small and slim, erect and trim." He was less than five feet high, almost blind, toothless, unwashed—but he had the tongue of a viper. The General, for his own amusement, had a replica of his own uniform made up for Sammy in miniature. In this array, the dwarf felt he was the equal of any of the Great Folks. He once walked into the Mansion, uninvited, for dinner, when the General was entertaining his uncle Captain Jim. The conversation turned to the supposed iniquities of the slave trade and privateering.

"Well," said the General righteously, "whatever else I've done, at least I've never gambled nor bet at a race track."

"I wish I could say the same." Captain Jim laughed.

"Why don't you, Jim?" said Sammy. "George does." *

Though George played no part in the war, he found a use, in connivance with Collector Collins, for the talents of those who had —first in the outlaw slave trade, and then, when it became too risky, in the equally illegal service of the rebel Spanish colonies of South America. He financed his operations through his fellow townsmen. They lent him their savings without asking how he invested them—preferred, indeed, not to know, so long as he returned them the traditional 25 per cent a year on their ventures. He did so well for himself—and them—that he became almost as rich as his uncle James. At the assessment of 1817, for instance, James was taxed for a four-wheel coach, a four-wheel phaeton, and two chaises, and his brother William for a coach and two chaises. But George owned a coach, a phaeton, a chaise, and a four-wheel

---

* With the possible exception of 'Fessor John, Sammy was the greatest eccentric in the town's history. He had a horse named Tobacco, but was too short to mount him, so taught the animal to squat like a camel at the mounting-block. When Parson Bates complained that he had no friend but his dog, Sammy told him doubtfully, "You might try getting another dog." In his old age Sammy was boarded and nursed by two maiden sisters named Ball. In his last illness they brought him a bowl of arrowroot gruel sent down by the kindhearted wife of Captain Jim. Sammy looked at it with the words, "Arrerroot! Why don't she send me a roast pig?" He grew a third set of teeth at the age of seventy, and died soon afterward, in 1837. He was buried in the mock regimentals given him long before by General George.

wagon; and while Captain Jim's coach was valued at $350, George's was worth $500. It was the finest equipage in town.

At this late date it is hard to unearth the facts about the slave trade between 1808, when it was driven underground, and 1820, when it became a hanging crime. Most New England traders honorably abandoned it in 1808. The few who continued did all they could to hide the fact by registering their ships under false names or foreign registry, and by destroying all papers that might incriminate them. When Collins lost his Collectorship in 1820 he burned all his records. His official correspondence with the Treasury, together with Ellery's complaints against him, were lost in a fire at Washington in 1833. Ellery's own copies are scattered; but even if they were complete, they would show only his half of the running fight with the deWolfs that he maintained for twenty-five years. Farmer John kept the records of the whole family, but destroyed those that connected it with contraband. General George is said to have buried his own ledgers in the garden of the Mansion, but they have not been found. It is a good guess that he owned more slavers than Ellery discovered. The quantity of molasses imported to town during these years is suspicious in itself. In 1818 enough arrived to distill one hundred thousand gallons of rum. Even allowing the twenty-seven hundred Bristolians the standard annual consumption of two and a half gallons per capita, enough was left over to buy almost a thousand Negroes.

The act which abolished the international trade in 1808 was complete as far as it went. To prevent smuggling in small boats, it even prohibited the domestic transport of slaves in vessels smaller than forty tons. But it carried no penalty. The act of April 20, 1818, placed on the suspected slaver the burden of proving her innocence; that of March 3, 1819, authorized the President to use the Navy in tracking down slave ships, and awarded half the value of any confiscated vessel to whoever informed against it; and that of May 15, 1820, declared any United States citizen who served aboard any ship in the international trade, whether she was American-owned or

foreign, a pirate, and so liable to death by hanging. The twelve
years between were the time of the trade's richest profits and most
inhuman cruelties. It was the time of the General's greatest afflu-
ence. He was elected to the Assembly; he was director of the Rhode
Island branch of the Bank of the United States. He was visited by
President Monroe at the Mansion, and ordered a silver basin and
ewer from England especially for the washing of the presidential
hands.*

Meanwhile Collector Ellery at Newport, still smarting from the
affair of the *Lucy* in 1799, did not lack information about the Bristol
lawbreakers. His informant was the extraordinary Parson Barnabas
Bates of the Baptist church in Bristol.

Bristol boys and girls used to chant this doggerel about the parson,
without the least idea who he was:

> Barnabas Bates put on his skates
> And skated up to meeting;
> When he got there he said a prayer
> And gave his skates to the Deacon.

The Baptist church had been built in 1814 on the west side of
the Common, by means of a seven-thousand-dollar lottery granted
by the state Assembly. The congregation were all poor people, and
there were not many of them. Bates, who had been parson at Barnstable, Massachusetts, was called to the Bristol pulpit in the same
year. He was a different sort of man from the three other divines in
town. His type—the politico-religious demagogue—has disappeared
from New England. He was a nimble, orotund little man about
General George's age, and English by birth. His sonorous voice and

---

* This visit, on June 30, 1817, was reported in *Niles' Register:* "The
President paused to partake of refreshments at the splendid mansion of
General deWolf. His path was strewn with roses, and on his departure he
was showered with the same by the ladies."

John deWolf described the visit in a letter to Captain Jim, who was in
Kentucky at the time, in these words: "The good old president of the U. States
visited us yesterday. He dined at George's. He showed himself very affable to
Mrs. deWolf your wife, who was presented to him."

dewlapped cheeks lent him an impressiveness which made up for his short stature. He wore important-looking spectacles, hung from a ribbon at his neck, and a flowing frock coat which seemed to make more of his person than was really there. Before he had been in town a year, the Masons elected him master of Saint Alban's Lodge, and he presided over the rituals in their hall upstairs above the "Town School," three doors up High Street from his stone chapel. In the fall of 1815 his sermons began to change. His congregation soon realized with horror that he was veering over to the newfangled Unitarian doctrine, which was popular in Boston but had yet to invade Rhode Island. At last, from the pulpit, he flatly denied the divinity of Christ. In 1816 his flock called a meeting to depose him, but he got wind of it ahead of time and filled the chapel with sailors from the docks and the Old Bay State, so there was no room for the congregation themselves. When the faithful dispersed, seeing he had stacked the meeting against them, he dismissed the sailors with two pennies apiece and locked the chapel door so no one could have access to the record book. For eight years, until he was finally eased out of town in 1824, the chapel was closed and the key was in his pocket.

Having lost his salary as pastor, he had to find another job. Collector Collins and three of the deWolf brothers recommended him to President Monroe for the vacant postmastership as "an undeviating Republican." They lived to regret the favor. Then, as now, the postmastership was a political appointment. It was less lucrative than the collectorship, but it carried considerable prestige. The Postmaster received no salary, but was allowed a commission of 30 per cent on postal receipts. Mail reached town by stage or packet. It was received and delivered at the Postmaster's office, which was usually his own house. The postage—there were no stamps—was paid by the addressee when he picked up his letters, at which time the Postmaster canceled them with his quill. Four times a year he forwarded the proceeds to Washington, less his commission. In one typical year Bates's commission amounted to $420. By way of contrast, Collins' legal take as Collector, in straight fees and a 3-per-cent commission on customs receipts, was a little over $3000. The Secretary of the Treasury himself received a salary of $3500.

Nobody knows more of what goes on in a village than the Postmaster, and it has never been easy to keep a secret in Bristol anyway. Bates used his position to spy for Ellery on the slave-trading conspiracy between Collins and George deWolf, and presumably received half the fines which the Treasury collected as a result of his information. During his four-year tenure at the post office, nine Bristol vessels were condemned as slavers. All except one belonged to General George.

No trader in his right mind would dare to smuggle slaves into an American port, but the Cuban market was insatiable. The technique of the trade had become more roundabout since 1808, but it was still essentially simple. Bates describes it thus in a letter of 1818:

> Cargoes suited to the African market are procured here in Bristol and taken aboard vessels suited to the purpose, and then cleared for the Havanna by the Collector. The master there effects a nominal sale of vessel and cargo to a Spaniard, takes on board a nominal Spanish master and proceeds to Africa. A power of attorney is always procured from the owner before leaving Bristol. When the vessel has made one voyage she can proceed on another without returning to the U. States. A new cargo is then generally sent out to her in the Havanna. There are several now out that have performed several voyages since they first sailed from here. There is one laying here ready for sea, called the *General Peace,* lately owned by Thomas Saunders of Providence. Thomas Russell of this town is her master, and attorney to effect the pretended sale. I wrote his power of attorney. The crew speak familiarly of their destination, and one man against whom I had a claim boldly told me that I must wait "till he could go and catch some blackbirds."

At the time of this letter, Saunders had just sold the *General Peace* to George deWolf.

The reason for a false sale to a Spanish subject was, of course, that Spain still permitted the slave trade to and from her colonies.

In 1817 the British government, which was always more zealous to suppress it than the American, paid Spain a bribe of £400,000 in return for a promise to forbid it by 1820—an act of humanity unparalleled in international politics. But the time for enforcement had not yet come (when it did, Spanish officials failed to honor the promise) and meanwhile importation was outlawed in the United States, but not in Cuba. To make sure that the pretended purchaser did not effectively get possession of the slave ship, he would be required to sign a paper promising her return on demand, and the "purchase" money would be placed in escrow. When General George, for instance, bought the privateer *Macdonough* from Captain Jim for use in the trade, he made Don José Wilson his attorney in Cuba, and through him ostensibly sold her to a firm of Havana slave traders named Disdier & Morphy. Collins removed her name from American registry and canceled her American bond. The purported price of $12,000 was placed in trust for the General at his Havana bank. Disdier deposited the following statement with the Town Clerk of Bristol, in English, and a duplicate, in Spanish, at the Ayuntamiento of Havana:

> Whereas Don José Wilson, attorney for the American brig *Macdonough*, of the burthen of 300 tons, has passed a bill of sale merely for the purpose of having her put under Spanish colours as the property of Disdier & Morphy, in order to enjoy the advantages which those colours now offer over the American:
> I hereby declare and acknowledge that notwithstanding the said Brigantine now appears to be the property of said Disdier & Morphy, she is still the property of said Wilson, as attorney.

Disdier & Morphy's fee for lending the General their name in this transaction was 10 slaves and 5 per cent of the *Macdonough's* profits. Since she bought her cargo of 400 slaves for as little as a single *onza* * the head and, thanks to the risk of seizure on the

---

* The *onza* was an ounce of gold, worth $16. It contained two doubloons, each of which contained eight Spanish milled dollars, or pieces of eight. Each dollar, in turn, contained eight reales, or "bits," worth 12½ cents.

Middle Passage, sold them for as much as $500 a head in Havana, General George probably cleared over $100,000 from a single voyage. He invested the money in a plantation of his own on the south coast of Cuba, called the Arca de Noë (Noah's Ark), where later, as will be seen, he made his home.

Other illegal slavers of the General's were the *Bello Corunes*, chased aground on Block Island by an Argentine privateer and looted by the Block Islanders; the hermaphrodite brigs *John Smith* and *Jacquard Packet*, which lost both captains of the fever in Africa; and the schooner *Rolla*, which, after an absence of almost two years, audaciously returned to Bristol, still under the American flag, with a cargo of palm oil, elephant tusks, coconuts, and figs—all legitimate African cargo and all consigned to the General.

The last Bristol slaver was the *Lisboa*, which arrived in the harbor under Portuguese colors in September 1819. Though her nominal master was a Brazilian named Alvarez, her real owner was the General. Clark Green of Bristol was enrolled as her supercargo and interpreter, though it is a mystery where he can have learned Portuguese or the African dialects. Bates promptly notified Ellery that she was loading trade goods, and Ellery forwarded the news to William H. Crawford, the Secretary of the Treasury:

> On the fourth of this month, I learned from an informant that a schooner named the *Lisboa*, under Portuguese colours, was in the harbor of Bristol with a cargo assorted for the slave-trade and with irons and chains to secure the slaves she might purchase on the coast of Africa, and that one Clark Green of Bristol, an American citizen, was secretely the master of her, and that it was expected she would sail the next morning. I sent for Capt. Cahoone, and directed him to proceed immediately up the bay with the cutter, and if he came across the schooner, to demand of her commanding officer her official papers; and if he refused to produce them, or failed to give satisfactory evidence that he had given bond according to law, to bring said schooner to the port of Newport for examination.
>
> Capt. Cahoone went up the bay, and returned the next day to report that he had seen the schooner still in the harbor of Bristol. He went on board, but found that her nominal captain, Alvarez, was not there. He waited on Mr. Collector Collins, who told him she

would not be ready to clear out under five days, and that he would not clear her out until bonds were given. . . . But, Mr. Secretary, suppose the Collector to strongly suspect from the cargo she has on board that the vessel is bound to the coast and kingdoms of Africa for the purpose of carrying on the slave-trade. Is he . . . *excluded* from examining what she has on board, and refusing to clear her? I know of no indictment under the Slave Act ever being brought in this state, and it seems that none will ever be brought.

No matter what his suspicions, Ellery had no right to seize the *Lisboa* as long as she lay at anchor. He was in a delicate position. Although he had overall supervision of Narragansett Bay, and command of the revenue cutter, Collins was his brother officer. Secretary Crawford was a southerner and could not be expected to intervene. Ellery recognized that the *Lisboa* could easily, between darkness and daylight, slip down the bay and out to sea without being seen by Captain Cahoone. That is what happened. In spite of his promise, Collins cleared her out one afternoon without demanding bond. She sailed immediately, before Parson Bates could post a warning over the Ferry to Newport. In reporting her escape to the Secretary, Ellery points out that Collins had made three long visits to Cuba "on personal business" since the close of the war, and leaves no doubt that the business was to promote the very traffic which he was sworn to suppress. He adds the discouraged note:

Our correspondence now contains all that I have learned about the inhuman, iniquitous and illegal slave-trade being carried on from Bristol. I have not mentioned the name of my informant, because of fears for his safety. His assertions, I am satisfied, are susceptible of legal proof. Since the departure of the *Lisboa*, I have received the following note from Mr. Collector Collins in Bristol:

"I exceedingly regret that this state is resorted to for the purpose of carrying on the illicit traffic in slaves. I wish you success in your exertions to put a stop to it, but I fear that so long as the American consuls at Teneriffe, Havana, etc., continue to wink at it, all exertions by myself or you will be unavailing."

Since the receipt of that letter I have not thought it worth while to correspond with Mr. Collector Collins about the slave trade. Indeed, so great is the profit in it that it will, in my opinion, proceed, even if bond should be obtained in every instance.

On that voyage of the *Lisboa,* her entire crew, except for Clark Green himself, died of the coast fever in an African lagoon and were buried by the very slaves they had intended to buy.

Though General George lost several vessels to the watchful Ellery, he lost none to the United States Navy. But the *Macdonough* had a narrow escape. Low in the water with a cargo of three hundred, she was overtaken by the cruiser *Ontario* after a chase that lasted almost the whole length of the Middle Passage. The commander of the *Ontario* knew his quarry, if only by her speed: she had once made the voyage from Havana to Newport in less than six days, and under jury rig at that. The *Macdonough's* captain knew that he knew her, and that no false colors would fool him. Crowding all sail, he slipped into the harbor of Havana hardly a gunshot ahead of the cruiser. Next year, however, renamed the *Enriques,* she was chased aground off Matanzas by HMS *Forrest,* and lost with her full cargo of slaves. Since General George was secretly her owner, he had to bear most of her loss.

The dangers of the trade were getting serious. To implement the acts of 1819 and 1820, Congress, by treaty with Great Britain and Spain, had authorized the American Navy, jointly with the British, to police the African coast. Commodore Matthew Perry, the brother of the great Oliver Hazard and of Captain Jim's son-in-law Raymond, commanded the American flotilla. (He was the same officer who later opened the ports of Japan.) Since Captain Jim's amendment to the treaty specifically forbade British cruisers to search American suspects, and vice versa, the General's slavers, on sighting an American cruiser, dropped the Spanish ensign and ran up the Union Jack; if they sighted a Britisher, up went the Stars and Stripes. Clark Green, shortly before his death on the Slave Coast, wrote the General a humorous letter about the African Squadron, in which he says, "I wish the cruisers were in some nice place like Hell or Texas."

But Perry, a Rhode Islander himself, was strangely blind to the presence of slave ships. In 1819, the very year when General George alone fitted out at least three, he wrote to Washington:

> I could not even hear of an American slaving vessel on the African coast, and am fully impressed with the belief that there is not one at present afloat.

II

While the African Squadron patrolled the eastern reaches of the Atlantic for slave ships, another task force of the Navy, beginning in 1822, was posted in the Caribbean to suppress piracy. This force, commanded by Commodore David Porter (father of the Civil War admiral) was popularly called the Mosquito Fleet. It was made up of nineteen vessels. Among them was the first steam warship, the galiot *Sea Gull*. Although many officers and men dreaded to serve aboard a vessel "with a boiler in her belly," the *Sea Gull* could pursue the pirates regardless of wind, and was shallow enough to follow them into the swamps and lagoons where they hid.

Pirates of the *Treasure Island* variety had infested the waters of the West Indies since anyone could remember. Many of them were citizens of the United States. Their numbers were swelled by the embargo of 1807 and the peace treaties of 1815. Soldiers and sailors of all nations, thrown out of work by the return of peace, flocked to join the buccaneers whose shoal-draft *flecheras* lurked in the lagoons and keys of Florida, the Bahamas, Yucatán, and Cuba. It was estimated in 1819 that ten thousand pirates were active in these waters, and that in the single year they captured or destroyed five vessels and $20,000,000 worth of cargo. They forced hundreds of innocent mariners to walk the plank. In 1821 an anonymous pirate who signed himself Richard Coeur de Lion, having peppered the Philadelphia ship *Orleans* with grapeshot and looted her of $40,000, and what was worse, induced her crew to join him, left aboard the drifting hulk a message addressed to the United States Navy:

> Between buccaneers no ceremony. I take your dry goods and in return I give you pimento. Therefore we are now even. I entertain

no resentment. The goods of this world belong to the brave and valiant.

Bristol merchants suffered several losses from pirates. The worst incident was in 1820, when Captain Jim's sloop *Collector*, outward bound from Matanzas, Ben Tilley's schooner *Milo*, and General George's brig *John Smith*, both inbound, were all captured at the harbor's mouth, in sight of the fort of San Severino and of Don José Wilson's lookout at Camarioca, by a launch manned by six Spaniards, two Englishmen, and one Portuguese. The pirates looted all three vessels, killed the captain and two men of the *Milo*, and burned the *Collector*. When Captain Simmons of the *Collector* reached shore the next day, he saw his own gold watch, along with the bags of coffee which had been his cargo, openly offered for sale in the Matanzas marketplace. The pirates had not even removed Captain Jim's stencil from the burlap. Simmons set after the pirate launch in a borrowed gunboat, but though he hunted her for two days he did not find her. There were times when American men-of-war, and even British or French ships, convoyed American merchant-men out to the open sea, beyond the reach of the pirates.

But there was a kind of piracy which had a faint color of legality: the fitting out of privateers for the rebel Spanish colonies of South America. Argentina was the first colony to revolt; she declared her independence in 1816. She was followed in 1819 by what was variously called the Republic of Gran Colombia, or New Granada, or the Cartagenian Republic. It included the present states of Colombia, Venezuela, Ecuador, and Panamá. The inspiration of the rebels, and their first president, was the great Simón Bolívar. His naval chief of staff was a Dutchman named Pedro Luis Brion, whose headquarters were on Margarita Island, off the Venezuelan coast.

Officially the United States were neutral. By a treaty of 1797 American citizens were prohibited from "taking any commission or letter of marque, and from arming any ship or vessel to act as privateers against the subjects of his Catholic Majesty, or the property of any of them, from any prince or state with which the said King shall be at war." An Act of Neutrality passed in 1819 confirmed this treaty, and made it an act of piracy for an American to outfit or serve on any vessel of the insurgent colonies. It was just as illegal for an American to join the Colombian rebels as it was for him to transport slaves, a fact which Spanish Minister de Onís pointed out to John Quincy Adams, Monroe's Secretary of State, repeatedly and in vain. American sympathies were with the rebels, and the cession of Florida to the United States in 1819 made it easier for the American volunteers to reach Brión's headquarters, for it removed the Spanish Navy from their path.

As soon as the republic of Gran Colombia was proclaimed, merchant ships began to arrive at Margarita, chiefly from the United States, loaded with arms for sale to the rebels. Most of them hailed from Baltimore and Charleston, but there were a few from the New England ports. Ashore, British soldiers thrown out of work by the defeat of Napoleon crowded to volunteer in Bolívar's army. At sea, the Gentlemen Sailors of the War of 1812, who had been idle since the Treaty of Ghent, offered themselves to the insurgent flag. A few, like Commodore Daniel Danells of Baltimore, enlisted as regulars in the Colombian Navy, but most served as privateersmen. Brion guaranteed 100 pesos a month, which was a little better than $100, to the commander of a privateer, and all hands had a share in her prizes, subject only to the customs duties assessed on arrival at a Colombian port. Many of the privateers were former slave ships. They were insured in Baltimore or New York and manned by adventurers from the American and Caribbean waterfronts. They were owned by American merchants, and registered and commissioned by Colombia; in 1824 the Colombian government even ordered two schooners direct from a Baltimore shipyard.

In cases where the high-minded Bolívar declined to accept the application of an American privateer, plausible commissions were forged at a small price by a gang in Galveston, which was then in Mexico, or by Louis Aury, a renegade Frenchman who operated a printing press on Amelia Island off the Florida coast. When the United States Navy, after the cession of Florida, drove Aury off Amelia, he set up shop on Old Providence Island, east of Nicaragua.

Besides his "navy," which flew the Argentine and Colombian flags at random, his empire included an "admiralty court" for the adjudication of prizes. Aury claimed to be a general in the Colombian forces, but the fact is that Bolívar disowned him and refused him permission to enter Colombian territory. Even so, provided a privateer did not attack American ships and could show a Colombian commission, no matter how dubious, she was not molested by the Mosquito Fleet.

The privateers not only preyed on Spanish commerce, but paid important sums in customs fees to the insurgent treasury. The presence of Spanish property on board a trader was excuse enough to seize her. The privateer *General Santander,* Captain Chase, brought $250,000 worth of Spanish vessels and cargo into the Colombian ports of La Guaira and Cartagena during the revolution, on which the Republic collected 45 per cent. The only loser was Spain, and sometimes the American underwriters who had insured the Spanish cargoes. In 1819 the New York insurance brokers, in a memorial to President Monroe, listed forty-five losses in the previous year to privateers under the rebel flag, illegally commanded by American citizens. In 1824 they demanded that he exact compensation from Bolívar, and Bolívar complied. They brought out that the *Santander* was owned, outfitted, and principally manned by Americans; that $70,000 of the Spanish property she had seized was covered by New York policies; and that Captain Chase, himself an American, had more than once seized American merchantmen on the ground they carried Spanish goods, had them condemned in Colombian courts or by Aury, and pocketed the proceeds of their sale.

It is surprising how many privateers under the red, yellow, and blue flag of Colombia had American captains. This writer has identified twenty-nine, but there were doubtless more. Most of them were named for heroes or battlefields of the insurrection. The *Bravo* was owned by Jean Laffite, the famous New Orleans pirate. The *McGregor,* Captain Tayer of Newport, had originally been the *Brutus,* jointly owned by James deWolf of Bristol and William

Gray of Salem during the War of 1812. Gray bought out Captain Jim's share and renamed her for a Scotch mountebank who commanded Aury's "army." The *General Paez*, Captain Chase, was the slaver *General Peace* which Parson Bates had denounced in 1818. The *General Ramirez*, Captain Smith, in spite of her Colombian commission, was taken at sea by the USS *Ontario* in 1821, with three hundred slaves stapled between her decks. The *General Padilla*, owned by George deWolf, had first been commanded by a Yankee named Thomas Severs. For some unknown reason, Brion dismissed him in 1821, and it must have been a serious one, for he needed every privateersman he could get. Shortly afterward he put her under command of Peter Bradford of Bristol. We shall meet Bradford later.

Most of the Colombian privateers were corvettes from thirty-five feet to a hundred feet long—narrow and sharp, schooner-rigged for quick handling, and armed with twelve- and eighteen-pounders on swivels. They were not built for long life. Their crews were usually Colombian or Florida Indians, with a sprinkling of Americans, all under the command of the American skipper who represented the owners. In theory, any American who served aboard was outside the protection of the law, and liable to be hanged by the government of any nation, for piracy was defined as "the crime against all mankind." American officials disowned them. John Randall, the American commercial agent at Havana, who could wink at most violations of the law, wrote to John Quincy Adams, "I disapprove of American citizens capturing Spanish property under the insurgent flag."

And when the case of the slaver *Bello Corunes*, mentioned above, reached the Supreme Court of the United States on appeal, the justices remarked, in disallowing the claim of Captain Barnes of the *Puerreydon*, who had chased her aground on Block Island,

It is a melancholy truth, too well known to this court, that the instruments used in the predatory voyages carried on under the colors of the South American states are among the most abandoned and profligate of men.

The sympathies of the American public were so strongly with the insurgents that a convicted pirate had only to pretend to be in the Colombian service to win a pardon from President Monroe. The French and British were more strictly neutral, if not pro-Spanish. A newsletter of 1819 reports:

> A pirate or privateer under the flag of Bolívar, president of Gran Colombia, has been captured by a French frigate and sent into Martinique. Her crew, 100 in number (36 claiming to be American citizens) are in close confinement, and, it is thought, will be hung, the commission being considered a forgery.

Sometimes the Americans fought on opposite sides. In 1824, for instance, the Colombian armed schooner *La Centella* captured the Spanish brig *Amistad,* and sent her into Cockspur Roads at Savannah for sale at auction. Captains Hopner and Ray were both Americans. In the same year the Colombian *Bolívar* took the Spanish *Ceres.* Both were products of the same Baltimore shipyard. When asked which side he favored, the shipbuilder answered, "If my customers choose to fight each other, and pit one piece of my handiwork against another, it's no business of mine."

General George invested heavily in privateering during the Colombian revolution, though he had only dabbled at it during the War of 1812, when it was not only legal but patriotic. There was little profit in hauling onions and blocks of ice to Cuba in exchange for molasses, for the end of the slave trade had killed the market for the rum which was distilled from it. He had become used to quick and enormous profits, and the whole town was used to them too. He had established his financial reputation in the slave trade, and had to keep going, for he was heavily in debt to his backers. He owned three ships, two schooners, nine brigs, and a sloop. At $15 a month, he chartered another schooner. The syndicate of traders who called themselves the Gentlemen of the Long Wharf were glad to be co-owners of his fleet, in fractions down to $\frac{1}{100}$ of a ship's value. Other townsmen endorsed his notes in return for a cut of his profits. Some, like his cousin Henry—long since retired from the Charleston slave-brokerage—touted his ventures in return for a share in them. Almost everyone in town, even the Negro servants, had lent him money. He kept accounts with Samuel Williams, the greatest banker in London, with Isaac Clapp in Boston, and with Guiteras & Morland in Havana. He still sat in the Assembly, and, at the annual muster on the Common, still reviewed the 4th Brigade.

His accomplices were Collector Collins ashore, and at sea two Gentlemen Sailors named Tom Jones and Peter Bradford. Both had served aboard the *Yankee* as Marines; Jones had been her commander on her fourth cruise. His origin was mysterious; he had arrived in Bristol from New York State at the start of the war, carrying his belongings in a bandana at the end of a stick, and attended by a three-toed Negro servant. He had fallen in love with a Bristol girl named Harriet Waldron when he saw her sweeping off her father's steps, and had married her. He was reputed to be the younger son of a Scottish laird named Ochterlony, who paid him to remain in America. It is certain that when he died in Bristol his body was shipped to Scotland in a tierce of spirits.

The General's enemies were still Parson Bates and Collector Ellery. In 1817, on information from Bates, Ellery caught Jones red-handed fitting out a Colombian privateer for George in Bristol harbor. She was a 145-ton brig named the *B. Collins*, without demanding bond, had cleared her for Puerto Rico on a sworn manifest which listed a cargo of potatoes, onions, and apples, a crew of fifteen, and defensive armament of a single gun. When Captain Cahoone of the *Vigilant*, on Ellery's orders, boarded her in Bristol harbor, he found she had four carriage guns mounted, five more in the hold, a crew of forty-five, and a cargo of ball, grape, small arms, cutlasses, and boarding pikes, with twenty cases of powder stowed below deck. She could be made ready for action in half an hour, and lacked only her Colombian commission. Cahoone, officially uniformed in blue swallowtail with epaulets and a black stovepipe hat with cockade at the side, ordered her down to Newport, where Ellery disarmed her and discharged her crew. He libeled the vessel and brought action against her captain. He won only half a victory, however; though the *B* was condemned to be sold, the suit against Jones was nol-prossed on orders from Washington. Neither Collins nor General George was named in the proceedings. At the vandoo, the *B* was bought in by a Cuban sea-captain named José Gonsalve, who, on his visits to Bristol, lived upstairs over the deWolf counting-house at the foot of Pump Lane.

Ellery died in bed at Newport, with his spectacles on his nose and a volume of Cicero in his hand, in February of 1820. He was ninety-three. The only signers of the Declaration of Independence who survived him were Jefferson, John Adams, and Charles Carroll of Carrollton. In two more months he would have completed his seventh term as Collector for Newport, and Collins his fifth as Collector for Bristol. His long fight with the deWolfs was over.

But the scandal he had denounced in Bristol could not be ignored in Washington. President Monroe was conscientious, if softhearted. In the appointments for his second term he failed to renominate Collins, and instead, to the dismay of the Gentlemen of the Long Wharf, named their enemy, the Reverend Barnabas Bates, to succeed him. For the four years of Bates's incumbency no slaver or privateer entered the harbor. By international law, a belligerent ship might enter a neutral port only in distress, and then just for the time needed for repairs. The Spanish consuls (one of them, Bernardo Malagamba, was stationed at Newport) were on the alert for violations. The General was obliged to sell his prizes on the inadequate markets of Colombia itself. But nothing prevented him from transferring specie at sea to his merchant ships, and so his profits, in spite of Bates, found their way to the pockets of the Bristol speculators.

Monroe renominated Bates in April of 1824, when his term expired. By that time Captain Jim was in the Senate. Though he had little use for his nephew George, he was loyal to the family interests and set about to have the reappointment rejected. Bates sent the President a list of the Bristol ships which had been condemned on his information, adding slyly:

I respectfully refer you to the Hon. James deWolf, Senator from Rhode Island, whose knowledge of the commercial interests of the District will enable him to confirm the truth of this list.

He was rejected all the same. Captain Jim announced his victory to his brother John in a letter of April 18:

> Confidential! No noise!
> Dear Brother:
> Thanks to my stars, I have not ranged about the wilds of life without finding friends. The Senate has been graciously pleased to *non-concur* the President's nomination of Barnabas Bates as Collector of the Port of Bristol, Sen. Knight and Messrs. Eddy and Durfee [the other Rhode Island Congressmen] notwithstanding. It has been a long and tough siege for me, but I beg you to keep still and show no sort of rejoicing—tickled inwardly as much as you please, but nothing more. Such a tissue of lies, calumny and abuse as the little Priest has invented against the people of our native town, you will be astonished. The vote was 17 for confirming to 26 against. You may depend on it, I have not spared him in the Senate. Show this to Brother William and have the laugh out. Shake your sides one or 2 hours in his house or some place where nobody will see you.
> As always, your friend and affectionate brother,
> James deWolf

Bates lost his job. He petitioned the Senate for a list of the charges against him, but received no answer. He vanished from town, taking the Baptist silver communion set with him. His congregation at last regained possession of the stone chapel.

In Bates's place, Monroe appointed an easy-going landlubber named Luke Drury, who had married a daughter of the Quakerish Levi deWolf. Drury was a frequent lecturer on temperance, and had the finest beard in town. He had written a textbook on geography, with maps. Though he was as upright as his father-in-law, and as poor, he could not be expected to take side against his wife's family.

Two months after the appointment, the town was visited by one of the General's privateers, and shuddered a long time afterward at the recollection. The best account of her visit is the story which

Dr. Smith, who was a boy at the time, wrote for the *Phoenix* in May of 1875. He called it

THE BRISTOL PIRATE

Early one summer morning, I think it was in the year 1823,[*] the residents of Bristol were startled by the report of cannon booming up from the offing of the harbor. The sounds borne toward the town on the rising sea breeze were echoed again from the opposite shores, and then, rolling away, died upon the quiet shores of Narragansett Bay. This of itself was no extraordinary event, as in those days it was customary for all vessels arriving from sea, or departing on their voyages, to salute the port. But the extraordinary character of the craft from which this firing proceeded attracted crowds of people to the wharfs to gaze upon the approaching stranger.

A large armed schooner, of the most rakish appearance, with all her ports open as if for instant combat, and the flag of the new republic of Bolivia [†] at her masthead, sailed up past the islands, and directed her course toward the upper anchorage, in front of the town. For a stranger, she seemed to show much familiarity with the channels and sailing courses; and without signalling for a pilot, moved up to her birth like one perfectly at home. Dropping her anchor and folding her canvas wings, the newcomer awaited the arrival alongside of the Custom House cutter, with the boarding officers of the port.

In the meantime, many were the conjectures and surmises expressed in the crowd, respecting this singular arrival. Some old sea captains, who were gazing upon her crowded decks through their spy-glasses, when questioned about her, shook their heads saying "they could not make her out, but there was no doubt she was a saucy craft, and a privateer at least, if she was nothing worse," and they "could not divine what had brought a vessel of her description into our peaceful waters." One old salt, I remember, begged the loan of a glass for a moment, and scanning the scooner from stem to stern, alow and aloft, returned the instrument with these words:

---

[*] It was Thursday, July 1, 1824.

[†] Dr. Smith's memory is mistaken. She was the Colombian privateer *General Padilla*, previously mentioned. Hereafter, for Bolivia, read Colombia.

"I say, Captain Browning,* that fellow *may possibly* be a Bolivian privateer! But I'm a horse marine, if a vessel with a crew made up of West India halfbreeds and Negroes is any better ● than she ought to be. And a craft that carries her name neither under her stern ports, on her bows, nor quarter rails, hails from no port in particular. Beside"—added the sailor—"I'll bet a month's wages, that chap has more than one set of papers and colors to sail on any occasion."

"Yes!" answered one of his shipmates, "and blast my eyes, Jack, if I don't believe the fellow's a free rover, anyhow;—and if you had the overhauling of his lockers, you'd mayhap find the red flag † and death's head and crossbones of them sea-rats lying in wait for honest traders among the keys and lagoons of Cuba."

While these not very flattering opinions concerning the new-comer were being canvassed by the crowd, the Custom-house boat, accompanied by the schooner's cutter, approached the shore. In the stern sheets of the latter was a tall handsome man, wearing the uniform of the Bolivian navy; and as the boat touched the wharf, he sprang to the land, and was immediately recognized as one of our own townsmen who had been absent for a number of years, and who had long since been given up for dead, even by his own family.

His name was Peter Bradford; and he was connected with the most respectable people of the town. His father,‡ a worthy sea captain, had been lost at sea, and Peter, left to the care of an indulgent mother, grew up to have his way in almost everything; and while yet a boy he had shipped on board the privateer *Yankee,* and remained a privateersman till the close of the war, when he disappeared from his native town, and had never returned till on the occasion above narrated.

For several days,§ while this suspicious vessel remained in our harbor, she and her mongrel crew were the objects of eager

---

* Beriah Browning.

† Contrary to general belief, the Jolly Roger was more often red than black.

‡ William Bradford, Junior, brother of Mrs. James deWolf and Mrs. Charles Collins. Peter was thirty-three at this time.

§ Parson Wight's diary, locked in a brassbound chest at Miss Agnes Herreshoff's in Bristol, notes that on that Sunday of 1824 "Capt. P. Bradford of the Colombian armed schooner *Gen. Padilla* listened attentively to my sermon."

curiosity and gossip of our townspeople; and many were the attempts to gain admission to her decks. But a strict guard was
• continually kept at her gangways, and none but a select few were permitted to ascend her sides. Among those, however, who were allowed to board her were my brother and myself, who, in company with the nephews * of Captain Bradford—boys like ourselves—had free access to all parts of the vessel. With the impulsive curiosity of youngsters, we ranged all over her. From a scrutininzing survey of her armed decks we entered the cabins and even the staterooms of the officers. Thence we found our way to the crowded berth-deck, and even into the lowest hold of the schooner. We conversed with, and asked a thousand boyish questions of such of the officers and men as chanced to understand English, and made ourselves at home generally.

The novel discoveries we made were of course detailed to our comrades on shore; and from one to another they circulated, till in a little while they became the talk of the town. Coupling the various circumstances together with their previous suspicions, but little doubt remained in the minds of our people regarding the true character of the vessel.

Among the crew was a young lad, who addressed us in English, and who, following us with his eyes as we hurriedly passed from one object to another, seemed desirous to speak with us. At length one day, when the officers were out of sight for a moment, he approached us and whispered:

"Boys, when I get a chance I want to have a long talk with you. But I dare not let the officers see us talking together. Watch the time when they are at dinner, and come to the bows for a moment."

When dinner was ready, a cabin boy invited us in the name of the officers to descend to the cabin and join them. The captain's nephews followed the boy; but my brother and myself declined the invitation, and sauntered carelessly toward the forecastle, where we were to meet the boy we knew awaited us.

His story greatly excited our sympathy. He said he was a Boston boy, and had sailed from that port about three years before,† with his father, on a voyage to Jamaica; that they had

---

* The sons of Golden Dearth. Mrs. Dearth was a third sister of the captain's father.

† Probably the brig *Laura*, Captain Shaw, destroyed by pirates in 1821. She was bound from Buenos Aires to Havana with a cargo of jerked beef.

fallen in with and been captured by pirates on the Bahama banks; that all hands, including his father, had been murdered, and the vessel, after being plundered, had been burnt; that he had been landed on one of the Lucayos,* at the rendezvous of the gang; from which he was taken by Captain Bradford, who chanced to land at the place; that Captain B. had, at first, promised to put him on board of some vessel bound to the United States, but that he had since refused to do so, and now kept him a prisoner on board. He said he had not set his foot on shore since he had left the island rendezvous of the pirates. The lad assured us that the vessel, though claiming to be a Bolivian privateer, was connected with the pirates of the West Indies, and with those who had murdered his father and crew. He concluded by begging us to assist him in escaping from her to the shore.

I can never forget the imploring expression of the poor lad's face when he begged this favor, or the words he used on the occasion.

"Boys," said he, "have you a mother?"

We told him we had.

"And do you love your mother?" he asked.

"Most certainly we do," we answered.

"And that mother loves you?" he continued.

"To be sure, she does," was our reply.

"Well, I too have a mother, I hope, in Boston, if she has not died brokenhearted since father and I sailed away. And I love my mother, boys, as dearly as you do yours; and how my return to her would gladden her widowed heart! Oh, if I *could* only escape from this wicked crew! Oh do, *do* help me in some way. I can't jump overboard in the dark and swim ashore," said he, "for the guards are continually on the lookout for deserters, and they would shoot me before I could leave the vessel's side. *Will* you help me?"

We assured him that we would. And children as we were, we determined to invent some plan by which we could rescue the unhappy boy; and before we left him it had been arranged that we would pull our little boat under the bows of the schooner the following night, and he should drop from the bobstays into her, when, covering him with a boat cloak, we should pull away again for the shore.

---

* A contemporary name for the Bahama islands.

This was the last time we were permitted to visit the schooner;
for when we approached her the next day, we were roughly
ordered to keep away; while the black sentinel, in broken English, threatened to fire upon us if we should come any nearer. But
our Boston boy was not forgotten; for letting some larger boys
into our secret, and getting the consent of our parents, whose interest we had excited by the boy's story, we waited till a late
hour on the night of that day, and pulled off silently into the
harbor, and without exciting the suspicions of the sleepy guard,
passed quietly under the bowsprit of the schooner. But the boy
did not appear as agreed upon. Again we passed under her bows,
and rested upon our oars. Still no one seemed to be waiting for
us. At length, I ventured to climb by the bobstays upon the bowsprit and peer over the bulwarks upon the forward deck. There
was no one there. The crew were below in their hammocks, and
only the sentinels, one at each gangway, were to be seen. Dropping noiselessly into our little boat, and sadly disappointed at
our failure, we pulled again to the dock, almost angry with what
we now believed the game the boy had been making of us.

The next morning a watering party was sent on shore, under
charge of the Boatswain's mate, a Floridian Spaniard who spoke
a broken sort of negro English. This fellow, it was soon discovered, was a great lover of rum. Some of our people took
advantage of his weakness, and while his men were pumping
water into the casks,* they tempted him into Pardon Handy's
store, and plying him freely with his favorite beverage, pumped
him for information. The mulatto, thrown completely off his
guard, became very confidential, and readily answered all the
questions put to him. I remember well the reply he gave to a
question of Captain Browning:

"Well, Boatswain, when you are on a cruise, what kind of
vessels do you take?"

His reply was—"We always takes de Spaniard *for sure*. And
we takes de Portugee—de French—de English, and *sometimes*,"
he added with a half drunken, confidential leer, "*sometimes we
takes de Yankee.*"

There was no doubt in the minds of all present that it was a
pirate vessel, though sailing under the new flag of Bolivia;

* The town pump stood at the corner of Hope and State Streets, at what
used to be called Loafer's Corner but is now Legion Square. It was only a
block upstreet from the deWolf wharf and counting-house.

and it soon became openly talked of in the town. Some persons were for taking measures for detaining the schooner and crew for judicial investigation, although a certain wealthy family of Bristol was supposed to be in some way or other interested in her voyages;—for bags of specie had been landed from her and placed in their possession.

As our little town had not the means of making a forcible seizure of the suspected vessel, it was proposed to send messengers to Newport and invoke the aid of the Revenue cutter and the authorities of that port. But what is everybody's concern is attended to by none. The measure was *only* talked of.

Of course the excitement now existing in the community could not fail to be known by those most interested; and in the afternoon of the same day, boats were frequently passing between the vessel and the shore, as if she were preparing to take her departure. In the meantime, however, there was no appearance of preparation aboard the schooner. That night proved to be a dark and stormy one. But after the townspeople had been some hours in bed, those living near the shore were awakened by the sound of several shots fired in the direction of the harbor. Accompanying these reports they thought they also heard cries as of some one in agony. But the sounds soon ceased, and nothing more was heard. In the morning, however, those who were earliest abroad discovered that the berth so long occupied by the suspicious craft was vacant. She had suddenly departed during the storm of the previous night, without even the formality of a custom house clearance.

Had there been any doubts in the minds of the most incredulous as to the true character of the vessel, they now ceased to exist. In still stronger proof of this, the incoming tide cast upon the beach at the lower end of the town the corpses of two of her crew. Both of them were multilated by musket shots. One was the body of the too communicative Boatswain's mate; *—and the other immediately recognized as that of the poor Boston lad we had tried to help to the shore. He had, no doubt, at the last moment, as the schooner was sailing out of the harbor, leaped into the sea, hoping to reach the land; but his escape was arrested by bullets through his legs, back and other portions of his

---

* The death records in the Burnside Memorial Town Hall contain this entry for July 8, 1824: "Drowned and shot, negro from armed schooner *Padilla*." They make no mention of Shaw.

body. It was doubtless the cry of the murdered boy that was heard accompanying the reports of the small arms. The Floridian, without doubt, was shot on the deck of his vessel, as his wounds were all in front. It was probably the penalty of his telltale tongue.

Scarcely had this murder been discovered than the town was thrown into the greatest excitement; and our Collector, accompanied by several of our influential citizens, hastened with all speed to Newport, to alarm the authorities, and if possible to prevent the escape of the schooner. But they were now too late. As they came in view of the open sea, the upper sails of the vessel were seen rapidly sinking below the horizon, to the southard of Block Island. Being evidently a fast sailer, it was deemed useless to pursue her with anything then lying in Newport harbor. Besides, she was too heavily armed, and would doubtless refuse to surrender if she could have been overhauled.

Some weeks after these events, and when they had almost ceased to be talked of, one of the members * of the wealthy family above referred to was suddenly called to the Havana. Finally it transpired that this hasty visit was in some way connected with Captain Bradford; and shortly afterward, a well-authenticated rumor that our suspicious visitant, while cruising among the keys on the north coast of Cuba, had been captured by a Spanish frigate: †—that the crew had been hanged at the yardarm of their own vessel, and Bradford himself taken for trial into the Havana. We also heard that while in prison, awaiting his trial under the tardy operation of the Spanish laws, he had sickened and died before the garotte could claim him. But fast upon the heels of this rumor came another, to the effect that Captain Bradford was not dead; but that through the influence of friends, the commandant and surgeon of the Morro castle, where he had been confined, had been bribed to connive at his escape,—that for a few days he simulated sickness;—and was afterward conveyed in a coffin from the prison,—not to the burying-ground, but to the shore of the island, when he was received on board a small boat, and rowed off to a snug trim-

---

* George deWolf sailed August 8 for Havana aboard his brig *Orozimbo*.
† July 20 she had blown up the Spanish brig *Marinero* two hundred miles off Savannah. Her Long Tom was split in the action; otherwise it is doubtful she would have been taken.

built Baltimore clipper which for several days had been lying off and on the coast in the vicinity.

What was the subsequent career of this man but little was known by his townsmen. But at one time after his escape he captured two drogers belonging to his old commander Captain J. O. Wilson, with whom he had sailed in the *Yankee,* who was residing on his Camarioca sugar estate. The drogers were loaded with sugar and coffee and bound to Matanzas. After having the cargoes of the coasters conveyed on board his own vessel, he ascertained from one of the skippers to whom the property belonged. But not having time to break bulk again and restore the plundered goods, Bradford wrote a very courteous and friendly letter to the planter (which letter, many years after, I had the pleasure of reading), deprecating what he had done, and excused the act by saying—had he known to whom the vessels belonged, he would not have captured them. The letter concluded by calling to mind some of the incidents of their lives on board the *Yankee,* and endorsed a draft on a well-known commercial house in the Havana for more than the value of the intercepted cargoes.

Several years after this last event, a Providence brig, bound to Jamaica, was chased by a suspicious-looking clipper schooner, off the east end of Cuba; but a West India tornado coming down upon them, the chase suddenly disappeared, probably capsized in the squall. The brig outrode the gale. But the clipper never more was head from. This was no doubt the last of our Yankee buccaneer.*

III

General George's luck came to an end in 1825. In June, he failed to deliver a promised cargo of sugar to Captain Sylvester Eddy's brig *Jacob* in Havana. The incident was small, but the news shook the confidence of the village. On July 6 his schooner *Eagle* reached Bristol with word that his sugar harvest had failed. The banks began to call in their notes; to meet, the borrowers had to collect their own debts from the General. In August he resigned command of the 4th Brigade (he was succeeded by Byron Diman, the family cashier)

---

* His entry in the Bradford genealogy reads: "Born 1791, died ? at sea, unmarried."

and announced he would not stand for re-election to the legislature. In October, Samuel Williams, his London banker, went to the wall for the huge sum of £700,000. The newspapers wrote confidently that the losses were spread among so many creditors that no single one would be badly hurt. It was unthinkable that the riches poured into town by privateering and the slave trade should have vanished in speculation, but the townsfolk who had trusted the General with their savings were frightened just the same. They took to sauntering past his counting-house, hoping for good news, and to calling at the Mansion to ask after Julia, his sick baby. They would ask him casually and cheerfully, as if they did not really care, when a venture would realize, or when Clapp in Boston might be expected to remit for the sale of a cargo. It took too much courage to demand payment outright, for the General's revenge for an insult could be terrible; besides, there was always the chance that he might double their investments, as he had often done in the past. In Bristol, the deWolfs have always been famous for coming back.

But the General took to staying away from the counting-house. Soon no one dared call at the Mansion, for it was said little Julia could not last much longer, and his grief had unhinged him. She died on December 6, behind the tall shuttered windows of the Mansion, and was buried on the eighth from Saint Michael's. That night, when the town was asleep, his coach, his phaeton, his wagon, and his chaise were loaded by lantern-light in the courtyard. Some of the furniture was too bulky, and there was no room for the books, the wine, or the heaviest plate. The presidential ewer and basin were left behind. When everything portable was tightly stowed, and the horses were hitched, and the Negro coachman was on the box, the General led his wife and six remaining children out the back door and started for Boston through the snow.

He had secretly taken passage for Cuba aboard Benjamin Tilley's schooner *Milo*, Captain Hatch. She was a hard-luck vessel, the same whose former captain had been killed by pirates four years before. On her trip in from Havana she had lost her fore and main topmasts in a storm, and had reached Boston, twenty-three days out, in bad need of refit, only two days before the General reached Boston himself. Hatch must have known he was compounding a felony to help the General escape, but he probably needed the $350 passage-money which was promised him. The *Milo* was a cramped and uncomfortable vessel of only sixty-seven tons, and no one would have suspected that the General and the luxury-loving Charlotte would have chosen her for an escape.

Charlotte spent the next afternoon loading the children and the carriages—even the horses—aboard the *Milo*. The General spent it in Clapp's counting-house. He signed the papers of bankruptcy, assigning all his American assets, for the benefit of his creditors, to his brother Charles, Junior, and to Clapp. They fell short of his debts by $300,000. He turned over all his shipping to the receivership. By the time he had finished, his family were aboard. Captain Hatch was waiting with sail up, and weighed anchor at eight in the evening, bound to Havana.

The news reached Bristol, by Chadwick's stagecoach *Napoleon*, the next morning. The General, writes his uncle John, "left a trail of execration behind him." The townspeople swarmed into the Mansion. They ripped the damask curtains from the walls and the chandeliers from the ceilings. The plate which Simeon Potter had looted at Oyapoc was looted all over again. The basin and ewer in which President Monroe had washed his hands were taken in part payment for wages by the crew of the *Orozimbo*. There was no police in the village, but Collector Drury and Squire Howe posted themselves in the hall, each with a copybook and quill. As each laden creditor passed out the Palladian doorway, they made out duplicate accounts of his claim and his recovery, and gave him one copy for a temporary receipt. (It was from these copybooks, years later, that the General's grandson was able to buy back some of the furniture.) All night, through the snow, tipcarts and lowgears trundled back and forth to the Mansion. By dawn it was an empty shell.

News that the General had skipped spread all over the country. Bristol banknotes were refused everywhere. (In those days, state

banks issued their own legal tender.) Lewis Tucker of Salem, who
was courting Sally Bradford of State Street by mail, wrote her:

> The failure of your swashbuckling General, who lives in that mon-
> strous great house, has given rise to much talk and conjecture; in
> consequence your Bristol money has been refused in this quarter.
> I was not surprised in the least, for when I was in Bristol, sweet
> one, I was informed that he was trading contraband on borrowed
> capital. This, with the failure of Mr. Williams in London, engrosses
> all the tongues of Salem.

The check for $350 which the General had given Captain Hatch
was refused by Guiteras, Morland & Co. in Havana. Two days before
Hatch presented it for payment, said the cashier, "the General had
driven to his coffee estate called Noah's Ark, without leaving funds."

Isaac Clapp, who should not have let the General escape in the
first place, wrote to Farmer John from Boston:

> It is impossible to look at Gen. deWolf's affairs without the most
> overwhelming regret. I am entirely at a loss how to proceed, except
> to suggest that his creditors delay pressing their claims for the
> twelvemonth to come.

But no one was able to wait. The General owed money to almost
everyone in town except his two cautious uncles James and John.
Even Captain Jim found that his gullible son Gentleman James had
raised a quarter-million from the New York banks on the prospect
of his inheritance, and entrusted it to the General. All he could
salvage was the ship *Anne*, which happened to be lying in New York.
He attached her before the receivers had time to do so, and turned
her over to his own creditors. Major William lost $50,000, but was
able to take over the Poppasquash house to help his son Henry,
who had lost even more. Henry was a man of honor, even though
he had traded in slaves; he passed his remaining days in poverty,
in order to repay his friends the losses they had suffered from his
advice. His wife even found it in her heart to forgive the General,
saying that he had only tried to bring back good times to the village.

Bristol faced complete ruin. The five banks in town lost $210,000,
which was about half their capital. Isaac Manchester lost $80,000,

his horse, his carriage, and his farm, when the General's own bank, which itself was almost ruined, foreclosed his mortgage. He spent the rest of his life peddling clams. Old salts like Timothy Coggeshall and Captain George Munro hired themselves out as farmhands, with no wages but the crops they might grow in their spare time, and the produce of their dunghill hens. For a month the currency of the Mount Hope Bank was refused, even in the Bristol stores. Captain Jim, the main stockholder, was personally liable for its banknotes, and finally had to sell enough of his out-of-town assets to redeem them all in gold. The General had mortgaged the Mansion to the Commercial Bank for $5,000—it is strange that he could borrow no more on a house that cost $60,000. The Commercial foreclosed, and Captain Jim bought it in for a hundred dollars over the mortgage. (Two years later he sold it to his son William Henry for $8,000, which was low enough to earn William Henry's gratitude, and high enough to teach him that a deWolf ought always to turn a profit.)

Colonel Nicholas Peck carried away ten tons of hay, worth four dollars apiece, from the General's barn; they were all he could find that others had not found first. He had to accept $2000 from his sons and let his wife sell her jewels. The Pecks had aspired to rival the Great Folks; their only consolation was that the Great Folks were suddenly a good deal smaller. The General had given Bishop Griswold a bad check for $100; from Cuba, he promised to make good in coffee; but the coffee never came.

Whole families left town. Henry deWolf's son Bill struck out for Fort Dearborn in Illinois, which is now Chicago. He lived to become one of its first citizens. George Coggeshall drove a team to Michigan and founded the town which is now Grand Rapids. The western migration, which drained other New England towns slowly, struck Bristol all at once. The fortune which John Smith had made from his quarter-share in the *Yankee* vanished overnight. He had endorsed the General's note for $10,000. To escape payment, he fled to Hartford, his wife's home town, taking his daughter Mary and his young sons George and Compton—the heroes of the *General*

Padilla. Hartford seemed like a safe place, being seventy miles from Bristol by the miry stagecoach road. But Farmer John, anxious to recover every asset, heard of the hiding place and warned the Hartford sheriff. Smith was thrown into jail for the General's debts. He was an old man now, and might have languished there till his death, but his wife somehow sprung him from jail and sailed him down the Connecticut River to safety in her father's sloop. I wish that Compton had described the escape, for it is recorded that Smith sat in the stern smoking his pipe, with his stovepipe hat on his head—it was the tallest in Bristol—and thumbed his nose at the jail as his wife handled the tiller. In the flush days, he had bought a quarter share in Don José Wilson's plantation at Camarioca. He headed for Cuba now, and built an *estancia* next door to his old skipper's. He dunned the General unremittingly—Noah's Ark was only a hundred miles from Camarioca—but the most he got was a marriage between his daughter Mary and the General's scalawag son Buckmaster. A poor bargain it was, though he would have been proud of the alliance in other days.

General George remained unassailable at Noah's Ark. Creditors from New York, Boston, and Bristol itself tried to attach the plantation, but since it was in a foreign country, it lay beyond their reach. Although his own widowed mother lived in destitution at home, the General needed to keep all he could, for he had a large family with expensive tastes.

For seventy-five years after the mainland colonies had revolted against Spain, Cuba called itself "The Faithful Isle"—*la Isla siempre fiel.* It is seven hundred miles from tip to tip. The colony of Bristol expatriates was scattered in coffee and sugar plantations each side of Havana. Captain Jim's Mariana and Mount Hope estates lay near each other west of the capital; his son Don Marcos inspected them on a yearly trip from home, and even married the daughter of a neighboring planter named Chappotin. The Esperanza, most remote of all, lay a hundred and fifty miles east, outside Cardenas; it was managed by George Howe, Captain Jim's nephew. Outside Matanzas Don José had long been established at San

Juan de Camarioca; when his daughter married the son of Captain Sabens of the slaver *Charlotte,* the whole Sabens family moved in too. John Smith's plantation lay next door. William Fales of Bristol, once skipper of the General's slaver *Little Ann,* lived in Matanzas itself. The colony was far from saintly: Sabens and Smith were accused of signaling to pirates and showing false lights to passing ships in order to wreck and loot them. Don José's daughter lived as "housekeeper" with the American Consul, Lewis Shoemaker, and Shoemaker himself, as late as 1831, connived at the escape of a Baltimore slaver named the *Pen.* As many as two hundred American vessels put in each week to Havana, and a dozen to Matanzas. Some of them had once belonged to the General, but their captains never came to call at Noah's Ark.

The General was not the man to mind their contempt. He and his wife were favorites of Don Francisco Dionisio Vives, the Royal Governor and Captain-General of the island, and of those Americans who did not know Bristol. In the early 1830s, when the highborn Quincy sisters of Boston visited Cuba, he went to call at their hotel, "in an elegant volante, and proved to be the soul of wit." Noah's Ark lay on the waistline of Cuba, where the north coast is only twenty-five miles from the south. The present highway from Havana to Pinar del Río passes near its ruins. Its walls were three feet thick, built of stone and plastered, with portholes for defense. From his patio he could walk in half an hour to his landing dock on the Gulf of Batabanó, well hidden from the sea-lanes; and on clear days he could see the Isle of Pines in the distance. The plantation was a pleasant place to spend an exile. The *Noticioso* was delivered daily, in time for a late breakfast, from Havana, forty miles to the northeast. Slaves were openly advertised for sale at the nearby markets of Artemisa and Candelaria.

The General sent his daughters Theodora and Charlotte to be "finished" in the United States, where they found American husbands of their own station. In 1833 his brother Charles, Junior, who had been his assignee, himself went broke in Bristol, and fled to join the family at Noah's Ark. It will be remembered that Mrs. George and

Mrs. Charles were sisters. In the loneliness of the Cuban exile, General George's last daughter married Charles' son. The young couple were double first cousins; they had only four grandparents between them instead of the usual eight. No children were born of this marriage.

The General grew homesick, as exiled Bristolians do. In 1844 Charlotte and he returned to the mainland. Incognito, they visited Saratoga and Niagara Falls. At Niagara they were seen by Don José Wilson, who had somehow found means to leave Cuba and tour the spas himself. He wrote to 'Fessor John in Bristol:

> I have recognized Gen. deWolf and his lady killing time at Niagara Falls, under false names. No communication passed between us, nor have I apprized the authorities of this delightful watering-place. This news is for your eyes alone.

Bristol was the one place where the General, no matter how artful his disguise, would be in danger. There is a legend in town, so stubborn that it must have some truth, that he rode into Bristol by Chadwick's stage *Napoleon*, with dark glasses on his eyes and a false beard on his chin. He hid out in the grass-covered mausoleum of his uncle Captain Jim, which Dickinson had blasted open two years before. No one would have suspected it as a hiding place, nor been likely to search it if he had. It lay only a stone's throw across Tanyard Lane from the Mount. Braddy deWolf, who had inherited the Mount from Captain Jim, had a wife as soft-hearted as himself. The tradition has it that General George, his hair as white and wild as King Lear's, his nose almost meeting his chin like the halves of a pair of scissors—he was an old man of sixty-five by now—rapped at his cousin's windowpane one night, as they were playing a duet in the Paul and Virginia room. He did not ask for shelter—indeed it was a sort of triumph over Captain Jim to sleep in his tomb—but he begged for a little food, for he dared not enter town to buy it. And that for a few days, while he remained their unwelcome guest, Polydore carried a silver-covered dinner-dish and a bottle of wine each day across the lane to the graveyard. And that Braddy, to get rid of him, sent him to Boston in his own chaise, with Polydore on the box and the blinds drawn, and put a check into his hand for passage on the next packet back to Cuba.

Whether the legend is true or not, General George deWolf died on June 7, 1844, in Dedham, Massachusetts, just short of Boston, at the inn where the stage changed horses. For twenty years more, none of his children set foot in Bristol.

Attempts to run slaves continued occasionally up to the start of the Civil War. At that late date, nobody but the most desperate was foolhardy enough to take the risk, and no such adventurers were left in Bristol. But in 1857 the *Wanderer*, owned by a fire-eater named Charles Lamar of Savannah, made two round trips to the Slave Coast, carrying six hundred Negroes 'tween decks under the most inhuman conditions. She was a 260-ton yacht, much resembling the famous yacht *America*. W. C. Corrie, her captain, was a member of the New York Yacht Club. On his second voyage he fell in with a British cruiser whose mission was to stamp out the remnants of the trade. Corrie promptly ran up the Club's ensign, and invited the British officers aboard for dinner. Over the very heads of his cargo, he responded to the toasts of the British captain in a speech, said the newspapers, "of considerable ability and impudence." It is impossible that his guests did not hear or smell the cargo beneath their feet. When the news reached New York, Corrie was expelled from the Club.

Although the trade had been a capital offense since 1820, only one man was ever hanged for it. He was a native of Portland, Maine, named Nathaniel Gordon. Aboard his ship *Erie*, of 476 tons, he was caught in 1861 off the Congo River by the USS *Mohican*, a steam sloop-of-war. He had the incredible number of 987 slaves stapled below. By that time, slaves brought as much as $1750 a head in the blockaded Confederacy. The *Mohican* took her into Monrovia, the capital of the young republic of Liberia. Three hundred of her cargo died before they could be unshackled. Gordon was returned in irons to New York, where he was tried and convicted. In spite of strong pressures, President Lincoln refused to reprieve him. He was hanged at the Tombs on February 21, 1862. Captain Jim and General George would have chuckled to know that the *Erie* had been built, many years before, by their old friend Caleb Carr in Warren.

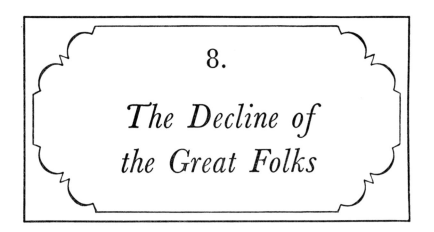

8.

The Decline of the Great Folks

AFTER General George's flight in 1825, none of his creditors was left with capital enough to maintain the fleet which he abandoned, nor to build the steamers which were fast supplanting sail. Oddly enough, the only family who lost nothing were the Usher brothers, grandsons of the missionary and cousins of Sammy. They had kept their specie at home instead of trusting it to the banks. They were able to buy up some of the General's fleet at bargain prices, and founded a general trade which outlasted all the deWolf shipowners. Until 1872 they were in business, buying any produce that was offered them. What the rust and smut don't take, the proverb went, the Ushers will.

Other New England seaports declined gradually, but the collapse of Bristol was instantaneous. George Munro and William Norris, two Gentlemen of the Long Wharf whom the General had bilked, opened a subscription book for a community restoration fund to be paid to them, as trustees, within a year. This was their prospectus:

> The unprosperous and decaying condition of the town of Bristol is seen and daily lamented by all its Citizens; and it is now time to ask and answer the question whether the place of our nativity shall be suffered to sink into decay and ruin, or whether we shall by some common effort attempt its resuscitation. The means are in

our power, and notwithstanding the miserable waste of capital we have lately experienced, there is something left; and we have men among us whose skill in business, whose habits of Industry and Economy abundantly qualify them for the management of Capital, and in whose hands it would be sure (if anything on Earth is sure) to be productive. We therefore, the undersigned, do hereby agree to invest the sums by us subscribed for the purpose of transacting such business as may be deemed most for the Interest of those concerned.

Nineteen men of the town responded. In sums from $500 to $3000 they risked all they had left. They were humble men, descended from the families who had settled the town long before Mark Antony deWolf had come from Guadeloupe: Church, Wardwell, Munro, and Tilley. They were farmers, shopkeepers, and sea-captains. There was not a slaver or privateersman among them. Captain Jim deWolf and Farmer John, who, having suspected the General in time, were still rich, did not subscribe. The only one of the Great Folks who did was the quixotic 'Fessor John. Teamwork comes hard to Yankees. It came especially hard to the frightened survivors of General George's fall. The committee raised only $26,000, which was a mere twentieth of the General's debts. The scheme to lift the village by its bootstraps failed, the subscribers' pledges were returned and the town, ruined by the General, sank into a torpor which lasted half a century.

Privateering and the slave trade had spoiled the village. The very isolation which had sheltered the outlaws became a hindrance to normal commerce. The opening of the Erie Canal in 1825 drew foreign shipping to New York at the expense of the outlying seaports; the Tariff Act of 1828 abolished the drawback on rum, which could now be distilled more cheaply in Cuba than in New England; and the watercourses of Massachusetts, within easy reach of Boston, were a cheap source of power for the wheels of cotton mills. The shallower ports could not handle vessels of deep draft. Bristol was left stranded on her peninsula. The forces which ruined the trade of such towns as Salem and Newport affected Bristol too; the General's failure only made the decline more sudden and more painful. The bankrupt Colonel Nicholas Peck wrote to his sons, "There is no heart left in us at all," and the gloomy blacksmith William P. Munro spoke for the town's conscience when, in 1832, he prophesied over his forge, "Bristol won't amount to beans till the nigger money is all gone."

For a time it seemed that Captain Jim deWolf's son William Henry, who had bought the General's mansion, might restore prosperity to the town. The one-tenth of his father's estate which he inherited in 1838 was a fortune in itself: a hundred acres on Poppasquash, one-sixth of the Kentucky lands, one-quarter of the ships and rigging, and one-quarter of the Cuban plantations.

In emulation of the Nantucket and New Bedford shipowners, he plunged into the booming whale fishery. The demand for whale-oil and sperm was inexhaustible, for they gave far better light than the old tallow candles. It was easy to convert a slaver into a whaler; the brick-based feed kettles made excellent trypots. The Reverend John Bristed * preached a sermon at Saint Michael's on the spiritual as-

---

* This divine, who succeeded Bishop Griswold, was no less extraordinary than his sainted predecessor. Born in England, he had practiced both law and medicine before taking orders. He was married to Magdalen, a daughter of John Jacob Astor the fur-trader, but was unable to live with her. Like her namesake in the Bible, he said, she was possessed of seven devils. She took up residence in New York, whither he traveled once a year by packet to dine with her. He was unable to endure heat. He always wore a sort of sport shirt, open at the neck. On the street he was followed by his servant Penny, armed with a turkey-feather fan, and before mounting the pulpit he sprinkled water on his wrists to cool himself out. In those days, each parishioner was expected to entertain the parson once a year at tea. Aaron Usher, newly impoverished, determined to spread him as good a table as any of the Great Folks. He killed his only pig and laid out all the butter, beans, and brown bread he could afford. After the costly feast, the minister thanked him. "Aaron, I'm glad to see how well you live."

Poor Aaron answered, "Mr. Bristed, if you want to see how we really live, come some time when you aren't here."

He could write such simple eloquence as this Easter invitation to Mrs. William Dimond:

Dear Madam: It is the delight of my heart to welcome those whom their heavenly Father invites to His own house and banquet. Your presence at the Communion on the approaching anniversary of His resurrection will gratify

Yours truly and respectfully,
John Bristed

His epitaph reads:
The affluent he attracted by his courtesy,
The poor by his benevolence,
And blessed all by the light of his example.

pects of the new industry, taking for his text II Kings, 5:7: "Go sell
the oil, pay thy debt, and live, thou and thy children, of the rest."
In the course of it he declaimed this verse, which may be parody or
poesy or piety, or a little of each:

> Ye monsters of the briny deep,
> Your Master's praises shout;
> Up from the waves, ye whalelets, peep
> And wag your tails about.

In 1838 the whaling fleet of Bristol, which had a population of
three thousand (it had declined since the General fled) numbered
nineteen vessels, most of them converted slavers and privateers. Nantucket, with six thousand inhabitants, sent out eighty-eight, and New
Bedford, with eight thousand, sent out more than three hundred.

William Henry set up a factory on the waterfront to convert the
expected oil into candles. The *Canton Packet*, owned by Nathaniel
Coggeshall, on a two-year cruise which carried her from Greenland
to the Indian Ocean, took 32,000 gallons of whale oil, 3000 of sperm,
and all the whalebone her hold would carry. The whale oil, tried out
from the carcass of the right whale, was worth 40 cents a gallon; the
sperm, from a cavity in the head of the sperm whale, was worth 90
cents (it burned with less smoke), and the bone, used for buttons
and corsets, brought 21 cents a pound. William Henry's own ship the
Governor Hopkins, in a single "plum pudding" cruise of a year, took
70,000 gallons of oil, and could have taken more if she had had room
for it. But the expenses of the voyage, even though more than half
her company were ill-paid Portuguese from the Azores, ate up her
profits. The average investment in a whaler was $28,000, and there
were few merchants in the prostrate village who could afford to
gamble such an amount for the uncertain and long-delayed profits
of a voyage. Whaling was a dirty business too. The generation of seamen used to the scrubbed decks of a privateer, or even a slaver, were
too squeamish for the grease of a whaler. In *Two Years Before the
Mast* Dana writes that "a thorough sailor despises whalers, and will
always steer clear of them if he can." The owners often paid no wages,

offering instead shares in the profits, if any; many whalemen were not sailors at all, but farmboys lured aboard by the chance of a rich catch or a find of ambergris.

The industry died a quiet death anyway, in the mid-forties, when gaslight and kerosene were discovered. Like the whalemen of New Bedford and Nantucket, the Bristol crews found work ashore. Some hired out to the steam-powered mills which began to supplant the distilleries of slaving days—a cotton mill, a sugar refinery, a rubber factory—and more, who could not endure confinement, in the onion fields. There were half a dozen old men at the end of the century who used to trudge to the outlying farm-lots with hoes over their shoulders; they were the stranded survivors of the whale fishery. They were proud. Though they had little heart for the fishery in their youth, they boasted of it in their old age. One of them was Viets Peck, the colonel's youngest son. In 1907 he took a ride in the first automobile seen in Bristol, bowling down Hope Street at fifteen miles an hour.

"Well, Captain Peck," the driver said to him, "I bet you've never been this fast before."

"Hell, young man," he called back through his beard, "I've gone faster behind a whale."

No new ships were built, and one by one the old fleet was sold, or foundered. At the time of the California gold rush in 1849, several aged Bristol vessels made their last voyages by ferrying treasure-seekers around Cape Horn to the West Coast. But the converted slavers had too little bulk for profitable whaling, and were not fast enough to compete with the Boston-built clippers of Donald McKay and Samuel Hall. Few forty-niners were patient enough to waste six months on a trip which they could make in three by clipper. The ship *Anne*, 220 tons, was one such vessel. General George had built her for the slave trade in 1807, during the time of Charleston's open port. Sam Norris, his neighbor, took her over for debt at the bankruptcy in 1825. He plied her in the coastwise trade, with indifferent success, and then sent her on two unprofitable whaling voyages in the 1840s. In 1849 she made one paying voyage round the Horn with a score of

Bristol bachelors who hoped to make their fortunes in the gold-fields, but when the fever began to subside, Norris surrendered her registration to the Collector of San Francisco, and left her to rot on the shoals of the Back Bay. He would have broken her up, but the cost of taking her apart was more than her salvage value. Whale oil seemed to have preserved her timbers. She lay keeled over for many years, with her name and hailing-port barely visible above the mud, until she finally fell apart. The old ships were almost indestructible, even when they were no longer seaworthy. Norris gave up the sea altogether, and became a traveling salesman for the Remington Arms Company, peddling rifles to the armies of Europe.

Though William Henry deWolf was the most promising of Captain Jim's sons—more likable than the arrogant Gentleman Jim or the glacial Don Marcos, and more energetic than the easy-going Braddy —he had no head for business. His inheritance began to vanish almost as soon as he touched it. He was too fond of rum and madeira to be much good at anything but hospitality. On Guy Fawkes Day, November 5, he would treat the whole village to a bonfire (it was called a burn-fire then) in the front yard of the Mansion, and himself touch off the effigy of the Pope. The flames often threatened the Norris house on one side of him and Chadwick's stable on the other. He was forever borrowing wineglasses from the Leonard Bradfords up State Street, though he seldom asked them to his parties. When he returned the stemware, which was not often, half of it would be broken off at the base. When President Jackson, dressed in a black suit and a white beaver draped in a mourning "weed," visited him in the summer of 1833, he brought out the silver pitcher and basin which General George had ordered for Monroe's visit in 1817. (He had bought them in from the widow of the *Orozimbo*'s captain, who had seized them for debt at the bankruptcy.) Another of his hospitalities was to treat his guests to the newfangled sport of sea-bathing, at Daniel Waldron's bathhouses at the foot of Constitution Street. Another was to sail them across the bay to Rocky Point for a clambake— and it is worth recording, as a footnote to history, that the clambake had been invented by a Bristol schoolteacher named Otis Storrs in 1825.

As inventions should be, it was the child of necessity. The *Phoenix* describes the occasion thus:

> He conceived the idea of taking his pupils across Narragansett Bay on an excursion. Some of the parents objected, but Mr. Storrs convinced them that no harm would come to the morals of the children. They sailed from Deacon Orem Spencer's dock, which he used for a wood-market. They crossed the bay on the good sloop *William Allen,* and anchored off Rocky Point, which was then a barren shore. After they had landed in boats, he discovered that he had neglected to provide any refreshment, so he concluded to make do with what the bounty of nature provided. He set the larger boys to kindling a fire of driftwood in the crevice of a large rock, heating some of the stones which abounded on the beach, and covering them with damp rockweed. The shore yielded clams in quantity, and the fish were eager for bait. Over it all Schoolmaster Storrs spread the *William Allen's* hatch-cover. The girls strolled round the fields, plucking fruit and berries, which were found in great abundance. The dinner was eaten with the fingers, amid great hilarity. All had enough and good enough, with plenty to spare. About five o'clock the company embarked for home, bursting spontaneously into hymns and popular ditties. Just as the sun was declining in the west, they landed on the wharf whence they had started. The experiment of a *clam-bake* was a success.

With part of his inheritance, William Henry even enlarged the Mansion. He had Russell Warren, by now an old man, add a Gothic library at one corner, and a ballroom at the other. The new ballroom was the start of his downfall. In 1844, when his youngest daughter Rosalie was eighteen, he engaged the Knickerbocker Ethiopians for the grand opening. These minstrels were not Ethiopians at all, but a group of New York bluebloods who traveled the country in blackface for the joy of amusing other gentlemen and their ladies. On stage they wore red-and-white-striped pants, curl-brimmed steeple hats, choke collars, tail coats, weskits, and fobs. Their repertoire consisted of songs, glees, choruses, and comic lectures, accompanied on the accordion, banjo, congo, tambo, and bone castanets. One of the minstrels was a curly-haired banjoist named John Hopper. At dinner before the minstrel-show, Rosalie sat beside him. They fell in love over her father's terrapin and champagne. Rosalie wore a high tortoise-shell comb at the back of her hair, and pantalettes peeped below the hem of her skirt. She had black ringlets hanging clear of her cheeks, and the slimmest waist in Bristol: Hopper bet he could circle it with his two hands. She blushed, but did not forbid him. He told her that his father was a solemn old Quaker lawyer in New York, which was glamour enough for a girl who had never been outside of Bristol. When the show began, she could not take her dark eyes off him; and his, across the row of shaded footlights, rolled at her from his cork-blacked face while he strummed the banjo to the tune of "The Old Arm Chair." Before the troupe left town next morning in Chadwick's stage, they had set a day for his return: not to the Mansion, for her father would never let her marry a minstrel, no matter how well born, but to the bridge at the north entrance to town, over Silver Creek. Her uncle and aunt Perry lived beside the bridge.

Mrs. Sam Norris, wife of the sea-captain, was a romantic lady. Rosalie confided to her that she planned to elope with John Hopper, and Mrs. Sam agreed to help. The day of the tryst, snow fell all afternoon. Rosalie smuggled her portmanteau across to the Norris stable. That evening, after tea, she told her parents that Mrs. Norris was driving her up to Silver Creek to visit with the Perrys.

"Well," said William Henry, "I shouldn't care to visit with them myself, but I know things are dull in Bristol for a pretty girl, so run along and come home early."

She threw a cloak over her shoulders and tied her bonnet, with the pleats well forward, on her head. But no sooner had her pattens clattered down the sandstone steps than he grew suspicious. Outside it was still snowing hard. It struck him that this was no night a girl would choose to call on her elderly relations. Calling out his own chaise, he drove after Mrs. Norris. He reached the bridge just in time to see Rosalie transferring to Hopper's, with her portmanteau already aboard. He lunged at Hopper through the snowflakes, but was a few seconds too late to head off the elopement. What he did to Mrs. Norris, history does not relate.

For a while the escape broke his heart, but he mended it with madeira. When Rosalie bore a son, and named him deWolf Hopper, after himself, he relented a little. Old Lawyer Hopper had been delighted with the marriage from the start. When little deWolf was still a baby, he would snatch him up from the carpet, stark naked, and swing him out the window by the heels, calling out to passersby on Broadway, "See what a fine grandson I've got."

William Henry tried to keep his other daughters locked up, with no more success. Mary ran off with a Dr. John Wheeler. Sarah Ann eloped with George Gardner, and Madeline with Benjamin Smith, both on the same night. Years later, Sarah Ann's daughter Nellie Gardner married her first cousin deWolf Hopper—both of them William Henry's grandchildren—but cousinly marriages were so common among the Great Folks that genealogists hardly noticed one more. DeWolf Hopper became a famous comedian, and had several subsequent wives. They said of him in Bristol, "To know him is to marry him."

After the four elopements, William Henry went downhill fast. His inheritance was all gone by 1847, nine years after he had received it. The townspeople were not surprised when he sold his one remaining whaler, the *Corinthian*. (She was one of the fastest sailers ever to hail from Bristol. In a smart breeze, she could make 15 knots. She was so deep that her keel, they say, stirred up the mud of Bristol harbor all the way out to deep water.)

The troubles of the Great Folks always interested, and often delighted, their neighbors. John Andrews of Bristol wrote that year to a friend:

> William Henry deWolf has busted up and made an assignment. He owes everybody, à la George deWolf. He has lately started for Matanzas in company with Miss Guess, for the estates of the family in the island of Cuba, leaving his wife behind. His brother Don Marcos is the same as ever, lording it in his temple on Poppasquash. One of his sons is studying the law, the other cultivating his mechanical genius. Race ginger now sells at 7¢ a pound.

Most of the deWolf wives have been more tenacious than their husbands. William Henry's wife, whose maiden name was Sarah Ann Rogers, was heroic. Before he fled, he had transferred the Mansion to her sole ownership, to save it from his creditors. She promptly mortgaged it for enough to pay his most pressing debts, and called him back from Cuba. She forgave Miss Guess for stealing her husband, and that must have been specially hard, for she lived on the opposite side of the Mansion from Mrs. Norris, who had helped her daughter elope.

William Henry might have ended his days in the stone poorhouse on Mill Gut, as Captain Jim had prophesied some of his sons surely would, if the Democrats had not won the election of 1852. President Pierce appointed him consul at Dundee, Scotland, in the same batch of nominations that made Nathaniel Hawthorne consul at Liverpool. William Henry had no visible qualifications for the post, except that he was an indigent Democrat. (Hawthorne had the same qualification, along with others.) He set out from the Mansion to take the packet from New York, confident that his future was secure at last. But he was taken sick before the packet had cleared the Narrows. She put back to New York, and he died in the arms of John Hopper, his minstrel son-in-law.

His widow survived him for twelve years. She sold off her horse and chaise to Nathan Warren, the expressman—he had bought the Wardwell Street stable on John Chadwick's death—and rented him her empty carriage-house. She locked up the drawing room where she had entertained President Jackson, and lived by herself in the kitchen. She rented the octagon library to Dan Tanner, the Negro barber. (Tanner always boasted that his razors were keen enough for any beard in town except that of Nehemiah Cole, the teamster; on him, he had to use a hacksaw first.) Every time she came in at her Palladian door, she had to pass the placard he had affixed to the iron fence:

> When you wish an easy shave,
> As good as barber ever gave,
> Just call on me at my saloon,

At morn or eve or busy noon.
I comb and dress the hair with grace
To suit the countenance of your face;
My room is neat, my towels are clean,
Scissors sharp and razors keen.
All that art and skill can do,
If you will call, I'll do for you.

The Bristol Female Charitable Society helped her surreptitiously. Each New Year's Eve, Minister Bristed at Saint Michael's and Parson Shepard at the Congregational church held a joint service. It was well known, though never admitted, that the collection went to keep the widow deWolf alive. Her brothers- and sisters-in-law at the Mount, those of them who had not left town with their legacies, kept her in pork and firewood, but long before she died they were all as poor as she.

When the railroad from Providence reached town in 1855, the stage line was forced out of business, and Warren could no longer afford to rent her carriage-house. To keep the property at all, she had to rent the Mansion itself. That June, under a grandiose stereotype, the *Phoenix* carried this announcement:

> Wm. Vars and Son, the subscribers, having leased the well-known mansion built by the late Gen. George deWolf and occupied by the late Wm. Henry deWolf, have entirely refitted the same, and added 25 lodging-rooms and an elegant banquet-hall.

This addition was a ramshackle three stories built over the rose-garden behind the house. For ten more years the Mansion, which was the pride of Bristol then as it is now, was a boarding house. Vars fitted it with gaslight. The onion-buyers, hair-goods salesmen, shipping agents, and the few Cuban visitors who still, as in busier days, spent their summers in Bristol, rocked out the evening on the sandstone portico with segars between their teeth, and then ascended General George's spiral staircase to bed. Subscription hops, at twenty-five cents a head, were held each Saturday in the ballroom where John Hopper had made eyes at Rosalie deWolf. On Guy Fawkes Day, Vars, to keep up William Henry's tradition, entertained the town with a free bonfire in the front yard. His family occupied three of the four bedrooms at the front of the house, and his servants lodged in the General's old slave quarters at the side. The fourth bedroom Sarah Ann kept for herself. It is said that she cooked all her meals over the fireplace, never went outdoors except to church on Sunday, and never spoke to Vars, his son, or his boarders. The townspeople admired her pride. Although she was one of the Great Folks, her poverty made her akin to themselves.

II

The years of the Civil War were the bleakest in the town's history, except for those between the bombardment of 1775 and the lifting of the British blockade in 1779. Although the population had almost doubled since General George's flight, the tonnage registered to the port was less, and not a single ship had been built or fitted out in town since 1856. Of the 5276 inhabitants listed in the 1860 census, 594 were of Irish birth, mostly families who had left Ireland to escape the potato famine, and now lived, almost as poor as they had been in the old country, as farmhands, servants, millhands, and coachmen. There were sixteen residents of Portuguese birth, mainly sailors picked up by the whalemen at the Atlantic islands, and now subsisting on their truck gardens. There was not a single Italian. There were thirty-three inhabitants named deWolf, seven of whom were colored. (In 1820, out of three thousand, there had been seventy-two white deWolfs and eleven colored.) From the harbor, the town looked about the same as it had in the General's day—the brick counting-houses, Captain Jim's granite warehouse, the spires of Saint Michael's and the Congregational church, the smaller houses and the half-dozen large ones which Russell Warren had built for the slave-trading deWolfs. Larger even than the churches, and burdened with taxes, they dominated the harbor from Don Marcos' and Major William's on Poppasquash to the Mount on Fox Hill, with General George's Mansion in the center of town. Everyone was poor, except Robert Rogers, Major William's son-in-law. Few ships rode at anchor, and most of the houses needed paint. The only new building on the waterfront was the arched-roof railroad station. Most of the new inhabitants lived wretchedly behind the town, on land which had been pasturage half a century before. It seemed that the time of William Munro's prophecy had arrived, for the slave money was all gone. Three hundred and seven youths of Bristol—eleven of them deWolfs —fought to liberate the race which their own fathers and grandfathers had enslaved, and twenty-three of them did not return.

Bristol's best-known hero of the Civil War was General Ambrose E. Burnside, whose whiskers have done more than his victories to preserve his memory. In the Town Hall which is named for him, his life-size portrait, in full uniform, gazes down on the staircase, with his plumage spread out from his chubby cheeks like a pouter pigeon's. Miss Maria Norris, the daughter of Captain Sam, was kissed by the general when she was young, and reported that his whiskers tickled. (She was also kissed by Napoleon III, and said that his actually *stung*.) Burnside was not a native of the town. When he moved there, he was a retired lieutenant-colonel who had seen no active service since the Mexican War. In 1856, when the voters elected him Surveyor of Highways, he was still a young man. In the words of the *Phoenix*, "He had a fine face, dark side-whiskers and a bearing of exceptional grace and dignity."

The highways, of course, were unpaved, and remained so until well into the twentieth century. The Surveyor's duty was to hire ox-teams to dump rock into the worst ruts and wait until it sank deep enough to require a new layer. During his leisure hours, in the barn behind his brick house on Hope Street, Burnside invented a breech-loading carbine, for which he received a patent. He formed the Bristol Fire Arms Company to manufacture it, using an empty shed for a factory and the harbor itself for a proving-ground. Captain Nat Herreshoff the boatbuilder, as a boy, watched him testing his weapon by firing at the striped buoy which marks the Middleground Shoal—"always missing," he reports, "but *ever coming nearer*."

When news of the bombardment of Fort Sumter reached Bristol, Burnside sprang to active duty in command of the First Rhode Island Volunteers. This regiment included a famous cavalry unit called the

"Trotting Twelfth," with which he shared the retreat from First Bull Run. Within a year he rose to Major General. For two months he commanded the Army of the Potomac. At Fredericksburg he made a frontal assault across the Rappahannock, even though President Lincoln rode out from Washington to dissuade him. In that worst defeat of the war, twelve thousand federal troops were lost. Lincoln rusticated him to the Department of the Ohio, but even there, way behind the lines, he got into trouble. Without a warrant, he arrested the copperhead Vallandigham, bringing down a storm of protest from the northern Democrats. He appears next before Petersburg, Virginia, where he dug a tunnel under the besieged city, loaded with enough mines to annihilate it. The explosion destroyed a six-gun Confederate battery; but storming the crater cost Burnside the loss of three thousand men, "like Shakespeare's 'enginer,'" gloated a Southern newspaper, "'hoist with his own petard.'" Two weeks later he received leave of absence, to await further orders. The war ended before they came. He returned to Bristol for good, with a sword of honor from the state and a vote of thanks from Congress.

He bought a farm on Ferry Road (it is now the site of the Nike) and built a house with a two-story living room surrounded by cubicles where his guests could sleep off the effects of his clambakes. Robert Holloway, the Negro orderly whom he brought back from his campaigns, looked after his needs. General Burnside became governor of Rhode Island and then United States Senator. President Grant visited him in 1875. After the formality of a call at the Mansion, he returned to Burnside's farm for the greatest bake in the town's history. It lasted from noon till midnight. Years afterward, Robert displayed with pride the cubicle where the President of the United States had sobered up.

The General, in retirement, drove a black horse named Dick, who lived to be thirty. Dick's only bad habit was to switch his tail over the reins, so as to loose his master's grip, and then bolt home to his oats. To correct it, the general erected a wire cage over the shafts, high enough so Dick could flick flies with his tail, but just low enough to clear the reins. It was an invention worthy of a Herreshoff. He took the cars to Providence three times a week. If Robert was late with his breakfast, or Dick refused to back into the shafts, he would telephone the Franklin Street depot (the telephone reached town in 1877) to hold the train for him. It was a distinction to have the train held, and still more to have a telephone. Telephones cost forty dollars a year. For that price, you could talk as often and as far and as long as you wanted to.

Another of Bristol's heroes, and a more bloodthirsty one, was Raymond Perry, a great-grandson of Captain Jim deWolf. He was born at Silver Creek, by the North Bridge, in the old house where Deacon Bosworth had held meeting in 1680 and from which Rosalie deWolf eloped in 1844. When he was three, he bridled a rooster and rode it around the barnyard till it dropped dead under him. At thirteen, he climbed out of bed one night, packed a shirt in his bandanna, and started for the Mexican War with his chum Leonard Bradford. His father caught him on Pump Lane, almost at Leonard's house. Raymond promised to stay home that year, if they would let him go to war next year. By then the war was over, so he made up for it by shipping aboard the Bristol schooner *Canvasback,* which hauled gold-seekers round the Horn to California. He returned across the Isthmus of Panamá on muleback; though the mule sank to its death in the mud, he met the *Canvasback* on the Atlantic side. On his second voyage he reached Canton. For amusement, he stationed himself on a bridge in the city, and cut off the queue of every citizen who tried to cross. It was a mortal insult to the Cantonese. Somehow escaping the mob which pursued him, he slipped into a temple and stole a gold statuette of Buddha—for a present to his mother in Bristol. The Chinese police placarded the city with red posters promising to boil the thief in oil if they found him, and they did find him, in his bunk aboard the *Canvasback.* Since he had painted his face yellow, to simulate the last stages of fever, they did not find the Buddha under his blanket. The ruse frightened the avengers long enough to let the schooner cast off.

Right after Fort Sumter, Raymond joined Colonel Ambrose E.

Burnside's regiment. That Bristol hero was too slow for him, so he switched to Sheridan's cavalry. Once he was left for dead on the battlefield, but revived. Once he forded the Potomac with 10 men to raid an outpost of the rebels, and came back with 125 of them. Because he had done it against orders, he was court-martialed. But success is a good lawyer; he was acquitted.

At the end of the war, Sheridan made him chief of the Galveston police. By now he was a major in the Army. Galveston had a sinful history almost as long as Bristol's. The carpetbaggers were looting the wharfs. When the carpetbag mayor offered Raymond a share in the plunder, Raymond threw him out the window. He shot two of the thieves at the wharf with his own pistol, and paraded their corpses through town on a wagon, as an example. That cleaned Galveston up for a while. When he was relieved of his office, the merchants of the city gave him a gold medal.

After that assignment, President Grant sent him as Consul to Santo Domingo. Down there, he found that American speculators were buying up land, and smuggling gold out of the country to debase the currency, in hopes that the United States would annex the island and raise the value of their real estate. General Ben Butler, the chief of carpetbaggers, warned him to keep quiet about what he saw, but Raymond went straight to the White House with his suspicions. He was prevented from seeing the President, who perhaps would have done nothing about them anyway. He resigned the consulship, taking the evidence back to Bristol with him. Butler sent two federal marshals after him, with a warrant for his arrest on the charge of murdering the Galveston looters.

Major Perry knew what they were after. He finished his milking while they waited. Then, pulling two pistols from his belt—he never milked without pistols—he asked them inside for a drink. One declined the invitation at once; the other went indoors with the major, who kept one of the pistols in his hand even as he poured out the whisky.

"Well, go ahead and arrest me," he said. "What's holding you up?"

The marshal never did arrest him. He jumped on his horse and followed the first one out of town, with Raymond laughing behind him.

Raymond Perry married twice. His first wife was a woman as stormy as himself. She was Fanny Blake Butler, who had had three husbands already. His God-fearing parents refused their blessings on the marriage, for they knew, as an old letter says, that she was a "cruel and wicked woman." He eloped with her anyway, and fell through the roof of her father's greenhouse in the process.

Cruel she was. She bore him a daughter who grew a beautiful crop of thick hair. Once, when the little girl got into the jampot, Fanny hung her out of the window for punishment, with the window-sash locked down on her curls.

Even when Fanny was borne to Captain Jim's deer-park graveyard, the Major did not lose his gusto. He fell in love with his pretty cousin Ellen deWolf, who was eighteen years younger than himself. But her mother fell in love with *him,* and broke up Ellen's romance by leading him to the altar herself. Raymond Perry was harnessed at last. He ended his days as a farmer on her estate. Instead of pistols, he carried lollipops in his pocket. The children loved him—his daughter and nieces and nephews—and begged for a ride when he drove to town, for he never failed to stop at Billy Briggs's little store on High Street for candy.

Unlike the Revolution and the War of 1812, the Civil War was fought far from the village. Except for the distant glamour of such heroes as Burnside and Perry, it left Bristol a dismal place, its population again declining, its commerce moribund, and its industry hardly born.

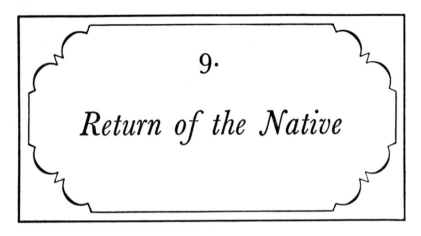

9.

Return of the Native

THE thrift of New Bedford built the Naumkeag Steam Cotton Mill on the ruins of the whale fishery, and the climate of Newport made it a matchless resort; but the tenacity of the deWolfs brought Bristol its second youth.

In 1865, at the end of the Civil War, Sarah Ann died. First as a bride and then as a widow, she had clung to the Mansion for thirty-seven years. The bank foreclosed at last, and it was sold at vendue. John Coy, the town crier, drummed the warning of the sale for two weeks ahead. W. H. S. Bayley, editor of the *Phoenix,* was the auctioneer. Though most of the village came to the sale at the foot of State Street (Pump Lane), he got only one respectable bid. Just as had been the case forty years before, there was no one in town who could afford to buy the Mansion, let alone maintain it. Vars, who had been running it as a rooming-house, dropped out at $6500. A young man with the unknown name of Colt then offered $7990—a small fraction of what it had cost the General to build, a little more than it had cost Captain Jim, $10 less than it had cost William Henry, and once more exactly $100 over the mortgage. Bayley slammed his gavel and struck it off to Edward Colt.

After the deed was signed, the village found out who he was, for he immediately transferred it to his mother. She had a name people did recognize. She was Theodora Goujaud deWolf Colt, no less than

General George's own daughter. As a child of five, in 1825, she had toddled after him into exile from the very house she now bought back. There was no one in town who had not heard of that night-flight. Some of the old-timers claimed to remember Theodora herself as a baby. Many who went past her iron fence on foot would have driven chaises except for the General. They felt that the Mansion belonged to the town—a feeling that still persists—and that he had tricked them all over again, though he had been dead a score of years, to reappear, so to speak, under a false name, and retrieve it for a fraction of what it had cost him to build.

Theodora was the widow of Christopher Colt, a brother of the Samuel who invented the revolver. She had met him, apparently, on the General's last surreptitious trip from Cuba, which had ended in his death. She had lived with her husband in Paterson, New Jersey, until he too had died, when she found, thanks to the success of the Colt revolver in the Civil War, that she had inherited enough to restore her father's house. With it, she resolved to restore his good name. She wrote to Bishop Mark Antony DeWolfe Howe, though she had not seen him since childhood, and was only his *second* cousin:

> I am human, dear Cousin Mark, *all too human,* and would not gloat over my *dear* cousins at Poppasquash and the Mount. Yet is it not just that Papa, after all the adversity and calumny of his life on earth, should, from his life in Heaven, know that his daughter redeems what rightfully was his? Perhaps it will take Bristol a little while, I do not say to *forgive* him, but to *understand* him. Meanwhile I do not forget our deWolf motto: He Conquers Who Endures.
> Your *affectionate* cousin
> Theodora Goujaud deWolf Colt

She had to face not only the resentment of the lesser townspeople but the reproof of her fellow Great Folks as well. She did not flinch. She succeeded in restoring an aristocracy in the village which ignored Newport, scorned Providence, and for half a century survived ridicule and calumny through its very self-approval. Its Bible was a genealogy of Mark Antony's descendants, compiled at her expense in 1900 by the Reverend Calbraith Perry, a great-grandson of Captain Jim. Her reign, and that of her children after her, covered roughly the Victorian and Edwardian eras. She herself was not unlike Queen Victoria, though a little more lively; and the son who succeeded her at the Mansion had the same zest for life as Edward VII.

Madam Colt, as she let herself be called, had dark hair, snapping eyes, a determined chin, and an amiability of iron. In her portrait, which hangs in the Colt Memorial High School, she wears a lace cap on her head and a lace mantilla from her shoulders to her bustle. Her hands are clasped about a fan, poised at the tip of her stomacher. Her face, enframed in earrings, may not be beautiful, but it is determined. "It was always *busy*," says one old-timer who remembers it.

Her son Edward died soon after he transferred the house to her, as if he had lived only for the restitution. In his place she made Francis deWolf her agent, and that was an artful gesture, for he was the son of William Henry and Sarah Ann.

"Thorough repairs," the *Phoenix* wrote, "are expected."

For $100 she sold off the crockery, spittoons, rocking chairs, and bedsheets which Vars had left behind. The lumber in his three-story annex at the back brought $400. She banished Dan Tanner's Tonsorial Saloon from the octagon. She bought up and demolished all the buildings on Wardwell Street, including Warren's stable and Burgess's Temperance House. She engaged the best mechanics in town for the restoration: James Freeborn to repair the carving, James Hoar to paint inside and out, and Geisler, the German blacksmith, to rebuild the iron fence and replace the broken glass in the lanterns over the gates. She installed a water-closet. She relaid the alley of marble from Hope Street to the portico, and planted lindens each side of it. When the work was finished she sent out cards to the other deWolfs, reading, with simple grandeur:

> ### Mrs. Colt
> Thursdays   Linden Place

She ordered salads of chicken and lobster, sherbets and champagne—delicacies not seen in the Mansion since the flush days of

William Henry—and hired George Easterbrooks to serve them in striped pants. She sat down each Thursday to await her guests. But the guests did not come; they sent their children instead. At Saint Michael's she sat humbly each Sunday in the hindmost pew. As early as 1868 she was giving *tableaux vivants* at Linden Place to raise money for a new organ. On the sidewalk, after service, she would greet the children whom she had feasted at Linden Place. She could never remember their names, or pretended she couldn't.

"Good morning, dear," she would say to each, "and which dear *are* you?" But the Great Folks themselves—and was she not one of them? —would smile at her and turn away without speaking. They remembered the Christmas of 1825.

Madam Colt had other troubles, but surmounted them all. Her sister, Charlotte Good, who lived with her, was a widow like herself, whose husband Edward had died on a Tuesday, years before. Charlotte believed that he would return on a Tuesday too, and spent that one day of each week at the Franklin Street depot waiting for him. One of the Colt boys eloped—was it a curse of the house? The two others were bright boys, and would make their way, but they both took a vulgar pleasure in shooting rats with a gang of disreputables called the Swamp Angels. Barry, the older, could talk like Cicero, but he was more convivial than Madam Colt thought right for his age. A glass of champagne gave him the voice of men and of angels. Pomeroy, the younger, she could see, would be a moneymaker. He sold papers on the morning cars to Providence, going and returning twice before noon, though he needn't have worked so hard, for his uncle the arms maker had left him $800,000. While Barry was convivial, Pomeroy was precociously amorous. She hired young Minister Locke of Saint Michael's to tutor them and then sent them both to college and on to law school. She took pride, as a descendant of Charles deWolf, that not one of the Jameses could boast a degree. Belle, her only daughter, did not do justice to her name; there were mockers in Horton's saloon who pronounced her name in two syllables.

Such trials Madam Colt learned to ignore, as she had learned to be ignored. She was devout. She read the Bible through each year, and knew the Book of Job by heart—Job, whose troubles were no greater than her own. Her greatest consolation lay in writing poetry. Her volume *Stray Fancies* (Boston, 1872) displays her aspirations and her learning. One poem lists the rulers of England:

> Ten sixty-six brought conquering Willy,
> Ten eighty-seven his Rufus Billy,
> In whose reign first Peter the Hermit
> Preached the Crusades without a permit.
> His brother Hal, who loved his ease,
> In eleven hundred King we see;
> But eating of too many eels,
> In thirty-five he ceased to be.

And so on until:

> In thirty-seven Victoria
> Took up the sceptre where it fell;
> O may she reign without a war
> And govern all her subjects well!

There is a ghoulish one beginning:

> Green and damp is the church on the heath;
> Greener and damper the people beneath.

And an ungrammatical one beginning:

> Dost remember the night, Annie,
> When the moon shone on high,
> And softly fell its rays, Annie,
> And kissed both you and I?

She distributed the volume among her fellow poets, and printed their acknowledgments as an appendix. Longfellow wrote her from Nahant:

Being interrupted by guests and the various distractions of a watering-place in summer, I have not yet had leisure to read your book carefully, but I have read enough in it to see the gentle and kindly spirit in which it is written, and to catch some of the playful fancies that flit along its pages.

Oliver Wendell Holmes mistook the author's sex:

Boston, Aug. 12, 1872

My dear Sir:

I was summoned here yesterday by a telegram announcing the death of a member of my family. I find the very handsome volume of poems, which I have looked over sufficiently to appreciate their playful tone and good spirit, but I cannot pretend to give a critical opinion of them.

With many thanks, dear Sir, I am,
In much haste, yours very truly,
Oliver Wendell Holmes

Gentle and kindly! Playful tone and good spirit! They were just the words she wanted to hear. From England came the stiff acknowledgment:

Mr. Alfred Tennyson begs to thank Mrs. deWolf Colt for her volume of poems, and for her kind words about himself.

The pious Whittier, whose Quaker conscience was his trademark, wrote her:

Dear Friend:

I thank thee for the gift of thy beautiful volume. I have not yet been able to read much of it, as my eyes trouble me, but I have been pleased with the tone and spirit of the pieces I have perused.

I am, most truly,
Thy obliged friend,
John G. Whittier

Her cousin Bishop Howe, to whom mercy was more precious than justice, wrote her:

You disclose more knowledge of men and things than falls to the lot of most ladies; and to weave such things into flowing verse is an ability which few of either sex possess.

There had never been a poetess in Bristol before—at least, not a printed poetess. The village capitulated and forgave General George because of his daughter's verses. On one of her Thursday afternoons, when her dining room, as usual, was crowded with children and no one else, a chaise stopped before Linden Place. Through the Brussels

window curtains, Madam Colt saw it; and so, next door, did old Mrs.
Norris. It was the chaise from the Mount. Out stepped sweet Mrs.
Bradford deWolf—Cousin Mary, as half the town called her. She was
poor, as all the Great Folks were now except Madam Colt herself,
but she was the arbiter of the town's society. The Mount coachman
tied his sorrel to the cast-iron hitching post and helped his mistress
up the walk of marble flagstones. Inside, Madam Colt hastily ordered
George Easterbrooks to set up a table for two in the drawing room,
away from the children, with a pint of champagne beside it in the
cooler. She ran halfway up the spiral stairs, and paused when the
bellpull tinkled. George opened the door. After a reasonable delay,
Madam Colt swept down the stairs again to greet her Cousin Mary.

After that, everything was easy. She moved up to the third pew in
Saint Michael's. Although the church was only two blocks from
Linden Place, she had Tom Downey, her coachman, drive her down
each Sunday with her children, for the unpaved sidewalks were foul
with the droppings of geese. She carried a black lace parasol over her
bonnet. Once, it is reported, she forgot to lower it when she entered
church, and swept up the aisle still holding it over her head. Her
clothes were said to come from the Maison Worth in Paris. She wore
a choker of real pearls. One Sunday she coughed so hard during the
sermon that it popped apart. The pearls rained like bullets on the
floor of three pews, and Minister Locke had to halt his sermon till
Bishop Howe's seven boys, who filled two pews of their own, had
retrieved them all.

Things like that were always happening in church. The Codman
sisters never arrived till the middle of the Psalms, and swept up the
aisle in cashmere shawls and feather bonnets that dated from before
the War. They never brought their offering to church, but made
Minister Locke call at their house for it, each of them giving him a
yellow-back that smelled of camphor. Somebody once set a prayer
book on Minnie Perry's bustle, and she balanced it there, all unconscious, until she turned to open the door of her pew. When Minister
Locke's daughter Mary once caught cold in the service, and made
him run down to the rectory for some Cherry Pectoral, the choir had

to sing the offertory three times over before he came back with it. The minister was unworldly to the point of folly. Walking up Church Street one day in the floppy hat and black Chesterfield which some of us remember, he was greeted with a cheerful "Hiya, Mr. Locke" by a man walking down.

The minister fumbled his pince-nez to his nose and said sternly, "George McGann, I buried you last week."

"No, sir; that was my brother Oliver. But I do favor him."

"Well," said the minister doubtfully, "I suppose you know best, but don't come back again."

Madam Colt regilded the tarnished glory of the Great Folks. She spent her winters at the Fifth Avenue Hotel in New York; most Bristol girls were lucky to get to New York once in their lives. She was rumored to be a close friend of Commodore Vanderbilt. Due to their friendship, it was said, the luxurious side-wheelers *Bristol* and *Empire State* docked twice a week at Franklin Street on their way from Fall River to New York. The steamboat *Bradford Durfee* stopped daily each way on her trip between Fall River and Providence. A steam ferry, supplanting the old horse-scow, plied across the channel to the Island. The Herreshoff family * operated the *Osprey*, a thirty-eight-ton carry-away boat to collect menhaden from the village fishermen and press it into guano, and in the eighties began to build the pleasure-schooners which have made their name famous to yachtsmen. The carrying trade ended in 1872, when the Ushers sold their onion fleet. The New York side-wheelers ceased calling in 1887, when the *Empire State* burned to the water's edge off Franklin Street, and Bristol ceased to be a port of entry in 1912. But while the Sound steamers lasted, they revived the hope that Bristol might become a great seaport again.

---

* Descended from the Prussian guardsman, they were the greatest geniuses in the town's history. Among other boons to humanity, they invented baking powder, anti-fouling paint, superheated steam engines, ankle-braces for skates, and the sliding seat for rowboats. In this generation, four of the seven were blind, but they could tell the speed of a boat by the feel of her hull-model, and pick up Block Island on the horizon ahead of anyone with two eyes. There was a saying in town, "You can't drown a Herreshoff"; they were almost amphibious.

Except perhaps for General Ambrose E. Burnside, Madam Colt was the town's most famous citizen. When President Grant visited Burnside in 1875, he did not neglect to call at Linden Place to wash up in General George's silver basin and ewer. (How they had survived the two bankruptcies is a miracle.) After Burnside died, President Arthur came to Bristol, in 1883, to dedicate a new town hall in his honor. This time Madam Colt had no rival. On a fine September morning, with the sou'wester blowing, he came up the bay from Newport on the revenue cutter. At the wharf he was greeted by Grand Marshal Samuel Norris, Madam Colt's neighbor; by Governor Bourn, who was a Bristol man too; and by her son Pomeroy, who served as colonel on the Governor's staff. The party stepped into the Colt landau for the drive to Linden Place. Tom Downey was on the box; the horses were decked with plumes of red, white and blue. Madam Colt awaited her guest on the portico of the Mansion. As the iron gates opened to admit him, twenty unimpeachable daughters of the Great Folks cast hydrangeas at his feet. Pomeroy, with his mustache waxed to a pinpoint, presented Arthur to her at the doorway. It was the greatest triumph of her life when the President of the United States took her arm and bowed her ahead of him into the house from which she had been hounded fifty-eight years before.

Pomeroy fell in love with Minnie Perry, the prettiest and wittiest of all the daughters of the Great Folks. She was doubly related to him, being descended both from Captain Jim deWolf and from his sister Abigail Howe. Cards were already out for the wedding when Madam Colt decided that Minnie's upbringing was not suitable for Linden Place: her father, though he sang a fine baritone, was famously shiftless in business. (He managed the iron works at Taunton, where Uriah Leonard had repaired King Philip's muskets, for the Boston-born Codman heiresses.) The engagement was broken, starting a schism which was to divide the town for the remainder of its long Indian Summer. A month later, Pomeroy married Dot Bullock, the violet-eyed daughter of the irascible Judge Bullock.* Though Dot

---

* Judge Bullock was not over-popular. His daughter Sylvia, a sister of Dot, declined to speak to him. When kindly Mrs. Sam Drury offered to heal the

was a deWolf on one side only, being descended from Farmer John, she was the great-granddaughter of the sainted Bishop Griswold, an ancestry which not even a double-barreled deWolf could disdain.

"Bride and groom," said the *Phoenix* in reporting the wedding, "are of commanding presence."

After fifteen stormy years and three children, Dot and Pomeroy caught each other in simultaneous peccadilloes. She delivered her ultimatum: a legal separation, a handsome settlement, and the ownership of Linden Place—or else, the scandal of a divorce. She gave him two weeks to choose, but he answered her in ten seconds. He welcomed a separation and could painlessly give her a fortune; but the Mansion she should never have. On those terms, they parted forever. She moved to a house at Hope and Burton Streets, picturesquely called the Anchorage, on the site of old Mark Antony's, which the British had burned. Pomeroy stayed on at Linden Place. Minnie Perry lived halfway between, and it is a wonder the town was big enough for all three. The Colt brothers set up their law offices in Tanner's octagonal barbershop.

The relationship between them was a good deal like that between their great-great-uncles Captain Jim and Farmer John. Pomeroy, like Captain Jim, was the brother of action. Barry, like John, was the brother of counsel. He looked like an ancient Roman, with a long flat cheek and a marble eye. He said good morning as if it were a benediction. He became first a lawyer, and then, in spite of his admiration for champagne, a federal judge. I remember asking him, as a boy, the difference between a Republican and a Democrat—in those days, in Rhode Island, almost everyone was a Republican. The Judge, in a voice trembling with emotion, explained to me, "They're like two boxes of strawberries, my boy. The Democratic box has some beauties

---

breach by asking them both to tea, Sylvia told her, "I won't set foot under the same roof with that man."

"Why then," said Mrs. Drury, "we can drink our tea in the garden."

At Judge Bullock's funeral, his neighbor Lem Clark Richmond, Junior, watched the obsequies from a rocking chair, with a cigar in his teeth and a toddy in his hand. As the hearse drew away from the house he exclaimed, loud enough so the mourners could not fail to hear him, "Well, there goes the old skunk at last. I won't be bothered by *him* no more."

on the top, but it's rotten down below. The Republican box? It may not look so fine on the surface, but it's *sound all through*."

When the brothers were growing up, the only industries in town were General Ambrose E. Burnside's carbine factory, Augustus O. Bourn's rubber works, and a small cotton mill, owned by out-of-towners, on the waterfront. Bourn's little factory on Wood Street, a stone building where the American flag was raised and lowered each morning and night, and the bell in the tower rang three times a day, was a genteel and certain place of employment for such village girls as were not needed in their mothers' kitchens. Augustus Bourn was not a business man, but a scientist. He had a chemist's interest in the strange gum which Bristol ships often brought back in lumps, as souvenirs, from South American voyages. It was spelled "caoutchouc" then, and pronounced like a sneeze. It had been only a useless curiosity until Charles Goodyear, in 1839, learned how to vulcanize it.

Bourn had built his factory in Bristol in 1864, the year before Madam Colt returned to town, and the year after the Herreshoff brothers, blind John B. and full-sighted Captain Nat, built their famous *Qui Vive*. He called it the National Rubber Company. Within ten years it gave work to twelve hundred citizens, who daily turned out five thousand pairs of boots. It brought an honest prosperity to the town and himself, from which he built, on Bishop Mark Antony DeWolfe Howe's potato patch at the end of Hope Street, a Gothic stone mansion with turrets and oriels. The name SEVENOAKS was carved on a granite tablet at the gate. Barry Colt and his bride lived in an octagonal house just behind it, and there was not even a fence between the two. The Bourn children picked apples from their own trees and brought them to the Colts' on baking day. Though Bourn was not Bristol-born, he rivaled any of the deWolfs in importance. In 1883 he was elected Governor of the state. On the same day that Madam Colt entertained President Arthur in the morning, Mrs. Bourn entertained him in the afternoon.

In 1887 one of the Bourn boys caught diphtheria. The doctor advised a change of climate. Since Governor Bourn had served the state well, and was a courtly and cultivated man, and a good Republican besides, President Harrison appointed him Consul-General at Rome. Bourn packed up his wife, his two boys, and his daughters Bessie and Alice. He boarded up the windows of Sevenoaks. He left the National Rubber Company in the hands of his friend Pomeroy Colt, with a power of attorney, and started to his post in Italy. It was already said of Pomeroy that he could make anything pay. In Rome Governor Bourn rented a villa which he called Palazzo Governore. Little George recovered. The girls were delighted by the Eternal City. They had not been abroad a year before the *Phoenix* printed this announcement:

> We hear that Miss Bessie, the beautiful and accomplished daughter of former Governor Bourn, is betrothed to Baron Eugene von Koenneritz, major in Queen Olga's regiment at Stuttgart. He comes of one of the most distinguished Prussian families, and is related to Prince Bismarck. She is a fine linguist and pianist. The wedding will take place after Easter at the Palazzo Governore in Rome.

But the affairs of the rubber works were in worse condition than the Governor knew. In his absence, the workers struck for their back pay. Pomeroy petitioned it into bankruptcy before Easter came. The court, who by coincidence was his father-in-law Judge Bullock, appointed him receiver. In the reorganization Governor Bourn's stock was wiped out. Bessie's wedding was canceled. The Baron remained in Stuttgart, for there could no longer be a dowry. The Governor hastened back to Bristol, where he found himself frozen out of his own company. Little Alice Bourn cried for a whole day. She had boasted of Sevenoaks to her friends in Italy, but now it seemed much smaller than the Palazzo, as Bristol itself was smaller than Rome. The Governor was never rich again, and Miss Bessie never married. In her last years, she had to sell Sevenoaks. Finally she took a job in the wire room of the factory which might have been her own. By that time, most of the workers were Italian. When a Yankee dared to pity her for working in a roomful of foreigners, she told him, "But I have always loved Italy. I was happy there. And these girls are so *obliging*. Why, they help me out in all kinds of little ways."

But the Italian girls themselves said they carried her bundles, and threaded her needles, and fetched her glue, only because it did not seem right, if you had been brought up to respect your elders as they had, that the old lady should have to work in a factory she might have owned, except for Colonel S. Pomeroy Colt—and might still have owned, if the Governor had abased himself to walk through the chicken yard and ask Barry Colt to intercede for him with his brother.

The factory which the colonel had picked up became the town's livelihood. In his lifetime the population of the village leaped from 4500 to 11,000, almost half of whom were the foreign-born—Irish, Portuguese, and Italians—who worked in his factory. By 1900 he had blown it up into what is now the United States Rubber Company. When he was elected President, and Sam Norris, Junior, Secretary, the Town Council ordered a parade in their honor on the day they returned from the board meeting in New York. The company was one of the trusts which Theodore Roosevelt denounced, but the town was proud of it. Indeed, the law would often have fared better in Bristol had it not been for the town's affection for the lawless.

Pomeroy Colt merged the five banks in the village, along with several in Providence, into a single bank, the largest in the state. For years after the town had outgrown its old one-family wells, its water supply was the Kickemuit River, up beyond Bungtown. Pomeroy floated a company to filter the tainted, malodorous Kickemuit and pipe clear water to every sink in town, and bequeathed his stock in it *to* the town. Up by the north bridge is the Carters' ancient house, with a finely carved garland over the second-floor window. An out-of-town antique dealer offered them fifty dollars for it; Pomeroy offered them the same not to sell it. He tried to buy back the furniture which his grandfather's creditors had salvaged on the disastrous night in 1825; but there he had less luck, for most of the creditors' descendants, poor as they were, were proud to have something he *couldn't* buy. And if half the town believed he had stolen the rubber works from Governor Bourn, the other half, which included himself, believed that by giving employment to the town he had repaid the debt of his grandfather General George.

Madam Colt lived long enough to witness his separation from Dot, but she was beyond caring. She died at Linden Place in 1901, seventy-six years after being driven out of it. Her last words, murmured into Minister Locke's ear, were the names of the sixty-two kings and emperors of ancient Rome, in strict order. The crepe which she had hung on the portico of Linden Place for the funeral of the murdered McKinley remained there for her own.

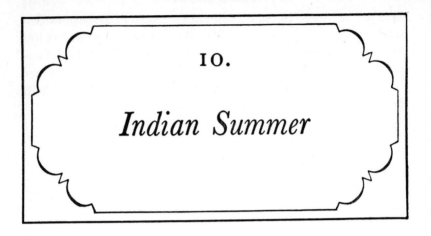

10.

Indian Summer

MADAM COLT's death removed the last restraint on Pomeroy's purse. He bought up the whole block between the Mansion and Bradford Street for a marble schoolhouse to her memory. He could not help making money, like Captain Jim and General George before him; along with Shakespeare and the ladies, money was his passion.

"If you don't love it," he would say in his gravelly voice, "you won't get it, any more than you'll get the ladies without loving them all."

His methods were murky, but his ends were beneficent. There was a phrase in Wall Street, "as twisty as Colt"—but no one in Bristol went to Wall Street. When his friend J. P. Morgan chided him for his amours, he defended himself.

"Pierpont," he said, "you're just as bad as I am, but you work behind locked doors."

"Pomeroy," answered Morgan, "that's just why doors *have* locks."

He had the bluntness of genius. When the advertising manager of the rubber trust asked him to suggest a slogan for the company's tires, he pounded his cane on the sidewalk of Hope Street and pronounced, "Tell them United States tires are *good* tires."

His slogan became familiar on billboards all over the country.

He worked mostly in New York, but came home for weekends **and** the Fourth of July. He liked to play artless games in the back yard of Linden Place, like "basket," where you swing in a laundry-basket strung on a broomstick between two chairs, and try to knock a dime off one of the chairs without falling out.

The teamwork between the Colt brothers is shown by the events of 1907–1908. That winter, Pomeroy laid plans to be elected senator by the state legislature. (It was not till 1913 that senators were elected by the people.) Like many men of great possessions, he craved the trust of his fellow citizens. He needed only a majority of the 109 delegates at the State House to win. One can only guess at the prizes which dangled before the members from the back-country towns, each of which, in the upper house, had as good a vote as Providence.

The other candidates were Wetmore of Newport, a Republican like himself, and Goddard of Providence, a Democrat who had no chance anyway. On the first ballot Colt led. A banquet was made ready at Linden Place to celebrate his expected victory on the second. But the stubborn Democrats, without whose votes neither Republican could be elected, continued to vote for Goddard. The deadlock lasted seven months, until it seemed that Rhode Island might lose one of her seats in the Senate. In the end, Goddard chose the lesser of two evils by releasing his votes to Wetmore, and Colt was defeated. But his town was still proud of him, and subscribed to a loving cup which Minister Locke presented at a consolation banquet.

"It is clear," Pomeroy told the press, "that the American people do not give men of large affairs the confidence which we deserve."

Defeat, for a while, unhinged his mind. Secretly he took to a sanitarium. His machines still fashioned soles and uppers, and his laborers cemented them together, turning out ten thousand pairs of sneakers a day. Barry watched over his brother as carefully as if he had been his son, making excuses for his disappearance and finally, when the news leaked out, bringing out bright prophecies of his recovery and imminent return. One day he did return, and went about his multifarious business as if there had been no interruption. He had resigned himself to his own defeat, but determined to elect Barry to the next vacancy at Washington. With Barry's respectability in front and his own money behind, he succeeded. Two years later the same politicians who had defeated one brother elected the other. Barry Colt served his term with distinction. He sat on the Immigration Committee. Just as his great-uncle James deWolf had barred British cruisers from searching suspected American slavers, he made sure that there was no interruption to the flow of cheap foreign labor for the United States Rubber Company.

Pomeroy Colt brought Bristol its Indian Summer. It was the time when every man—except the foreigners—had his own shaving mug in a slatted rack at the Tonsorial Parlors; when gaslight drove out oil and was driven out in turn by electricity; when the railroad had supplanted the stagecoach, but had not yet been supplanted by the automobile; when the ailing believed in nostrums like Massasoit Salve, Thompsonian Remedies, Talbot's Tropical Preparation, and Prussian Wash (cures all warts in two weeks if used ten times a day); and when the hale subscribed to such periodicals as *Clarke's Weekly Counterfeit Expositor* and the *Saturday Evening Gazette and Ladies' Toilet*. When Spencer Rounds, the builder, advertised "scrollwork and house-moving a speciality." When the butter was kept in the well, and Sunday breakfast meant fishballs, brown bread, and beans baked overnight inside the stove in a gray and brown crock with molasses oozing under the lid. When the townspeople, three hundred strong, crowded into Henry Easterbrooks' news store each evening for the city newspapers, almost collapsing the floor. When a dime bought a dollar's worth, and the spinster storekeeper called Miss Bazaar could sell you a whole family Christmas for a two-dollar bill.

It was the time when the last tax-ridden mansions—all but one— which Russell Warren had built for the Great Folks crumbled or burned. Captain Charles's had been quartered through its cross-halls in 1847 and moved in four pieces, with the bird-of-paradise paper still flapping on its walls, to make room for a sawmill. The house which Captain Jim gave his son Francis had burned in 1860, killing two firemen. Henry deWolf's had blown down in the gale of '69, along with the vase-shaped elm which stood beside it. The Mount itself burned on a snowy Saturday in 1902; that night Mrs. Willy B. deWolf, the owner's widow, gave a party at the Belvedere, with champagne, to celebrate. The Reverend James deWolf Perry, Captain Jim's great-grandson, had prepared his next day's sermon for Saint Michael's from the text "And the fire of the Lord came down upon the mount." He had to preach a new one extempore.

Don Marcos's temple on Poppasquash burned in 1926. The insurance company refused to pay, for wads of excelsior, soaked in kerosene, were found among its fallen columns. But the columns themselves, copies from the Choragic Monument of Lysicrates, were copied in turn for the stone front of the Junior High School which stands by Silver Creek. Major William's lacy house next door to the temple, most beautiful of all, but beyond the purse of his descendants, was shattered by the gale of 1938 and had to be pulled down. None of the slave traders' houses is left except the simple farmsteads of Farmer John and the Quakerish Levi, and the Mansion of General George.

Indian Summer was also the time when the village, like many others in New England, finally became a mill-town instead of a seaport, and when the foreign population first outnumbered the Yankees. As in most New England seaports, there had been a minority of foreigners from the start. Captain Papilion, who settled with the Proprietors, was French, and so was Daniel Morice, who had come from Haiti. The deWolfs themselves, migrating from Guadeloupe, could fairly be called Frenchmen; and the Herreshoffs were half German. The chief strains now are Portuguese, Irish, and Italian.

The Portuguese-Americans of Bristol came mostly from the Western Isles, as the Azores used to be called. Even now, when two meet for the first time, each asks the other which island his family came from; only the snobs come from the mainland. The first one on record was Jack De Costa, who shipped aboard the *Yankee* in Fayal on her third cruise. He was a bachelor then, but by the census of 1830 had acquired a family of nine. In that census, the guest list of transients at the Old Bay State boarding house, which had been Parson Lee's mansion, consisted of twenty-six seamen, fifteen of whom were white and eleven Negro. Only four were Rhode Island-born; there were two from Massachusetts, one each from Maryland and Virginia, one from England and one from Italy, two each from Ireland, Cuba, the West Indies, Africa and the South Seas, and three each from the Azores and the Cape Verdes. A law of 1817 required that two-thirds of an American ship's complement must be citizens, but it was evaded by giving Yankee names to foreign sailors, and two at the Bay State, though born in the Western Isles, were named Francis Moore and Henry Brown.

The Portuguese did not arrive in waves, like the Irish and Italians, but increased by a heavy birth rate and a natural accretion from the islands only halfway across the Atlantic. They began as farmers and fishermen, as they had been at home. Although they were Catholics, they went mostly to the Baptist and Methodist churches. (There is a big Portuguese church in town now, with services in the mother tongue once a week, for the few who still speak it.) They were gentle, hard-working, and prolific. In the days when the *Empire State* called at Bristol, her hundred staterooms were stripped of their linen each morning by an enterprising group of Portuguese laundrymen, as soon as her passengers had entrained for Providence and Boston. They carried the bedsheets and pillowcases in a lowgear from the Franklin Street dock up to a fine spring back of the town, near Captain Jim's decaying mansion, and had them washed, ironed, and dried in time for her return trip the following night. Manuel August, who came from the Azores to Bristol in 1883, was first a ship's carpenter at the Herreshoff boatyard, and later train inspector on the Providence cars. His daughter Elizabeth in 1914 became the first Portuguese girl to graduate from the Colt Memorial High School. (Few of the immigrants could afford to keep their children out of work so long.) She is married to a prosperous grocer now, and knows little more of the trials of the Portuguese pioneers than the Yankees know of King Philip's War. When I asked her how the nationalities that make up Bristol's population today differ from each other, she told me they hardly differ at all, except, she added, that "the Italians have more life than the Portuguese."

As Father Fauque reported, there were Bristol Irishmen aboard the *Prince Charles of Lorraine* in 1744. When Hubbard, the Crown agent, fled with the British fleet in 1779, he left behind his gardener, an Irishman named Guin, whose widow was still extant in the War of 1812. Except for her, there were no Irish in town until the potato famine of 1846 drove thousands from the old country. In 1847 a New England committee raised money to send food to Ireland and bring back as many immigrants as could crowd aboard the relief ships. Usually the men came alone, to try out the new life for a while before risking their families in the unknown country. James Duffy, for instance, came out by himself in 1847. By the next year he had made enough in the Bristol onion fields to send for his wife, his five children, and his brother-in-law. They came out in the steerage of the clipper *Mortimer Livingstone,* Liverpool to New York in twenty-eight days, with their crockery and bedquilts, and took packet from there to Bristol. By that time there were thirteen Irish names on the tax rolls, but only a single complete family besides their own. Pat Hammill was here already, without his wife, and the Widow Ellersly, whose pig got into Saint Michael's, as related earlier. There was no priest. Mass had not been said in town since 1817, when a French bishop had come from Boston to baptize Captain Morice's wife. The newcomers had to walk five miles to Warren for the Sacrament, for none of them owned a horse, and the stage did not run on the Sabbath. If there was snow on the ground, the men trudged ahead to break a path for the women and children. By 1852 there were three hundred Irishmen in town. So many of them had to make the Sunday journey that Father McCallion of Warren offered to drive his gig down, and they set him up an altar on sawhorses in an empty house behind a saloon on Thames Street. It was not till 1855, the year of the railroad, that the first Catholic church was built. The men worked as coachmen or farmers for the Great Folks, at no higher wages than the freed slaves had got, and their wives and daughters hired out for housework. Madam Colt herself employed three Irish girls at Linden Place.

The Yankees, far from being worried by the increasing numbers of the Irish, welcomed a new supply of cheap labor that could speak their own language (which the Portuguese could not), and regarded them as lovable and comic characters. Some of them were, indeed. There was no abashing an Irishman. One young fellow was bold enough to send this love letter to pretty Annette Munro in 1882:

> Respicted Miss:
> Excuse me the liberty I take in handling the pen for your benefit, and indeed there is no quill of goose that can express the devotion of my heart to the sweetest jewel of a girl that walks the streets of this town. My heart beats at the thought of ye since the morning I see ye in the window of your sleeping apartment with a blue ribbon to your hair. Oh, twas the color of your eyes.
> It is not of immejit marriage I would be speaking; but my father —the Holy Virgin and all the saints preserve him in life!—is an old man, and will soon be leaving me a neat little cottage, a cow, calf and pig, foreby $80.07.
> If your father and mother and yourself agree, please sit tomorrow morning in the same window, and my heart, as the Pite says, will start and tremble under your feet, and blossom in Purple and Red.

But he forgot to sign it. He might have been horsewhipped if he had. As late as 1912 it was regarded as an outrage that A. P. Nerone, the respected Irish-Portuguese shoeman, sued Senator Colt for an unpaid bill.

Michael Callan became coachman for Bishop Howe, Tom Downey for Madam Colt, and Pat Hammill for Captain Rogers on Poppasquash. When Pat needed a raise, he knew better than ask his boss for it. He had a friend in Rochester, New York, write him a letter offering him a job out there for five dollars more a month than the captain gave him. The captain offered him ten dollars not to leave him. Pat bought the old Congregational parsonage on State Street with his savings, and there he and his wife raised eleven children. The captain, in his old age, depended more and more on him. After their daily business at the bank and post office was done, Pat would drive the open carriage, with Captain Rogers in the back seat, up to his own house, to look in on the children. The captain, who had no children, did not begrudge him that. But sometimes he would stay inside for an hour or two, and the colder it was outdoors, the longer he stayed. Captain Rogers, freezing by himself, might call, "Patrick, Patrick!" as long as he cared: Pat took his time about coming out. In the end he had a fight with Father McCabe at Saint Mary's, and was buried from home instead of from church. He rests now, surrounded by the children, under a splendid granite obelisk at Juniper Hill, the beautiful cemetery planted on Levi deWolf's old cornfield. It is only a little smaller than Colonel S. P. Colt's, and he is the only Irishman up there.

The first generation of Irish wore itself out with work and childbearing, as the early Yankees had. The second never raised the same big families, but during the Indian Summer rose to eminences undreamed of by Madam Colt or her sons. Frank Hammill became Probate Judge, First Councilman, and Republican leader at the State House. Luke Callan, who became a general himself, rebuilt all of General Ambrose E. Burnside's roadways with his own crushers and rollers, and drained them properly. Eddie Leahy, whose family were forty-eighters, became Moderator at Town Meeting—and often it needed moderating—and Judge, and finally Senator at Washington, where he died too young, after losing his only son in the Second World War. It seems impossible that, within living memories, Irishmen were called foreigners.

The last wave of immigration was Italian, and it arrived expressly because of the rubber works. There are gaffers still alive who remember when there were no Italians at all in town, except for one who brought a trained bear each summer and another who brought a monkey. The first arrivals were Antonio Desiderio and his wife, who came in 1889 from Scafati, a village between Naples and Pompeii. (The word itself means "excavations.") In Scafati they have a famous fiesta each Annuniciation Day, in honor of Our Lady of Mount Carmel. Brunos, Maisanos, Romanos, and della Mortes were other pioneers, and they dispute the Desiderios' primacy as fiercely as *Mayflower* descendants argue among themselves, and with just as much reason. A young shoemaker named Luigi Malafronte came soon after the Desiderios, and married their daughter—theirs was the first

Italian wedding in Saint Mary's. He opened a bar, which later grew into a bakery and grocery store. He advertised in the *Phoenix* foreign delicacies of which the Yankees had never heard, and dared not taste, such as *acciughe in salamoia* (anchovies in brine) and *liquore Strega*. He set up as Immigration Agent and Interpreter, and became the representative of the White Star and Cunard Lines, making all arrangements to bring out the families of Italians already here—and, when they reached town, feeding and housing them till they found jobs and helping them take out citizenship papers. Each summer he set up a papier-mâché shrine in his back yard on Wood Street, with a statue of Our Lady of Mount Carmel under the arbor. Many Italians, and some Yankees, gathered there on Sunday afternoons to eat his pizza and drink the zinfandel which he pressed each October from his own grapes. He became the patriarch of the Italian colony. He sent many of his compatriots to study English with Miss Evvie Bache, who taught school on State Street in the daytime and was eager to make a little money in the evening. The della Morte bakery might have perished for want of trade except for those lessons. The Yankees never quite approved of Miss Evvie's teaching foreigners the language, though she was descended not only from the Bradfords but from Benjamin Franklin as well, for as soon as the della Mortes could speak English to their customers, business began to fall off in the established bakeries like Charlie Spooner's.

The first real wave of immigration from Italy came in 1894, when Terence McCarthy, the manager of Colonel S. P. Colt's rubber works, dropped wages to a dollar for a nine-hour day. The employees had the audacity to strike, whereupon the company set up a labor agency in Naples to recruit replacements. Bidding for labor in foreign countries was against the law then, as it is now. It is said that posters appeared on the street corners in Naples urging the citizens to come to Bristol, but I have never seen one. It is certain, however, that many drafts came, in quick succession. Here is the recollection of a day in 1894 by one Yankee, who was a little girl then:

"We peeked through the window of the Franklin St. depot, and

THERE THEY SET. Must have been a hundred of them, all *over* the place: women nursing their babies, and *everything*. Sausages in fishnet bags. Big cheeses like *we* had never seen. Great big bedquilts all tied up in knots, and people sitting on them, and lying on the seats —why, on the floor!—and *everything!* Were they going to work for Colonel S. P. Colt? Well, I don't know what happened to them, and didn't want to know, but there was a load in the depot that morning all right."

Mr. "Had" Munro remembers the same day:

"One morning I looked up, and going by the house was about seventy-five or a hundred of the awfulest looking tramps you ever saw. And they had a leader, or *padrone*, or whatever you call it, and they were marching up from the depot to the rubber works. And they were in their old clothes just as they come from Italy: hunting jackets and feathers and all. They all had mustaches and some had rings in their ears. They were Italians, come to work for Colonel S. Pomeroy Colt and Terence McCarthy."

But Jeremiah Romano, descended from one of those pioneers (his very name is a symbol of the new pattern in town; he works for Prudential Life and ran the town's 275th birthday, a few years back), disputes Had Munro's account:

"I don't believe they wore earrings," he says. "And they hated the word *padrone*. Why, they came to the US to get away from *padrones*. And what Mr. Munro doesn't know is that mustaches were a sign of dignity in those days. Back in Italy, and maybe right here in Bristol, you could hardly get married if you didn't have a mustache."

Because they came in such numbers, the Italians lived more wretchedly than the Portuguese before them. The *Phoenix* wrote sneeringly:

> Several tenements in town, owing to the incoming foreign population, are much crowded. One on Thames St. is reported to contain a family of 16, with 26 boarders. One in the eastern part of town is said to be occupied by 25 persons, all males, without furniture, all sleeping on the bare floor, as contented as if it were a bed of down.

The immigrations were not without violence. In the same year, 1894, a knife battle broke out on Thames Street between Portuguese and Italians over the honor of three girls. At Mrs. Robinson's bar, the Crow's Nest, a general fight, with no national lines drawn, was quelled by one-armed Police Chief Hoard and his assistant, Uncle Ben "Tighthole" Munro. Hoard was more sympathetic than most Yankees to foreigners, for he had married a Portuguese girl named de Costa, perhaps a granddaughter of the Jack who served aboard the *Yankee*. At the entrance to the rubber works, Mrs. Desiderio, normally a placid lady, shied a glass bowl at an Italian dancing teacher named John del Grego for lending forty-three dollars to her nephew Salve Rinaldi and attaching his wages as security.

Salve Rinaldi is a patriarch now. His wife, "Auntie Kate" to a good part of the town and still pretty at her age, is the first Irish girl to have married an Italian. Salve has forgotten the fight now, and perhaps was too young then to understand it. But he remembers the early hardships. He treated me to a glass of zinfandel in his parlor on Congregational Street, and described them with gusto:

"They thought we wore horns, like devils. Why, an Italian they wouldn't let walk on the sidewalk. And the boys and girls pasted us with snowballs, so that Chief Hoard had to hire extra cops outside Byfield School and the rubber works. He may only have had one arm, but he was a tough chief. Some of the snowballs had horse chestnuts in them too, and even rocks. They called us Dagos. The Portuguese people they called Guineas—or maybe it was the other way round. But that is all over now."

Although most natives resented the influx, no politician of either party could resist the temptation of the foreign vote. In the back rooms of barbershops and saloons they conducted classes in the proper marking of ballots. The Italian voters were more partial to the Republican machine, which was controlled by Yankee heelers, and the Portuguese to the Democratic, which was controlled by Irish. Elections in the foreign district east of the Common were held in the Train of Artillery Hall. Ballots were secret, of course, but when several of the new citizens abruptly lost their jobs at the rubber works it was charged that Colonel Merton Cheesman, S. Pomeroy Colt's hatchet-man, had hidden himself with a spyglass in the ropehole under the belfry and seen them mark their Xs under the Democratic star. Since he commanded the Train of Artillery, no one had a better right to be up there.

The victims of Indian Summer were the Yankee yeomanry—the descendants of the shopkeepers and the mariners who had trusted General George yet regained nothing from his daughter or his grandsons. They were snubbed by the Great Folks and elbowed aside by the foreigners; there were thousands like them in all the old seaports of New England. They were the kindly folk who spent their evenings round the parlor lamp, who kindled the stove on Thanksgiving Day and let it go out at Easter—though you could freeze fore and aft if Easter came in March. They read prayers to their children every evening, and meant them too; and snuffed out the candle on the table in the upstairs hall when each last child was in bed. They kept a set of best china for the minister's yearly tea. They laid braided rugs in the kitchen as well as the parlor, and beat them every day. They said "God bless you" when you sneezed. Whenever the town of Taunton was mentioned, they exclaimed, "Tent'n, good Lord!" for no known reason. The men, too proud to work in a mill, kept shop themselves or built ships for the Herreshoffs. They spent Sunday afternoon fishing or digging clams. Their women spent it at the North Burial Ground, visiting with each other and with those who had gone before, knitting beside the family stones, sharing their gossip and complaints while their tethered horses munched the lush grass and their children fished in the pond, and the flowerbed of red, white, and blue flags waved in the cast-iron stars which they had set last Decoration Day at the headstone of each soldier, were he never so forgotten. They were not the Great Folks, and might have been rich but for General George deWolf. Though they dwelt comfortably on the bosom side of Dives' gulf, and knew some of the Great Folks roasted on the other, they did not refuse them the drop of water. If Maitie Minsher of the Great Folks ogled them at the depot, they forgave him, for they knew he was a widower. When he bequeathed his champagne to whoever would adopt his wife's cat, they nodded their approval, though they never tasted champagne themselves, for Maitie had shown innate good breeding.

II

Like Simeon Potter before him, Colonel S. Pomeroy Colt became the patron saint and sinner of the town, which had never seen much difference between saints and sinners anyway. It got to calling him Uncle Pom, or just plain Unkie. He had a passion for statuary. He planted Linden Place with reproductions of Praxiteles. He offered Rodin's naked Eve for the front of the Colt Memorial High School, but the embarrassed Town Council declined it. He built a drive around Poppasquash, with life-size bronze bulls on marble pedestals at the gateway, and tablets carved with the invitation:

COLT FARM PRIVATE PROPERTY PVBLIC WELCOME

Farther out, he threw a bridge over Mill Gut, and set the Venus de Milo and the Discobolos on the buttresses. Minnie Perry called the Colt Drive Wall Street, for its bulls and bares.

On his Poppasquash farm was a whole shedful of extra statues, and a big stone barn where he bred Jerseys. He named the cows after the girls he liked: Nancy Dear, or Darling Ruth. There were a dozen cows in the herd. A girl's reputation did not last long when her name went up on the stanchions, but most of them did not care.

Overlooking the western arm of the bay he built a half-hidden shingled casino. At the head of the dock a bronze dog, pedestaled on a puddingstone boulder, gazed out to sea. At the driveway a statue of Ganymede proffered a cup. Inside the casino were a bowling alley, a two-story dining room, and a parlor with a lighted niche containing a statue of Silenus and his goatskin. On Sundays after church (Unkie always went to Saint Michael's when he was home for Sunday) his guests drove carriages or automobiles, or pedaled their bicycles, out to the casino for lunch. The girls changed into Annette Kellermanns, which were a shocking costume for the day; but a girl who wore more would be laughed off the dock. Unkie, in a white waistcoat, sat smiling on a bench as they trotted toward the the springboard. If they had good figures, he slapped their behinds as they passed him; if they didn't, he just tapped them with his goldheaded cane. At half past one he would call them ashore. "Children, let's go up and milk the Squantum cow."

Then it was back across the road to the casino, where Silenus's bronze goatskin, at the flick of a switch, poured milk punch from the Squantum Club into the merry goblets; and then, swaying, into the dining room set for fifty. Minnie Perry always sat at his right, and the prettiest younger girl at his left. It was like Belshazzar's Feast in the old engravings. The writing on the wall was far up, below the casement which opened from the ladies' dressing room. It said:

> 𝔑𝔞𝔶, 𝔫𝔞𝔶, 𝔤𝔬 𝔫𝔬𝔱 𝔰𝔬 𝔰𝔬𝔬𝔫;
> 𝔓𝔞𝔯𝔱𝔦𝔫𝔤 𝔦𝔰 𝔰𝔲𝔠𝔥 𝔰𝔴𝔢𝔢𝔱 𝔰𝔬𝔯𝔯𝔬𝔴.

In town, those Sunday lunches were said to be "orgies." Of the branches of the Great Folks, the descendants of John and William and James—except for Minnie Perry—stayed severely away. The Levis were not invited. Though the Herreshoffs had twice intermarried with the deWolfs, they were too taciturn to be asked.

(There was a jingle in town:

> Here's to dear old Bristol,
> The home of the onion and clam,
> Where deWolfs talk their heads off to Herreshoffs,
> And Herreshoffs only say "Damn!")

But a few Abigails consented, and all the Charleses were there, along with New Yorkers and other out-of-towners who were not Great Folks at all.

Linden Place was a century old in 1910. Unkie gave it a birthday party. The guests were received by his sister-in-law Mrs. Senator Colt, his daughter-in-law Ethel Barrymore, and his sister Belle.*

---

* She had married a deWolf first cousin nicknamed Hungry Frank, a grandson of General George. He was fleshless as a vulture, and whiskered besides. The Swamp Angels feared and hated Hungry Frank. The day his beard caught in the cranksleeve of his scarlet Mors, they stood jeering at him on Hope Street till J. F. Huestis the mechanic and Seabury Manchester the barber combined to release it.

Minnie Perry came, but Dot, though she was his legal wife, was not invited. The town peered through General George's iron fence at the Great Folks, drinking champagne among the statuary of the garden. There were thirty-nine pieces of Will Paine's homemade fireworks that night, including tourbillions, Bengal lights, and North Pole batteries. They ended with a flaming portrait of the Mansion itself, crowned with the dates 1810–1910.

> With its brilliant display [the *Phoenix* reported next day] and the electric fountain throwing its spray fourteen feet in the air, the scene resembled the magic of the Arabian Nights, and will be recorded as the most brilliant social affair in the annals of the historic old town of Bristol.

Unkie died in 1921, with a lovely nurse sitting at each side of his bed. His obelisk is the highest monument in Juniper Hill. On its face, the frisky colt which was his symbol crunches one spear between his jaws and balances another between his forelegs.

His death ended the Indian Summer of the Great Folks. Three years later the Mount Hope suspension bridge was built over the Ferry, tying the peninsula to Newport as it was already tied to Warren. The isolation of Bristol was ended. As if the town resented connection with the rest of the world, the suspension cables gave way before the first car crossed, and the whole roadway had to be lowered into barges on the water below until new cables were spun. Bristol has become a way-station instead of a terminus. Three centuries and more have passed since Massasoit welcomed the Pilgrims; it does not seem a long time.

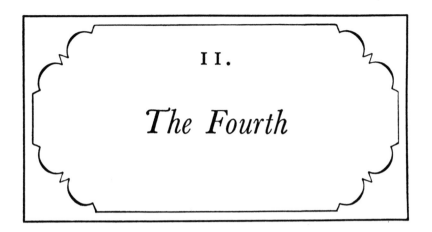

II.

The Fourth

THE present population of southern New England is a blend. In Bristol, the distrusts had pretty well mellowed by the end of Indian Summer. Nowadays every issue of the *Phoenix* reports a wedding between couples of the different stocks which history has brought to town: Irish-Yankee, Yankee-Italian, and Irish-Portuguese. (For an unknown reason, the rarest is one between the two Latin strains, Italian and Portuguese.)

The institution which, next to marriage itself, does most to unite the town is its famous Fourth of July. There is not another like it in the country.

Independence Day was observed there before independence was won. Major Mackenzie of the Royal Welsh Fusiliers wrote in his diary for July 4, 1777, in the British redoubt across the Ferry:

> This being the first anniversary of the Declaration of the Independency of the Rebel colonies, they ushered in the morning by firing 13 cannon, one for each Colony, we suppose. At sunset the Rebel frigates fired another round of 13 guns each, one after the other. As the evening was very still and fine, the Echo of the Guns down the Bay had a very grand effect, the report of each being repeated 3 or 4 times.

The first official celebration was in 1785, just after the Revolution. Parson Wight, who had lately been mustered out of Washington's army, led the village in prayers of gratitude for the nation's delivery, and his own. He continued to do so each Fourth until he died in 1837. Each year the celebration grew a little larger and louder. By 1790 the Train of Artillery, in blue capes and red-plumed hats, was firing its cannon on the Common at sunrise. The tradition lingered for a century and a quarter, in spite of the danger to nearby buildings —stray wadding several times set fire to the shingle roof of the Baptist church—until, in 1915, a misfire almost killed one of the guncrew. Then the sunrise salute was abandoned for good.

For the fiftieth anniversary of the Declaration, in 1826, the Town Council made a special appropriation of $30. Since General George had bankrupted the town only a few months before, the sum was not as niggardly as it sounds. Patriotic citizens raised it to $65 by subscription. While the militia were still in bed the uptown and downtown boys were out in the darkness, blowing fish-horns and conch-shells, and setting off firecrackers imported from China. By nine the streets were crowded with sailors from the idle ships, the colored population of Goree, and the town's burghers. Fathers carried their children in their arms, for baby carriages had not been invented. A procession marched through town, headed by the Train of Artillery, from the Court House on the Common to the Congregational church on Bradford Street, where, says the Warren newspaper,

> The service was enlivened by appropriate music from a select choir, and Parson Wight made a fervent and impressive appeal to the Throne of Divine Grace, and returned the unspeakable thanks of a grateful people to the God of Battles.

The smartest pupil in Madam Waldron's dame school recited the Declaration of Independence from memory. Twenty-seven veterans of the Revolution sat together in the box pews. Farmer John deWolf was one of them, along with the three Negro survivors: Cato Reynolds, who had been Lafayette's orderly; Bristol Peck, the servant of Captain Sion Martindale; and John Casco, the fiddler for the troops. When the parson described how a British ball had knocked off his cocked hat during the battle on the Island, Casco stood up and shouted, "It's the truth, boys; I was there and seen it."

After the service the parade marched to Horton's hotel on Pump Lane, and there disbanded. Most of it drifted up to the Common to watch a mock battle between the Train of Artillery and the Light Infantry Company. Some of the more convivial citizens, with a few visiting Mussels from Warren, stayed on at Horton's for a fine dinner.

> After the removal of the cloth [wrote the reporter] several toasts expressive of the good will of both towns toward each other were quaffed in generous wine, and songs sung which went to show the prevalence of liberal sentiments among the patriots of each.

It sounds as if the patriots got drunk. The incident caused a revulsion against liquor among the townspeople. In 1835 the Fourth was taken over by the Young Men's Temperance Society, headed by Collector Drury. Until 1848 the dinners took place at Burgess' Temperance House, where the Critter was never served. In those years the festivities included a sermon on the evils of drink, and the choir was formed from an organization called the Cold Water Army, who sang this song as they paraded Hope Street:

> A pledge we make no wine to take,
> Nor brandy red that turns the head,
> Nor whisky hot our guts to rot,
> Nor fiery rum that ruins home;
> Nor will we sin by drinking gin;
> Hard cider, too, will never do,
> Nor sparkling ale, the face to pale,
> Nor brewer's beer—its curse we fear.
> To quench our thirst we'll only bring
> Cold water from the well or spring;
> So here we pledge perpetual hate
> To all that can intoxicate.

Human nature reasserted itself. In 1850 soup was served to all comers. It was brewed from a stock of Galápagos turtles which had reached Bristol aboard the Ushers' brig *Maria*. One of these monsters could feed a hundred people. Ever since, Bristol's Fourth has belonged to fun-loving boys and reminiscent homecomers. Bristolians regard it as next in importance to the Day of Judgment. At the coronation of Edward VII in Westminster Abbey, Hungry Frank deWolf and his wife, who had been Belle Colt, heard a voice behind them exclaim, "There's never been anything like this except the Fourth in Bristol." When they turned around they saw the speaker was their official but unspeakable-to sister-in-law Dot, so protocol forbade them to agree out loud.

There is no one like a retired hero to inspire a patriotic parade. The Bristol Fourth had two of them in succession during Indian Summer: General Ambrose E. Burnside and Private Ed Anthony. Over three-quarters of a century, they worked around the calendar to prepare for the great day.

General Burnside, by the time he died in 1881, had made the Bristol Fourth famous. He imported orators from New York and Washington. He sent to Boston for fireworks. In 1876, the centenary of independence, he got the Navy to order a man-of-war to the harbor; the custom has not lapsed since. She was the steam sloop *Juniata*. Yachts and excursion steamers came from all over Narragansett Bay to share in the celebration. On the Night Before (it is never called the night of the third) every house in town was lighted by Japanese lanterns. In the parade, the general, as chief marshal, rode old Dick. A hundred sailors marched behind the Train of Artillery band, and the town sergeant carried a standard which Proprietor Byfield had presented in 1724. That night the fireworks on the Common included

> Hexagon wheels of changeable colors, mutating to Roman candles which discharged jets, streamers, rockets and gold rain

to say nothing of

> The representation of a beautiful Vase in mosaic work, with clusters of candles throwing stars and *bouquets de feu*.

Ed Anthony, who succeeded the general in command of the celebration, had been his "scout"—or, as he would be called now, his bodyguard—during the war. He claimed that he was once chased through a peach orchard in Georgia by a whole regiment of rebels, and escaped them by hiding under a porch where Robert E. Lee was holding a council of war.

"If they'd known I was there," he would say, "they'd have cut my heart out."

Ed Anthony lived in a white house at the turn of the Back Road with his sister Medora. Neither was married. It was said that a legacy from Captain Jim deWolf kept the two of them alive, long after the deWolf children had squandered their inheritance. Each spring Ed was the first man in town to get his onion sets into the ground. Winter and summer he wore the same blue peacoat, with a black string tie and a dirty roll-collar shirt. He explained that the coat kept out the cold in winter and the heat in summer. He never walked, but always dog-trotted, even on the mile trip from his house to the Town Hall. Each year he carried a Christmas tree down to Saint Michael's Sunday School, still at a trot. He never knocked on a door, but announced himself by an Indian war-whoop from outside. He loved lemon-balls, the bigger the better. Once, on the Fourth, the committee had one specially boiled for him, as big as a fist. John Church, the Town Clerk, had to break it with a hammer into pieces small enough for him to suck.

He was a great marksman. With his own hands he built a target of white quartz behind his house, rowing the stones over from King Philip's throne on Mount Hope, heaving them into his skiff till the bow was out of water, then climbing into the bow himself. In this position his oars barely reached the water, but he claimed it was easier to row downhill than up. He practiced marksmanship with a ship's cannon. If the balls fell into the water, he retrieved them with his skiff, but this became costly, for he could not find every one. Thereafter he used rocks for ammunition. Each summer he gave a shoot for the Train of Artillery, fifty muskets strong. He and Willy B. deWolf, Captain Jim's grandson from the Mount, once, with telescopic rifles, strung up two ducks each with one bullet, by waiting for the birds to get in range and then firing at just the right instant to send the bullets through all four heads at a distance of three hundred yards.

He vowed to collect thirty treasures before he died; the thirtieth was to be a wife. But since the twenty-ninth was to be a hen's tooth, he never married. The rich Codman sisters gave him a helmet-shaped coal-scuttle—or was it a scuttle-shaped helmet?—which had belonged to William IV. He coveted LeBaron Bradford's collection of shells; Bradford promised them to him for a wedding present, as his thirty-first treasure.

Even with his target finished, and his museum as full as it would ever get, he could not help tinkering with nature. Along his fenceline he set tall poles, each braced in a cairn of white stones and topped with a cartwheel. He knew that the fishhawks would build their nests on the wheels in spring. Even now, the *Phoenix* dates the arrival of springtime not from the calendar, but from the day when George Fish, the scoutmaster, reports the first fishhawk on Ed Anthony's cartwheels.

He was chairman of the Fourth of July Committee for thirty years, until he died in 1914 from lifting a rock that was too heavy for his heart. No sooner had one Fourth ended than he started work to make the next one even better. A whole year beforehand he began begging the Navy for the largest ship it could spare. He blandished governors and senators into attending the parade, negotiated for out-of-town fire companies for the afternoon squirt on the Common, planned costumes for the Antiques and Horribles, bargained with carnivals for the two-day concession, and started to fatten the porker which he donated each year to the Greased Pig Contest.

If the Fourth happened to fall on Monday, there would be special excursions across Narragansett Bay on Saturday for a shore dinner at Rocky Point. (Ah, Rocky Point, Mother of Clambakes! There were seven trips a day by Continental Steamboat, and the fare but 40 cents. Ah, empty islands in her path: Prudence, Patience, Hope, and Despair! The Queen Anne dining hall of Ocean House would seat two thousand; it claimed to be the largest in the USA. Her clambakes, so far refined from the impromptu of Schoolmaster Storrs! The stones were heated only by hickory-wood; under the sailcloth, but a single bucket of water was needed to steam the dripping rockweed. The celebrants sat at benches on each side of the long table, and if a gentleman cared to remove his hat, there was a continuous shelf on iron posts right down the center, where derbies could be laid between the cruets. When President Hayes visited her, 250 bushels of clams disappeared at a sitting. Her amphitheater for dancing! Her Forest Ice-Cream Saloon, her bowling alleys, her rink with patent roller-skates and full band of music! Her Coliseum, with minstrel entertainment! Her bathing beach, with suits to let! Her veranda by the sea, picture gallery, reception cottage for the ladies, merry-go-rounds, and alligator pond! Ah, Jerry, her Indian fish-and-chowder cook! Ah, her indigestion!)

In most years, the Fourth began at sunset of the Night Before. Nobody expected to sleep that night. The sputter of lady-crackers, the roar of cannon-crackers, the report of pink-wrapped torpedos, and the din of fish-horns hardly let up till dawn, when the church bells took over. On one Night Before the gang called the Swamp Angels stole a buggy on the Neck, stuffed it with hay, and ran it blazing through town. On another they found a hundred empty tar-barrels lined up outside the Highway Surveyor's shed. They split into three groups; two started small diversionary fires at the Neck and the Ferry, to get the fire companies off the track, then the main body set fire to the shanty, rolled the barrels up to the Common, and set *them* on fire. Next year the Town Council ordered the police to jail anyone who started a bonfire on the Night Before. That sounded like tyranny to the Swamp Angels, who never had firecracker-money of their own before pig-killing time, and to some other independent citizens too. Storekeepers, farmers, sailors, lawyers, and even Minister Locke joined the Angels just before midnight in front of the First Councilman's house to protest—he was Colonel S. Pomeroy Colt, and the house was Linden Place. They were armed with anything that would make a noise or throw a blaze. Charlie Thompson, the Bristol historian, was there.

"At the stroke of midnight," he recalls gleefully, "we let loose with salvo after salvo of shotguns, horse pistols, and cannon crackers— six- and ten-inchers. You never heard anything like it in your life, everybody hollering and cheering. Hundreds of Roman candles shot up all over the place. We set bombs under the green tubs filled with flowers, and the tubs rose into the air and vanished, flowers and all."

After that the Council gave up trying to enforce the curfew on the Night Before. But no matter where they set the deadline, the boys always feel they have a challenge to outwit the law. As lately as 1953 some of them set fire to the official bonfire at Mill Gut on the night *before* the Night Before.

On the morning of the Fourth, the parade began at eleven—it still does—or as soon thereafter as everyone could be "marshaled." It was headed by a platoon of police, as soon as there were enough police to form one. In belted knee-length blue coats and gray coal-scuttle helmets, they swung their truncheons in time to the bands. Behind them rode the chief marshal and his staff, dressed in Prince Alberts and top hats. A chief marshal was judged by his mount, and spent much time cantering back and forth along the line of march, ostensibly to keep the parade moving, but really to show off his horsemanship. The staff had to be content with inferior horses, mostly rented from Josiah Peckham's livery stable, and later, when automobiles drove him out of business, from the Poor Farm. The Poor Farm horses were as big and round as the town waterwagon, and made little attempt to control their flatulence. They might shift if a cannoncracker went off between their hooves, but otherwise they were shockproof.[*] Luigi Malafronte, however, who served in 1908, had a white circus horse which could dance in time to music. And more recently, many remember the palomino ridden by Matt Brito, and the sombrero which set it off.

After the staff came the barouches of the local and visiting dignitaries, and then the comrades of the Grand Army of the Republic from the Soldiers' Home on the Back Road, lining both sides of a bonton, leaning back from the long benches to wave their campaign hats to the crowd. Then came Ed Anthony, dressed as Uncle Sam

---

[*] When one of Unkie's sons, however, circa 1905, set off a cannon-cracker *with a pinwheel* in it under the mount of Colonel Merton A. Cheesman, the horse reared and bucked Chezzie off, to the delight of the crowd.

and driving the forty-foot Historical Float, with thirteen girls aboard
to represent the original states, and four matching whites ahead, their
ears sticking through holes in their straw hats, and each led by a
boy got up as a Minute Man. Then came the military—Train of Artillery, First Light Infantry, detachments from the warships and
from Fort Adams at Newport, and visiting militia in Continental uniforms, each with its own band. After them were the fire companies,
with sirens blowing. The firemen walked beside the pumpers, carrying flower-filled cornucopias in their red shirtsleeves. The King
Philips were the only company with a distinctive uniform. They wore
blue pants with red piping, and had the motto ON TO THE RESCUE embroidered on their caps and belts. Beginning at the turn of the century, the Portuguese and Italian societies marched, each with its
national flag. Their bands were the best of all. Last were the Antiques
and Horribles, a group of short-legged children dressed up as elephants, Zulu chiefs, giants, skeletons, and dragons. At the head of
each division was a subsidiary marshal, an American flag, and a band.
The tune which each band played at least once in the parade was
"Why Don't You Marmaduke Round Here?" No one knew what the
title meant, nor what the words were; it was vaguely supposed to
derive from Marmaduke Mason, the expert cobbler.

Summers when Lipton had challenged for the *America's* Cup,
the harbor was full of yachts, and yachtsmen, Sir Thomas among
them, rolled along the sidewalk of Hope Street.

Every house flew the flag, and the proudest was Miss Evvie Bache's,
which had only sixteen stars in the field.* Those of the Great Folks
who lived on the route held open house, though nobody but the
other Great Folks dared walk in without an invitation. Outlying
deWolfs would sift in to watch from the piazzas of their relations—

---

* Miss Evvie kept the last dame school. Her fee was fifty cents a week.
She loved children, and understood them. When one of her pupils refused to
spell "pig," she knew why: he had small blue eyes, blond bristly hair, and a
flat nose.

"Just because you spell 'pig,' Jim," she told him gently, "doesn't mean you
are a pig."

"Why didn't you say so to start with, Miss Evvie?" the boy sang out. "P-I-G."

the descendants of Don Marcos from Poppasquash, of Farmer John from Ferry Road, of Henry from the Neck, and of the prolific Bishop Howe from the Back Road. Mrs. Middleton, with her daughters, all three cocooned in white, were driven in from Major William's by their Negro handyman, whose name was also William deWolf. The best location was Minnie Perry's at High and Union, for you could see the parade on its way out, and then, by running down to Hope, catch it on the return. But the best punch was served at Lizzie Diman Cabot's on Hope Street, and the best candy at Maria Norris's, next door to Linden Place. As the parade passed, the guests would run out, punchglass and orange cake in hand, to the mounting block and hitching post which stood in front of every doorway. Their loudest cheers were always for Ed Anthony.

In most parades the Colt brothers rode together in Captain Jim deWolf's old coach, which Unkie had bought from Willy B. at the Mount. It was not the great traveling-coach, which Ben Mann and Polydore used to pilot to Washington, but the light chaise for short-distance use, in which Mrs. Braddy deWolf had called on Madam Colt. Once the floor fell through beneath the two brothers as the ancient vehicle passed Minnie Perry's piazza. Between the cannon-crackers and the bands, Tom Downey did not hear their calls for help. For half a block their heads were out of sight, and their two august pairs of legs trotted with the buckskins, till laughter from the sidewalk warned Tom to pull up. When the brothers were extricated they laughed too; that is the kind of brothers they were. And after the parade disbanded, the marchers, hundreds strong, were welcome at Linden Place, to sing "The Star-Spangled Banner" with the Portuguese-American band and a girl soloist from one of the churches, to hear Barry's forensic voice read the Declaration of Independence, and to drink Unkie's punch. Like the chorus in an opera, the files passed up the marble walk to the portico. There would be a punch-bowl on each flank in the vaulted hall, with George Easterbrooks and his helpers behind it. Most of the patriots, having drunk once to the Colonel's health, went out the back door, around by Wardwell Street, and up again, at the tail end of the procession, to drink the

Senator's. The GAR, who were the guests of honor, were as spry as any. Until late in the afternoon they could be seen reeling out to the bonton which waited to carry them back to the Soldiers' Home. They might stop in at Speedy Chadwick's saloon, where Willy B. deWolf would ease their fatigue by unstrapping their wooden legs, and strapping them on again when they were ready to go. And if pension day happened to coincide with the Fourth, they might line up at a certain shuttered house on High Street, and not get home till midnight. It was not often they got a free ride to town, so they made the most of it on the Fourth.

In the afternoon, if you had children, you took them to the circus on the Common. Mother had laid out a cold lunch, and Father took a drink that afternoon, if it was the only day in the year he did so. On the steps of the Baptist church the Swamp Angels had set up a refreshment stand: jawbreakers and hard pink cookies and a pail of lemonade, with a dipper in the middle and half a dozen tin cups hung on the rim. Their pitch was the chant:

> Cold lemonade
> Made in the shade,
> Stirred with a stick by an ugly old maid.

The circus—or, as it was called in early days, the Caravan—was set up in the northeast corner of the Common, with orders from the Council not to encroach on the baseball game or the firemen's muster. It is a mystery how room was found for all three, to say nothing of the crowds who came to watch them. The children naturally preferred the circus, which offered such attractions as these:

REYNOLDS' WORLD UNITED SHOWS! A VERITABLE NOAH'S ARK OF WILD BEASTS! INCLUDING GIANT ALBINO CAMEL FROM THE SAHARA DESERT! THE ROYAL ROMAN HIPPODROME! THRILLING REVIVAL OF ANCIENT CHARIOT RACES, CAMEL RACES, &c &c! THE MAMMOTH ELEPHANTS BALDY AND QUEEN JUMBO! ALL PRESENTED UNDER ONE VAST CANOPY OF WATERPROOF CANVAS!!

Sometimes the circus arrived by sea, from the Island—Baldy and Queen Jumbo swimming, and the rest of the troupe aboard the horse-scow.

The middle-aged watched the baseball game against Warren, standing in rows around the diamond. There were no bleachers, nor even any ropes to keep them off the field; the players had no uniforms, but wore their everyday clothes.

Old-timers loved to watch the stream-throwing contests of the fire companies off at the southeast corner: Hydraulions, King Philips, Ever-Readys, and Defiance, the one remaining bucket-tub. On a hot afternoon the pumpers who manned the heavy bars would take off everything but their pants, for they built up a three-hundred-pound pressure in the canvas hose before they would let go.

The Fourth was a day of reunion, as it still is. If you have a cousin out of town, or a fellow islander from the old country, the Fourth is the day you ask him home. If you live away yourself, it is the one day of the year you make sure of returning, as Archie Hawkes, in his nineties, flew on from California every year and put up at the Belvedere. In 1895, for instance, the veterans of the whale fishery assembled.

"Fifty years ago," one of them told the *Phoenix*, "the brig *Governor Hopkins* sailed from Bristol on a plum-pudding voyage. There are only four survivors of that gallant crew, not counting the hands we picked up in the Western Isles. We were welcomed at the depot by our venerable shipmate Thomas Springer in time to review the parade, after which we were driven to his residence. We arrived eager to partake of the sumptuous dinner prepared by his daughter. As we drew near the house she gave us the usual salutation, 'THERE SHE BLOWS!!' which we quickly answered with 'WHERE AWAY?' After dinner, pipe-smoking and speeches were the order of the day, and the time passed pleasantly until the next morning, when we took our departure."

Anyone who felt like it could join the parade. There were sometimes more marchers than spectators. Oskytel Clark made his own white uniform for the day, with a cap like a postman's; he looked as fine as Admiral Dewey. Sam Slocum would appear by nine o'cock at Gooding's Corner, halfway to the Neck, in an immaculate suit of white marseilles and a frock coat doubly starched. He carried a silver-tipped baton, wore a flower in his lapel, and sported a gilded stickpin in his tie and brilliant rings on all his white-gloved fingers. He never got far from the corner, on his way to town, before one of the Swamp Angels sneaked some lighted lady-crackers into his pocket; in spite of which he always reached the Common in time to fall in behind the Train of Artillery band and strut behind them through the parade, keeping time with his baton like a drum-major. Willy Green from the Poor Farm marched in the parade every year—not in it, exactly, but beside it, in the gutter. For the Fourth he always wore his "other suit," which was white. He sported a red, white and blue streamer in the band of his straw hat, and a last year's badge marked COMMITTEE in his lapel. He was a stubby little fellow, with pink eyes in his chubby face. He would start out in line with the mounted staff at the head of the procession, but his legs were so short that he soon fell behind and wound up opposite the Dom Luiz Felipe Portuguese-American band, in the last division. He held a harmonica to his mouth. If anyone on the sidewalk asked him, "Whatcha playing, Willy?" he took it from his lips long enough to call out, " 'Yankee Doodle,' " but since he had short breath and few teeth, it is likely that he made no music at all.

The Fourth was the briskest day for peddlers like the barrel-man and the basket-man. It was a superstition that the former would bring rain in the afternoon, and the latter fair weather. One man came down from the City, as Bristolians call Providence, in a brimless Canadian cap with eartabs. He inched through the crowd, calling, "Balm of Gilead, Balm of Gilead! Daddy makes it and I sell it!"

Mr. Wright, the hull-corn man, hawked a three-gallon can of what looked like unpopped popcorn but was soft enough to eat with molasses. He lived on the Neck, in the disputed territory which Warren stole from Bristol. He wore a full-length linen duster and a curl-brim

derby. Everyone knew his wife would not let him come home till he
had sold the whole canful and brought her back three dollars. He had
no trouble getting rid of it on the Fourth. As for the tramps, they
not only got their usual handouts from the softhearted, but often
filched a ham from the sink-room or a chicken from the coop. Captain
Goff of the police had a setter named Tige who could diagnose a
tramp by his smell and point him like a bird-dog till his master arrived to usher him out of town; but on the Fourth Tige marched behind the captain in the parade.

Off the route of the procession, the saloons were crowded all day.
Blondie Rawson's was so noisy on the Fourth that a man couldn't hear
himself think. In one corner at the back were four bulldogs in continuous battle; in the other were two Negro minstrels from Providence, one playing the piano and the other singing. (The one who
sang bore the extraordinary name Valorious Glorious George Washington Hathaway Peck Stout.) In the middle of the mahogany bar
stood a washboiler full of well-salted chowder. At one end a parrot
clung to the rim, swearing; at the other, two monkeys skidded on the
varnish, jabbering at each other.

But the sun never set on the Fourth that Wash Gorham, the old
whaleman,* did not stagger out of Blondie's in time to pay his yearly
visit to Mrs. Andrew Sherman on High Street. He would climb un-
steadily over the rail and tell her, "Now, Sade, let's you and me sing
our favorite hymn, and if I go before you do, I want you to see they
sing it at my funeral."

And the neighbors, rocking on their own piazzas, would hear the
strange duo, the irredeemable bibber and the motherly housewife,
raise their voices together.

---

* Wash, who descended from the John Gorham to whom Massasoit sold
one hundred acres, made his living by cutting grass and sweeping horse-
chestnut leaves off people's sidewalks. The guests at Minnie Perry's said
they would rather listen to him than to Ralph Waldo Emerson. He once said
to Minister Locke, "Mr. Locke, I do love you so!"

"Well, Wash, if you loved me you'd quit drinking whisky."

"Now, Mr. Locke, you can't ask anyone to love you *that* much. It's plumb
stuck-up."

"Pass me not, O gentle Savior,
Hear my humble cry;
When on others Thou art smiling,
Do not pass me by."

All the vanished patriots, I think, come home again each Fourth to watch the parade, along with twenty or thirty thousand others who crowd into the old town. Nowadays there are a dozen divisions. The hand-pumpers have given way to gasoline. Even the division of antique automobiles must seem way in the future to General Ambrose E. Burnside and Ed Anthony; and Parson Wight, before returning heavenward, must rub his eyes at the wiggling rumps of the drum majorettes. But he would not scold them, for in Bristol everything is forgiven on the Fourth.

Close to the front of each year's parade ride the five members of the School Committee. Though they are charged with the future of two thousand children, and spend more than half the taxpayers' money, they get no pay for their work. Their chairman at this writing is a cheerful Italian-American named Vincent Saviano, who does not look old enough to have served his adopted town for twenty-five years. His story is a sample of the change that has overtaken Bristol since the Indian Summer. I might not have asked him for it except for hearing one of the Great Folks read the names of the seniors at the high school and exclaim, "Why, there is hardly an American in the bunch!"

He was wrong; they are all American.

Vincent's father, Gabriele Saviano, was a cabinet-maker in the village of Pomigliano d'Arco, four miles south of Naples. He made about a dime a day on workdays, which were not many because of all the fiestas. Vincent was born there in 1896. It was rumored that in America gold lay in the streets, waiting to be picked up. America seemed as far as Mars from Pomigliano d'Arco, till someone wrote Gabriele from there that so long as he stayed home he was, as Vincent puts it, "working for peanuts."

In 1901 Gabriele made the passage alone on a little steamer loaded with marble, Naples to Boston in thirty-six days, with storms every day. He left his wife Lucia at home with their three boys. When he landed there was no gold to be seen. He was out of a job for nine months. Then he heard of Bristol, where Luigi Malafronte found him one for $1.50 a day, cementing soles to uppers with a brush in Colonel S. Pomeroy Colt's rubber works. It was not his trade, but he made fifteen times the wages of Pomigliano d'Arco. The Yankees laughed at him in the streets. The boys threw snowballs at him; he had never even seen snow before, except once on the top of Vesuvius. In the stores he had to point for what he wanted, for he did not know a word of English.

In two years he had saved enough to send home for his wife Lucia and their three boys. He knew they would miss the warm climate and the easy life, as he did. But, as Vincent says, "Italy is all right, but if it was any good we wouldn't be in America. It was the comforts that made up for the fun."

Lucia made a dollar go a long way, and Gabriele's salary rose when Superintendent McCarthy found he was an expert carpenter. The day began at six and lasted for ten hours. In the summer-long layoffs each year, there was time to build a house for whoever could afford one— and he never had to look for customers—with his sons to help him: Gabriele himself as the carpenter, Jim as the mason, Joe as the plumber, and Vincent as the electrician. The boys were on vacation too, from public school. In Pomigliano d'Arco, they might not have gone to school at all.

Lucia was taken sick in 1909. Vincent—he was thirteen then—had to give up high school and take a job in the rubber works alongside his father. Nights, he took the train to the School of Design in Providence, to study electric motors. In the First World War he spent two years in the United States Army.

Between his two trades, Gabriele earned enough to buy the tenement on Wood Street which he had rented ever since his family had come over. Now, as the boys married off, he could rent their floor to tenants, and put by a little more. All of them were married by 1921, when Lucia died. Each of them asked him to move in with them, but by now Wood Street was home to him. He could not leave it. So Vincent and his wife Giulia broke up *their* tenement to move in with him. He died in 1953 at eighty-seven, still hardly able to speak English or write Italian, but he had given the boys the education he himself had missed.

Vincent was elected to the School Committee in 1932. He had never got through high school himself, but he made sure that his children did.

His oldest son is Gabriele, named for his grandfather, as is the custom of Pomigliano d'Arco. He went on to Brown and to Yale Medical School. He served as captain in the Medical Corps in Korea. His wife is Lois Law, the daughter of an Englishman. Vincent, Junior, the next son, spent the Second World War in the Navy and then worked his way through the College of Pharmacy. He is a latex chemist now in the granite building which Governor A. O. Bourn built in 1864, where his grandfather first cemented soles to uppers. His wife is Irene Martelly, a French-Canadian girl from Warren. The third child is named Lucia, after her grandmother. She worked as a make-up artist in New York until she married Leger Morrison, who is a graduate of Columbia Teachers' College and professor of accountancy at Bryant College in Providence. Giulia, the baby, is seventeen now. Last June she took her diploma from her father's hands, under the portraits of Madam Colt and the Colonel. I hope that she marries a boy of Italian lineage and keeps alive the stock that ventured to leave Pomigliano d'Arco half a century ago.

Though Vincent himself is chairman of the School Committee, he is still on the payroll at the rubber works, on the night shift. He winds motors as big as 350 horsepower. Back in 1949, they gave him a gold watch for forty years' service, and he begins to wonder what they will give him for fifty.

"It's quite a life," he said, sighing, when he sketched me the family story, "and I've enjoyed every minute of it. I hope there's more of the same to come. You and I aren't old yet, you know."

I reminded him that for all Captain Jim deWolf's five millions, not one of *his* children had had the education his own were getting, and that every one of them was broke ten years after their father's death. With a wrinkle of his black eyebrows, he said, in an accent which has not really shaken off Pomigliano d'Arco, "I'd rather give my children an education than leave them a thousand dollars—forget about the million—because no one can take it away from them. Now I didn't have enough, and my old folks didn't have any. But my kids, they've got enough to hold them."

"Come back to the old folks," I said. "How could they come from a place where they didn't have to work hard—or at least it wouldn't hurt them if they didn't—and work harder than the people who were here already?"

He thought for a second.

"I believe it was the combination of newness and necessity, like everyone here being dressed up in good condition. Everybody had rugs, and a stove, and lived like the Joneses. To get the money you had to work for it, and a little harder than the people who had some to start with, like those ones they used to call the Great Folks. Once my people had the nerve to leave Pomigliano d'Arco, they had all the more responsibility when they got here. The trouble was, they stuck together. Had to, maybe. Why, they wouldn't buy a lollipop except in an Italian store. They wouldn't know the word in a Yankee one. Let me tell you: twenty years more and there won't be any more Irish or Porchagee or Italian or Yankees. We'll all be American. Why, what else could they call us? That's what we are right now. What's the difference where you were born? We all hope to go to the same place. What I'm telling you is progress."

In 1883, during the Indian Summer of the Great Folks, Minister Locke wrote a prayer which always bears repeating. I, who am his grandson, know that he foresaw the progress Vincent Saviano means, for he told me so.

PRAYER FOR OUR COUNTRY

Almighty God, who hast given us this good land for our heritage, we humbly beseech Thee that we may always prove ourselves a people mindful of Thy favor and glad to do Thy will. Bless our land with honorable industry, sound learning, and pure manners. Save us from violence, discord, and confusion; from pride and arrogancy, and from every evil way. Defend our liberties, and fashion into one happy people the multitudes brought hither out of many kindreds and tongues. Endue with the spirit of wisdom those to whom in Thy name we entrust the authority of government, that there may be justice and peace at home, and that through obedience to Thy law we may show forth Thy praise among the nations of the earth. In the time of prosperity, fill our hearts with thankfulness; and in the day of trouble, suffer not our trust in Thee to fail. Amen.

INDEX OF PERSONS
AND SHIPS

Howe, George Locke.
    Mount Hope; a New England chronicle. New York, The Viking Press, 1959.

    viii, 312 p. illus. 22 cm.

    1. Bristol, R. I.—Hist.   1. Title.

F89.B8H84   974.55   59–5643 ‡

Library of Congress

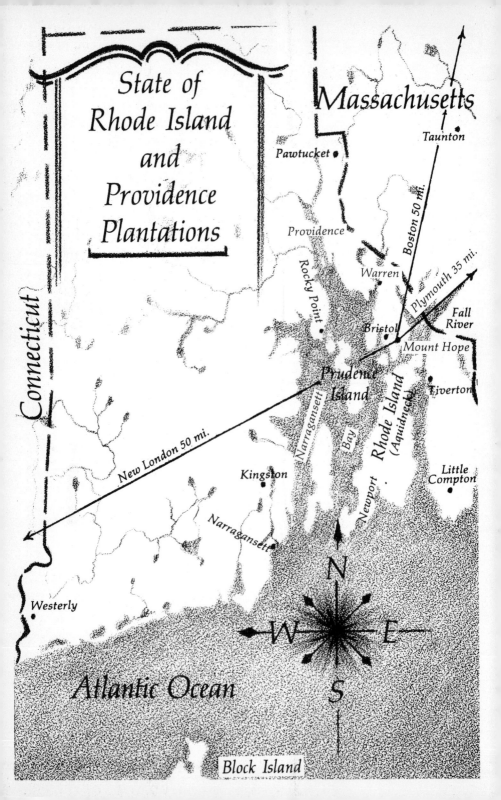